Transforming Dreams

Transforming Dreams

Learning Spiritual Lessons from the Dreams You Never Forget

Kelly Bulkeley, Ph.D.

John Wiley and Sons, Inc.

New York • Chichester • Weinheim • Brisbane • Singapore • Toronto

Published by John Wiley & Sons, Inc.
Published simultaneously in Canada

Library of Congress Cataloging-in-Publication Data:

Bulkeley, Kelly.
    Transforming dreams : learning spiritual lessons from the dreams
  you never forget / Kelly Bulkeley.
        p.   cm.
    Includes bibliographical references and indexes.
    ISBN 0-471-34961-5 (pbk. : alk. paper)
    1. Dreams. 2. Dreams—Religious aspects. 3. Dream
  interpretation.   I. Title.
  BF1091.B93   2000
  154.6'3—dc21   99-32356

Printed in the United States of America

10 9 8 7 6 5 4 3 2 1

For Conor
and
In memory of Brownie

Contents

Acknowledgments

This book has grown out of the many wonderful conversations I've had with friends, students, clients, research volunteers, and members of my family. I thank all of them for their generosity in sharing their dreams with me.

I also thank the teachers and colleagues whose critical comments and insightful suggestions have guided me in the process of researching and writing this book. The notes at the back of the book provide references to their works.

Finally, I would like to thank my agent, Ling Lucas, my editor, Tom Miller, and all the staff at John Wiley & Sons for their guidance, encouragement, and general good cheer.

In most of the dream reports described in this book, I have made slight changes to certain details in order to safeguard the privacy of the dreamers. Any such changes are bound to distort certain aspects of the dreams, but I've done my best to keep these distortions to an absolute minimum.

Readers of contemporary nonfiction sometimes wonder if the authors are making up their examples or are fabricating narrative details to make their books more dramatic and exciting. I assure you I have not done that. My academic training is in the field of religion and psychological studies, and I have followed the basic research methods of that field in gathering, analyzing, and describing the dream reports I present in this book. Other than making the aforementioned changes to preserve the dreamers' privacy, I have presented the dream reports as simply and directly as I can, with no fictional embellishments of my own creation.

Ultimately, you must judge for yourself the legitimacy and significance of these extraordinary dreams. One thing that distinguishes dream studies from other academic fields is that everyone has direct access to the object being studied. This isn't true for most areas of scholarly research: If you don't have an electron microscope, you can't personally verify the claims of a molecular biologist. If you don't know how to read ancient hieroglyphs, you can't independently evaluate the arguments of an archaeologist. If you've never done field research in a faraway place, you can't confirm for yourself the accounts of an ethnologist. But everyone does have dreams, and this means that each person has the resources needed to test the claims of a book such as this one. I hope that as you read the following pages you will rely on your own dreams, as well as your reason and your common sense, in evaluating what I have to say.

Introduction

The religions of the world have found a way to disagree on almost every subject under the sun. They've clashed over everything from the nature of the soul to the reality of God, from sexual morality to what foods people should and shouldn't eat. But on one small point most religions do agree, and that's a point about the nature of dreams. Nearly all the world's religions share the belief that some dreams are true revelations of the Divine, bringing people into direct contact with some kind of transpersonal being, force, or reality. Not *all* dreams are believed to have this power; most traditions emphasize that the majority of dreams are related to ordinary daily events and have no unusual, heaven-sent meaning. But almost every religion in the world recognizes that at least once or twice in their lives people have dreams that are *different*, that have a special energy, vividness, and intensity to them. The Mohave Indians of the American Southwest call these dreams *sumach ahot*, or "lucky dreams," while the Jamaa church people of western Africa call them *mawazo*, or "holy dreams." Medieval Islamic theologians referred to them as "clear dream visions" sent directly from God, and ancient Hindu philosophers spoke of them as "dreams under the influence of a deity."

These unusual types of dreams are not merely the relics of ancient religious superstition. People in today's society experience dreams that are virtually identical to the dream revelations reported in a wide variety of religious traditions. Although many individuals in the modern world use nonreligious language to describe their dreams, the dream experiences themselves always have a vivid intensity that sharply distinguishes them from more ordinary types of dreaming. These are the dreams people never forget—the dreams they can't help but remember, the dreams that linger in their memories and haunt their imaginations throughout their lives.

Psychologist Carl Jung referred to these momentous experiences as "big dreams," and he said that such dreams could, if people learned to appreciate their meanings, become "the richest jewels in the treasure-house of the soul." Unfortunately, many people in modern society have no idea what to think or do when they experience a big dream. They worry that having such strangely vivid and powerful dreams must mean there's something wrong with them. "Where did *that* come from?" the dreamers nervously ask themselves. "I've never experienced anything like that before, whether I was awake *or* asleep."

For many years now, I've been studying these kinds of extraordinary dream experiences, trying to understand where they come from, what functions they serve, and how their meanings can be interpreted. My deep interest in this subject began, not surprisingly, with my own dream experiences (I've since learned that many dream researchers also got started in this way, with an interest in their own dreams). I would probably have become a stockbroker or a lawyer if it weren't for a series of harrowing nightmares I suffered while I was a teenager. These terrifying dreams were so intense, so weird, so absolutely alien to my whole view of the world that I felt I had no choice but to heed their call and set out on a quest to understand their meanings. I initially turned to psychology because psychology seemed to be the most authoritative source of information on dreams and nightmares. But even though I learned much from psychology, I was soon disappointed by how much I could *not* learn from it. I found that mainstream Western psychology is sharply limited in its understanding of extraordinary dreams in at least three ways: First, psychology focuses primarily on pathology, on what's wrong with people; it concentrates so much on illness, disease, and malfunctioning that it has little to say about how certain unusual dreams might contribute to people's fundamental growth and development. Second, psychology aims at defining the normal, the ordinary, the average; it therefore has little interest in those dreams that deviate from the theoretical norms, in those dreams that have unusual, extraordinary, or seemingly "impossible" qualities. And third, psychology assumes from the start that humans are independent, self-contained organisms and pays little attention to the possibility that at least some dreams may be influenced by forces and powers that transcend the normal bounds of the individual human mind.

I definitely appreciated the many important facts I learned from modern psychological research on dreams—but they weren't facts about the kinds of dreams I most wanted to learn about. As I pursued my increasingly passionate exploration of the vast and mysterious world of dreaming, I decided the best path to follow was one that combined psychology with what is truly the original field of dream study—religion. From the dawn of history, humans have regarded dreaming as a valuable source of spiritual wisdom and insight; and to my great joy, I found that ancient religious approaches to dreams were the perfect complement to modern psychological approaches. In the world's spiritual traditions, I discovered inspiring visions of human growth that went beyond psychology's tepid definition of health as the mere lack of illness. I found that spiritual traditions celebrated extraordinary experiences like big dreams as vital sources of wisdom, rather than as pathological aberrations to be dismissed. And I found that the world's religions had many intriguing and thought-provoking theories about the possible influence of transpersonal powers on people's dreams.

When I tell people that I did my graduate training not in a psychology department but at a divinity school (first at Harvard and then at the University of Chicago), they are invariably puzzled and sometimes even a little hostile. "Are you some kind of religious fanatic?" they ask. "Are you going to tell me that all my dreams come from either God or the devil?" Well, no, I respond with a smile, that's not my thing. I wasn't raised in a particular church or religious tradition, and to this day I'm not a member of any formal religious institution. If anything, I'm a kind of "born-again pagan," enjoying the presence of the sacred in mountains and trees, rocks and rivers. But I was convinced by my divinity school training that the collective teachings of the world's religions contain many important insights about the nature and functions of dreaming, and I've come to believe very strongly that the best approach to the study of big dreams is one that integrates psychological and spiritual perspectives. I've used this approach in my scholarly research and also in the experiential dreamsharing groups I've led for the past fifteen years. In these groups I've helped people discover for themselves how a combination of psychological and spiritual methods is indeed the best way to understand and appreciate the haunting power and the mysterious wisdom of their big dreams.

Transforming Dreams shares with readers the basic principles of my approach, showing them how to make better sense of their own most vividly remembered dreams. The first part of the book, "Tales," describes four of the most striking forms that big dreams take: dreams of reassurance, dreams of making love, nightmares, and dreams of death. The second part, "Pathways," lays out the practical methods of exploration that I have found most helpful in discerning the deeper meanings of big dreams. These practical methods include reflecting on a dream's strongest sensations, sharing dreams with other people, following particular images and themes across a series of dreams, and creatively expressing the energies of dreams in waking life. *Transforming Dreams* is written for people who simply want to know more about their own big dreams, and it is also intended for the various professionals (psychotherapists, social workers, educators, pastoral counselors, spiritual directors) whose work might benefit from a greater familiarity with the most extraordinary and mysterious realms of the dreaming imagination.

I am not assuming that the readers of this book share any particular religious faith or spiritual world view. Big dreams come to *all* people—to religious believers, to die-hard atheists, and to all those people who don't belong to any formal religion but who feel a yearning to discover greater meaning and purpose in their lives. In the coming chapters, I will respect the healthy skepticism some readers may feel toward the subject of dreaming, and I will also try to honor the sincere religious convictions of other readers who feel their dreams have truly divine origins. My focus in *Transforming Dreams* is on the big dream experiences themselves, and I feel confident in promising readers that no matter what belief system they hold, these vivid and utterly unforgettable dreams have the power to deepen their self-knowledge, broaden their emotional awareness, and open their imagination to new realms of vitality, freedom, and creative possibility. More specifically, readers will find in this book evidence for the following ten affirmations about the ultimate goal, or *telos*, of big dreams:

1. Big dreams bring greater consciousness into being; they are a channel by which feelings, sensations, thoughts, and intuitions enter into people's waking awareness, expanding their understanding of themselves, of other people, and of the world around them.

2. Big dreams prompt people to try new ways of looking at things; they reveal new possibilities, envision alternative scenarios, and compel the dreamers to think about realities they have ignored, forgotten, or resisted.

3. Big dreams reassure people in times of crisis; they strengthen people's self-confidence, reconnecting them with deep sources of life-affirming energy and renewing their hope when they are facing a challenge they fear is insurmountable.

4. Big dreams arouse people's passions and stimulate their desires; they reveal to people what their deepest and most fervent wishes are and give them a vivid, tangible experience of how good it feels to satisfy their wishes.

5. Big dreams warn people of dangers to their well-being; they alert people to threats, obstacles, and conflicts that are blocking their future growth, thus making them more vigilant about potential problems both in the external world and within their own psyches.

6. Big dreams help people come to terms with death. They renew people's emotional connection to loved ones who have died, giving them profound insights into the eternally mysterious relationship between living, dying, and being born anew.

7. Big dreams motivate people to develop greater spiritual self-awareness. The intense realism of certain dream experiences—the feeling during the dream that it was *really happening*—forces people to ask profoundly spiritual questions about the very foundations of their existence: What is real, and what is illusion? How can I tell the difference between truth and deception? Can I live with the possibility that I may never be absolutely sure which is which?

8. Big dreams nurture the abilities to think symbolically and to tell stories. They help people see their lives as ongoing narratives, as tales in which they are simultaneously author, hero, audience, and critic. Big dreams guide people toward the paradoxical discovery that sometimes the greatest truths can only be expressed by means of symbol, fiction, and story.

9. Big dreams revitalize the power of memory. They cultivate people's appreciation for the power of time, helping them see how their past experiences have shaped the realities of their present and have opened the doors to the possibilities of their future.

10. Most important, big dreams expand consciousness by compelling people to ask this question: *Where do these dreams come from?* What is the ultimate source of these strangely transformative experiences, which seem so alien to ordinary waking consciousness and yet which deal with the most intimate and personal concerns of their lives? Big dreams literally force people to confront the living reality of *other* powers, powers that originate far beyond the sphere of normal reality and conventional reason. Big dreams, by their very nature, invite people to grow beyond themselves.

PART ONE

Tales

CHAPTER ONE

❧

Dreams of Reassurance

Bottom (awaking): *I have had a most rare vision. I have had a dream, past the wit of man to say what dream it was. Man is but an ass, if he go about to expound this dream. Methought I was—there is no man can tell what. Methought I was—and methought I had—but man is but a patched fool if he will offer to say what methought I had. The eye of man hath not heard, the ear of man hath not seen, man's hand is not able to taste, his tongue conceive, nor his heart to report, what my dream was. I will get Peter Quince to write a ballet of this dream. It shall be called "Bottom's Dream," because it hath no bottom.*

—William Shakespeare,
A Midsummer Night's Dream

Think for a moment about how vulnerable our dreams make us. When we go to sleep each night, we lie down, close our eyes, and withdraw virtually all sensory attention from the outside world. We remain in this condition for several hours at a time, utterly motionless and completely absorbed in our own private realm of feeling and experience. This is a terribly dangerous position in which to put ourselves. Our prehistoric ancestors, when they were asleep, were obviously much easier prey for saber-toothed tigers than when they were awake, just as the slumbering Bottom was helpless against the mischievous scheming of Oberon's woodland fairies, and just as we today are more vulnerable to burglars and rapists when we are asleep in our beds at home. Why have we humans evolved with the instinctual need to enter this essentially defenseless condition for eight or so hours every night of our lives? What adaptive benefits do we receive that make it worth sacrificing our normal abilities to defend ourselves from external attack?

The Mysteries of REM Sleep

In recent years psychological researchers have discovered at least a few answers to these questions. Dreaming, we now know, is closely related to the stage of the sleep cycle known as *REM sleep,* so named because of the "rapid eye movements" that are its most visible external sign. Although some dreams come from non-REM phases of sleep, the most emotionally vivid and visually complex dreams seem to occur during REM sleep. Based on this evidence, we can assume with some confidence that the time at which big dreams most likely occur is in the midst of a REM phase.

People usually have four or five periods of REM sleep during an ordinary night's sleep, and in each of these periods truly remarkable changes occur within the brain. Out of the slow, languid brain wave patterns that characterize sleep during non-REM periods, there is an abrupt explosion of electrochemical activity in REM sleep: Neural systems all over the brain suddenly come to life, and flashes of intense, supercharged energy burst out in rapid staccato rhythms. Researchers have long marveled at the sheer power of the brain's activities during REM sleep, a power that easily matches, and at time exceeds, the electrochemical energy generated by the brain during waking consciousness. Indeed, if you had nothing but the readings from a brain-wave-measuring device (an EEG, or electroencephalograph) to go by, you could not tell whether they came from a person who was awake or a person who was in REM sleep—the brain's total output of energy in the two conditions is indistinguishable.

The chief conclusion of this research is that the brain does not simply "turn off" when a person goes to sleep each night. On the contrary, at regular points during an otherwise quiet and restful sleep, the brain kicks into its highest gear, creating the neurological conditions that underlie those strange experiences of image, emotion, and sensation that people, on awakening, remember as dreams.

This basic pattern of alternating periods of REM and non-REM sleep is a feature found in all mammalian species. From cats and cows to elephants and mice, the sleep pattern of all mammals involves a cycle of REM and non-REM periods. By contrast, fish and reptiles have no REM sleep, and birds have only the briefest flashes of REM-like brain activity during their sleep. Researchers take this as evidence that REM sleep has played a significant role in the evolution of the mammalian brain, a brain that is more complex, sophisticated, and flexible than that of nonmammals.

Another important fact to emerge from current research is that in all mammals the percentage of REM sleep as a total of each night's sleep is highest in infancy and early childhood. As mammals grow up and reach adulthood, the percentage of time they spend in REM sleep decreases to a much lower amount, at which it remains throughout the rest of their lives. We humans spend more than 50 percent of our sleep in REM during infancy (and in the womb—fetuses experience REM sleep, too). But by the time we grow into mature adults, REM sleep accounts for only 20 to 25 percent of our total sleep. This common pattern of relatively greater amounts of REM sleep in childhood provides further evidence that REM sleep is directly involved in the growth and development of the mammalian brain.

After the initial discovery of the connection between REM sleep and dreaming, many researchers tried the experiment of waking up subjects every time they started to enter a REM phase to see what would happen if a person were totally deprived of all REM sleep. Not surprisingly, the subjects became very cranky and agitated. As the experiments went on, the REM-sleep-deprived people had increasing difficulties with thinking, learning, remembering, and dealing with emotionally disturbing experiences. For obvious moral reasons the researchers conducting these experiments could not push their human subjects beyond a certain point. But in studies using animals as subjects, long-term REM-sleep deprivation has been associated with serious damage to the brain and central nervous system.

The researchers conducting these studies found that an interesting thing happened when the deprivation ended, when the human or animal subjects were allowed once again to sleep through the night without interruption: The subjects experienced a large increase in their total amount of REM sleep over the next few nights, a kind of "rebound" effect indicating that their brains were trying to make up for the deprivations of the previous nights.

It is clear from these crude but enlightening deprivation experiments that we humans *need* to have REM sleep. We cannot function, and perhaps cannot survive, without our regular nightly doses of REM sleep.

Making Sense Out of Nonsense

More-subtle scientific experiments have been conducted in recent years to figure out what types of waking-life experience might cause an increase in REM sleep. These experiments have shown that if people are given new learning tasks, are asked to remember a large amount of new information, or are exposed to a highly upsetting emotional stimulus (for example, watching a medical school training film showing how to dissect a human cadaver), they experience a large increase in the amount of REM sleep during their next night's sleep. And if the people are deprived of REM sleep during that next night, they are much less capable the following day of performing the newly learned task, of remembering the new information, or of dealing comfortably with a repeat exposure to the emotional stimulus.

Many, many questions remain about how sleep and dreaming have developed and about what specific functions they serve. But based on the present state of scientific research, we are sure of at least this much: Sleep and dreaming have developed over the course of evolution as a way to promote the growth and maturation of the mammalian brain. REM sleep helps humans respond effectively and creatively to waking-life experiences that are new, challenging, and/or frightening. Dreaming enables humans to process new information, to maintain a high degree of mental flexibility, and to cope with emotionally upsetting experiences. This is the reason why humans willingly leave themselves so utterly defenseless for nearly one-third of their lives. Dreaming is the brain's way of making sense of everything people have experienced during the previous day and of preparing them for whatever new experiences they may face in the day to come. The evolutionary benefits of having a quick, alert, well-tuned brain are tremendous, and these benefits more than justify the cost of periodically making a person more vulnerable to external attack. After all, humans have used their high-powered brains to invent things like fences, drawbridges, and burglar alarms to protect their slumbering bodies while they journey each night to the distant and mysterious realm of dreaming.

Scientific Skepticism and the "Lab Effect"

A few researchers have taken current knowledge about REM sleep and have drawn a very skeptical conclusion from it. These researchers argue that the evolutionary functions of REM sleep do not depend on the conscious remembering of dreams: People could pay no attention whatsoever to their dreams; they could forget every single one as soon as they woke up, and their REM-activated brains would still accomplish the basic job of processing information, consolidating memory, and reestablishing emotional balance. Francis Crick, the Nobel prize–winning codiscoverer of DNA (deoxyribonucleic acid), has gone so far with this reasoning as to suggest that consciously remembering dreams might not be merely irrelevant, but actually harmful to people's health: "In this model, attempting to remember one's dreams should perhaps not be encouraged, because such remembering may help to retain patterns of thought which are better forgotten. These are the very patterns the organism was attempting to damp down." Crick believes the core function of REM sleep is to clean out the many faulty neural connections that are accidentally formed in the brain each day. If this is indeed REM sleep's main function, Crick says, then remembering a dream would be reinforcing a connection the brain is actively trying to eliminate. It would be like one person in a family taking the garbage out each night, and another person bringing it right back in the next morning.

Although I disagree with Crick's theory, I believe he does raise a key question: Why *do* people remember any of their dreams? More to the point of this book, why do people have some dreams *they can't possibly forget*—dreams with such vibrant imagery and intense emotional impact that they haunt the dreamers for the rest of their lives? Is there any evolutionary value to people's big dreams, or are these experiences mere epiphenomena of REM sleep with no real meaning or purpose?

Researchers have found it very difficult to study the more unusual and extraordinary types of dream experience, and for good reason. The traditional venue of scientific dream investigation, the sleep laboratory, has the unfortunate effect of making people experience boring dreams. Various studies have shown that people sleeping in a sleep laboratory have fewer aggressive dreams, fewer sexual dreams, and fewer nightmares than do people sleeping in more natural settings. Indeed, people who are frequent nightmare sufferers and who volunteer to be research subjects often feel safer when sleeping in a laboratory—they know that someone will be carefully watching over and protecting them all night long. This heightened sense of safety prevents them from having as many nightmares as they usually do when they sleep at home. One leading dream researcher, J. Allan Hobson, has freely confessed that "the most interesting dreams always occur outside the laboratory."

What is now called the *lab effect* has forced dream researchers to grapple with the same paradox that quantum physicists discovered earlier this century: There is no neutral standpoint from which to observe an object. Things cannot be studied experimentally without their being affected or altered to some degree. Thus, if people are brought into the sleep research department of a large hospital, have wires attached to their heads, eyes, torsos, and genitals, sleep in strange beds in strange rooms, and are informed that at various points in the night they will be awakened by people they don't know and asked a series of intrusive questions, researchers should not be surprised if the people have dreams that are tamer, more guarded, more conventional, and more homogeneous than the dreams they experience in other settings.

In my own research, I have taken a decidedly low-tech approach to investigating those types of dream phenomena that are systematically excluded by the lab effect. Using both personal interviews and written surveys, I've simply asked people to describe their most memorable dreams, whether they came to the people last week, last month, last year, or way back in their childhood. In this way I've gathered hundreds of reports of dreams that people say they can still remember with crystal clarity, dreams they insist were unlike any other they had ever experienced, dreams that, as Bottom marveled, are "past the wit of man" to account for. To be sure, these dream reports are not as systematically controlled as those collected in a sleep lab, and there's a serious risk that the people to whom I've spoken are either remembering only selected parts of the original dream or actively embellishing their descriptions to make the dreams sound more exciting. But that's a risk in the sleep laboratory, too, where researchers have to trust that their subjects aren't holding back on certain details out of embarrassment and aren't adding in new details to please the investigators.

Researchers have yet to find a way of getting inside another person's dreams, so all researchers are in the position of having to trust the dreamer's subjective account of what he or she experienced. In the end I believe the best way of developing a good, solid understanding of big dreams is to bring together the findings of *all* forms of dream research, looking carefully at the full variety of dream types and patiently sifting through the particular (and possibly fabricated) details of each individual dream report in order to discern the broader patterns, themes, and meanings that emerge in all of them. That's the approach I take in this book.

The Ancient Warrior Chieftain

Elena was twenty-one years old and had recently graduated from college. She had just started a new job as a systems analyst at a high-tech start-up company, and she was very excited about the bright future that lay in front of her. But suddenly she began experiencing strange sensations in her chest, and when she went to the doctor, she received news that brought her life to a screeching stop: She was suffering from a serious, and probably fatal, heart condition. Because the condition had been discovered so late, she needed to have major heart surgery as soon as possible. Even with the surgery, the doctor warned, Elena might not have more than a year left to live.

This sudden confrontation with mortality shook Elena to the core. In the anxious weeks leading up to the surgery, with her parents nervously fussing around her apartment trying, with little success, to hide their own fears, Elena had a dream:

> I am standing on an open plain that appears to be lightly covered with a brilliant, golden blanket of grass. On the exterior of the vast land, I can make out large, luminous rock formations, which seem to frame the dream as if it is a window that I'm peering into. Then I notice a young Native American girl. As my gaze falls upon her, I realize in an instant that it is myself I am seeing, but at a very young age, possibly six or seven years old. She is dressed in a simple brown leather dress, and her eyes and confidence draw me to her. She appears to be without fear, aware only of herself and the land around her. Then I see there is a hand resting on her shoulder. When I look up to see who it is, I literally stop breathing for a second because his presence is so powerful that I actually lose my sense of who or where I am. He is like an ancient warrior or chieftain who has seen many battles in his life. His skin is worn and aged from the sun, and he wears a traditional Native American robe, brightly colored with red, yellow, and orange beads, and has a huge headdress made of eagle feathers. His face is painted in stripes of yellow and red. The young girl and the old warrior stand together in silence and stare up into the sky. When I finally tear my eyes away from them, I realize they are looking up at an eagle, which is circling overhead. The eagle continues to glide along the wind like it is light as a feather. As I look up with them, I have this overwhelming feeling of peace, warmth, and security.

Is a dream like this an arbitrary piece of neurological nonsense, the kind of mental garbage that researchers like Crick claim has no real meaning or value? Elena didn't think so. When she woke up, she immediately connected the dream to her fears about the heart surgery, and she realized she suddenly had a powerful new sense of hope and optimism. Although she was still terribly worried about the surgery, the dream brought a host of *new* feelings and emotions into her awareness, putting her anxieties in an entirely different perspective. She now felt a deep, unshakable confidence that no matter what happened with her surgery, no matter what the future held, there was a powerful *presence* in her life that would always watch over and protect her.

As it turned out, the heart surgery was successful. After a few months of rest and recuperation, Elena was able to go back to work and resume her normal life.

In the midst of a terrible waking-life crisis, this young woman had an incredibly vivid dream that *reassured her*—that gave her new hope and new energy for the future. A large number of the big dream reports I've heard over the years have this same effect of comforting and reassuring a person who is suffering from a major crisis or going through some kind of difficult life transition. These extraordinary dreams have the effect of totally transforming the emotional attitudes of people, giving them a deeply reassuring confidence that they *will* overcome the challenges confronting them, whether it be a serious illness, a divorce, a job loss, a car accident, a fire, a move from one home to another, or any other event that deeply threatens a person's sense of emotional stability.

Dreams of reassurance are found in every period of recorded history and in cultures all over the world, and they have always been revered as gifts from the gods, as revelations of divine aid and consolation. However, a person doesn't have to buy into any particular religious world view to appreciate the value of these dreams. Stating the point in nonreligious terms, reassurance dreams rally the emotional resources of people at a time when they are suffering a severe challenge to their well-being, if not to their very survival. These dreams renew people's courage, revitalize their spirit, and reorient their attitude from despair to optimism. Whether there's any value to remembering dreams in general, these particular dreams have a clear and unmistakably positive effect on people's lives, bursting upon consciousness to help them at precisely those moments when they are feeling most vulnerable and endangered.

It is worth looking more closely at Elena's experience to see exactly how her dream creates such a beneficial transformation in her emotional outlook. The dream has four basic parts:

1. Elena finds herself standing in the midst of a beautiful golden prairie, open and expansive yet well protected by the strangely luminous rocks; the atmosphere is rich and fertile, alive with possibility.

2. She sees the Native American girl, whom she recognizes as *herself.* In this young girl's eyes, Elena sees an alluring confidence and fearlessness, and their mutual gaze draws them closer together.

3. With a literally breathtaking shock of discovery, Elena sees the aged warrior. With his hand resting on the young girl's shoulder and with his brightly colored clothing, headdress, and face paint, the warrior appears to Elena as a radiant embodiment of wisdom, experience, and strength.

4. *Then,* Elena follows the eyes of the girl and the chieftain up to the sky, where she sees a majestic eagle soaring through the air. As she and the two others silently watch the eagle's flight, Elena is suddenly filled with "this overwhelming feeling of peace, warmth, and security."

All four parts of Elena's dream work in harmony to generate a deeply transformative emotional experience. The first part of the dream sets the overall tone by creating a symbolic environment that is both free and safe, stimulating and protective. The second part gives Elena the opportunity to view herself from a different perspective and to realize that the young girl's feelings of confidence and fearlessness are *her* feelings, too. Although Elena's waking life is dominated by anxiety and despair, the young Native American girl literally "re-minds" her that she has a deep and powerful core of strength within herself. In the third part, the stunning appearance of the old Native American warrior carries the emotional reassurance to a new level of intensity by revealing that the young girl's fearlessness is grounded in age-old traditions and hard-won life experiences. The warrior is an inspiring figure of elder wisdom, there to support the young girl (and Elena) toward the future. And in the fourth part, the dream reaches its climax in showing that the awesomely powerful warrior is not the ultimate source of strength, but that even he must give respect and honor to the power of the soaring eagle, circling in the air overhead, flying high and free.

Each part of the dream builds on the others, adding new layers of imagery and new dimensions of meaning, to create the wonderful sense of hope and optimism that filled Elena when she awoke. The dream's complex narrative design and elegant interweaving of symbolic form and emotional energy produced an effect that truly changed Elena's life.

Dreams like this are worthy of the name Jung gave them—"jewels of the soul."

Wishful Dreaming

Karen was a forty-seven-year-old part-time librarian in a small suburb of Boston. She and her husband had been having marital troubles off and on for several years, but Karen was hoping that a marriage counselor recommended by a friend would be able to help them sort through their differences. Then one day her husband suddenly announced that he had met another woman and wanted a divorce. Karen was devastated by his abrupt abandonment of their marriage, and she tried to persuade him to wait and see if the counseling could help them. But after a long, angry night of arguing with her husband, Karen realized that there was no possibility of reconciliation. Their marriage of fifteen years was over.

When she went to bed that night, Karen tossed and turned for hours, too hurt and grief-stricken to sleep. Toward morning, she finally drifted off and had this dream:

> *I feel absolutely wonderful, and weightless. I'm no longer in my body, but now I have the shape of an embryo. I'm high in the clouds, floating. Every time I breathe, I float upward from one cloud to another. I'm filled with an incredible happiness and joy.*

When she woke up, Karen couldn't believe she had experienced such a strange and wonderful dream at a time of so much painful emotional turmoil and suffering. She immediately recognized the dream's connection with the end of her marriage, and she understood that the dream was opening the way to a new kind of life, a life that would rise up out of the desolate ruins of her failed relationship with her husband. Karen realized that in all the years of trying to keep their marriage together, she had been denying her own needs. She had been so overwhelmed with fearful worries about what she might *lose* from a divorce that she had never realized how much she might *gain*, what new possibilities might be born out of the "embryo" of the present crisis. That's precisely what her dream showed her—that despite the loneliness and despair of the present moment, she was now free to soar into the future, unburdened by the emotional weights that had held her down for so long. "The dream was such a wonderful experience," Karen said afterward, "like I was with God. I wish I could have this dream again!"

Dream theorists through history have noticed that dreams tend to revolve around people's deepest wishes and desires. Sigmund Freud, the founder of modern dream psychology, based his entire psychoanalytic theory of the mind on the fact that when a very strong wish is frustrated in waking life, people often dream of it at night. A dream like Karen's would seem to be a perfect example of a Freudian "wish-fulfillment" dream, in that it portrays an image of how Karen wishes her life could be: She wishes she could "rise above" her sad feelings about the divorce. Freud took a dim view of such dreams because he felt they revealed an infantile unwillingness to face the cold, hard facts of reality. Freud argued that people could achieve true emotional maturity only by renouncing their wishes, surrendering their happy but illusory dreams, and devoting themselves instead to a rational mastery of the physical world.

Although I agree with many of Freud's insights into the nature of dreams, I disagree with his unduly harsh claims about wishful dreams. The extremely vivid and memorable dreams of Karen, Elena, and many other people do not obstruct their abilities to face waking reality. Rather they enhance them—Karen's and Elena's dreams made them feel *more* hopeful, *more* energetic, and *more* self-confident than they were before. The transformative emotional power of their dreams strengthened their adaptive resources at just the moment when they needed help the most. If these are wish-fulfillment dreams, they are wish-fulfillments *in the service of greater waking-life courage and vitality*.

Even if Freud's legitimate concerns about self-delusion are accepted, the beneficial effects of such dreams should not be underestimated. The worst danger posed by a major life crisis or trauma is that people will give up hope and will become so despairing and overwhelmed by their problems that they no longer have the capacity to imagine that their lives could ever get better. In such times some people are blessed with tremendously powerful dreams that reassure them that there *is* hope and that beyond the terrible sufferings of the present there *are* possibilities for a better life in the future. Their energies are renewed, their emotional balance is restored, and their courage is revitalized. Most important, these dreams give the dreamers a broad new perspective in which to see and understand their problems. Rather than being trapped *within* the crisis, they are able to stand outside it and see that their individual lives are connected in a deeply mysterious but absolutely reassuring way to other powers and other realities.

Interpreting Dream Symbols

It is worth pausing for a moment to reflect on the meanings that have emerged in these first two dreams. People sometimes complain that dreams are too jumbled and mixed-up ever to be understood. Why don't dreams just say what they mean in plain, simple language? If dreams are supposed to have such valuable and beneficial effects on people's lives, why aren't they easier to figure out?

As the examples of Elena and Karen illustrate, dreams express themselves in a language of symbolism. What appears jumbled and mixed-up to the conscious, rational mind is, for better or for worse, the natural way in which the dreaming imagination operates. This is why the ancient Greek philosopher Aristotle said that interpreting dreams requires an ability to "see resemblances." To interpret a dream is to discern the resemblance between symbolic images in the dream and various aspects of waking life. The resemblance may not be immediately obvious, but that usually says more about the limits of consciousness than about any inherent failings in the dreams themselves.

If you went to visit a foreign country, you wouldn't expect the people there to automatically begin speaking in your native language just to make life easier for you. No, if you really wanted to get to know that country, you would take the time and make the effort to learn *its* language, to learn the form of communication natural to that land. The same is true in trying to understand dreams, which at first sight can seem totally baffling and incomprehensible. Patient, careful reflection almost always shows that, beyond the apparent nonsense, people's dreams do in fact relate sensibly and meaningfully to the most important concerns of their waking lives. It is true that there's no simple, one-step method to interpreting a dream, and it's also true that every dream has many different levels of meaning to it. Dream interpretation is not like solving a math equation, with a plain, clear-cut, unambiguous answer at the end of the process. Interpreting a dream is more like viewing a painting, or reading a novel, or listening to a piece of music: It's a process that requires both reason and intuition, both logical analysis and empathetic imagination. Instead of sharply defined answers, dream interpretation reveals new connections and fresh possibilities; it deepens self-awareness and broadens perception of the world; it leads people a little bit farther down the path of conscious growth.

I want to emphasize that dream interpretation is not a random or arbitrary process. There are better and worse interpretations of a dream, and I've found that using a few basic principles can help people make interpretations that are accurate, comprehensive, and meaningful for their lives.

1. *The dreamer knows best what a given dream means.* Only the dreamer has direct access to all the images and the feelings in the dream, and only the dreamer is familiar with all the memories and the associations that make up the dream's broader context. This may seem an obvious point, but unfortunately much mischief has been done through the centuries, and right into the present day, by self-proclaimed experts who say they know how to interpret dreams better than the dreamers themselves.

2. *The best interpretation of a dream will account for as many of the dream's details as possible.* I call this the principle of "internal coherence." An interpretation that brings together more of the various elements of a dream is better than an interpretation that only refers to a few isolated pieces of the dream. This principle is based on the observation that almost everything appearing in a dream (and especially in a big dream) is meaningful in some way or other. It often happens in dream interpretation that a seemingly trivial item—the color of a room, the shape of a table, the type of shoes a character is wearing—turns out to have a crucial symbolic meaning that adds an important shading to the overall interpretation. Naturally, problems can occur if a person tries to force all the details of a dream into a fixed or predetermined interpretation. But on the whole, the interpretation that accounts for the most details is the best interpretation.

3. *An interpretation should try to make as many connections as possible between the dream's contents and the dreamer's waking life.* This is the principle of "external coherence," and it is grounded in the fact that dreams are created out of images, ideas, and feelings from the dreamer's daily existence. A good interpretation strives to discover the connections between those waking-life sources and the various symbolic strands of the dream. Sometimes the connections relate to the dreamer's experiences from the previous day or two, like a recent conversation with a friend or a television show watched just before going to bed. Other times the connections involve events from farther in the past, such as a childhood family vacation or a failed high school test. And in other cases the connections refer to events in the future, like an upcoming presentation at work or a planned trip. One key test of a dream interpretation is how well it contextualizes the dream in the dreamer's life and how well it accounts for the waking world origins of the dream's imagery.

4. *A good dream interpretation will be open to new and surprising discoveries and will look beyond the obvious* (what consciousness already knows) *to find the novel and the unexpected* (what consciousness does *not* know). If the interpretation of a dream leads to the reaction, "That's no big deal, I already knew that," then the interpretation probably isn't a very good one. Big dreams rarely if ever come to tell people things they already know. On the contrary, they usually

come to reveal brand new perspectives on people's lives, to give them new ways of seeing and thinking about the world. Often the surprise in a dream comes in the form of an unexpectedly revitalized emotional conviction—the dreamer thought he or she knew something before; but now, thanks to the experiential impact of the dream, the dreamer *really* knows it.

If readers take nothing else from this book, I hope these four principles will give them enough guidance to try to understand their own big dreams. Later chapters of the book will describe more advanced methods of dream interpretation that build on these four principles.

Faith

Scientific researchers who study dreams are often embarrassed by the more bizarre or unusual aspects of people's dream experiences. For many researchers the idea that dreams can really bring people into contact with transhuman powers and realities is an affront to the modern scientific world view. The goal, in the view of these researchers, is to get beyond the foolish superstitions of primitive peoples and to rationally explain dreaming in terms of natural physical processes, without reference to gods, ancestral spirits, or other divine beings.

The problem, however, is that any honest attempt to understand what's going on in people's most memorable dreams inevitably leads to issues of religious faith. Dreams of reassurance like those experienced by Elena and Karen almost always involve the clear sensation of being connected to something *more*, to something greater, stronger, and more powerful than the dreamer. This vivid feeling of *spiritual presence* is an integral feature of most big dream experiences, and a truly scientific approach to the study of dreams would take these feelings seriously, rather than dismissing them as primitive or irrational.

I've devoted a great deal of my scholarly research to investigating the role of dreams in the world's religious traditions. In nearly every one of these traditions, I have found reports of people experiencing incredibly powerful dreams that have reassured them in a time of major life crisis. Again, there is reason to be cautious about the accuracy and truthfulness of these reports, as some of them are clearly aimed at promoting a particular religious movement or ideology. But as with the descriptions of big dreams from contemporary people, I believe the smartest method is to look at a variety of traditions and to try to find the most common elements and the most uniquely distinctive qualities that emerge in their portrayals of these kinds of dreams.

One of the most striking dreams from the biblical tradition is Jacob's vision of the heavenly ladder in Genesis 28:13. This intensely memorable dream of reassurance shares many of the basic qualities found in the dreams of Elena, Karen, and other people in contemporary society. Jacob had just tricked his blind father, Isaac, into giving him the blessing that should have gone to his older brother, Esau. Esau was enraged at this treachery and made a secret vow to kill Jacob. But their mother, Rebekah, overheard Esau, and she quickly arranged a marriage between Jacob and a young woman in a distant village, giving Jacob the opportunity to escape before his brother could murder him.

So Jacob left his home in the town of Beersheba and fled into the wilderness. One night during his solitary journey through the deserts of ancient Palestine, Jacob lay down, placed a stone under his head for a pillow, and went to sleep:

> *And he dreamed that there was a ladder set up on the earth, and the top of it reached to heaven; and behold, the angels of God were ascending and descending on it! And behold, the Lord stood above it, and said, "I am the Lord, the God of Abraham your father and the God of Isaac. The land on which you lie I will give to you and to your descendants; and your descendants shall be like the dust of the earth, and you shall spread abroad to the west and to the east and to the north and to the south; and by you and your descendants shall all the families of the earth bless themselves. Behold, I am with you and will keep you wherever you go, and will bring you back to this land; for I will not leave you until I have done that of which I have spoken to you."*

Jacob awakened from the dream filled with wonder, surprise, and fear. "Surely the Lord is in this place; and I did not know it," he said to himself. "How awesome is this place! This is none other than the house of God, and this is the gate of heaven." Jacob picked up the stone he had used for a pillow, placed it on top of a pile of other stones to create a shrine, and carefully poured a stream of pure oil on top of it. As he did this, Jacob made a sacred vow, saying, "If God will be with me, and will keep me in this way that I go, and will give me bread to eat and clothing to wear, so that I come again to my father's house in peace, then the Lord shall be my God, and this stone, which I have set up for a pillar, shall be God's house; and of all that thou givest me I will give the tenth to thee."

When Jacob originally fled Beersheba he had many reasons to worry about his future. He was leaving his family and his home behind and heading for an unknown land, to marry a woman he had never met. Even though he had been given his father's precious blessing, the deceptive way in which he had received it couldn't help but make Jacob wonder if God might have turned away from him. Jacob must also have been thinking about his enraged brother, Esau, who was probably pursuing him through the desert at that very moment. And perhaps Jacob was also thinking of his forefathers Cain and Abel and the tragic result of their fraternal quarrel. Alone in the wilderness, troubled by these many worries and fears, Jacob went to sleep and had the amazingly powerful dream of reassurance. The glorious vision of the angels of God ascending and descending on the ladder revealed to him a mysteriously powerful connection between earthly and heavenly realities. God's words of comfort, consolation, and guidance gave Jacob a profoundly revitalizing confidence that God would always be there to protect and care for him.

Without a doubt, the story of Jacob and his dream of the heavenly ladder has been shaped by the theological interests and biases of the authors of the book of Genesis. There is no way to be absolutely certain that Jacob really had this dream (or that there was even a real person named Jacob). However, the Bible story bears striking similarities to the kinds of dreams described by people in today's society: At a moment of grave personal crisis, when the future seems fraught with uncertainty, a wonderfully vivid dream comes to reassure the dreamer that hope is still alive and that the caring presence of a transcendent power will remain to guide him or her through the present crisis.

Whatever the truth of its theological or historical claims, the story of Jacob's dream has a deep *experiential* truth that resonates clearly with many people's dreams in the modern world, more than three thousand years later.

The Spontaneous Creation of New Religions

In many of the world's cultural traditions, important religious beliefs and practices originated as thankful responses to the Divine for bestowing the gift of an especially powerful and reassuring dream. Indeed, whole religious movements have grown out of particularly striking dream experiences. What sparks these dream-inspired religious movements is often a combination, within a single individual's dreaming imagination, of an acute *personal* crisis and a terrible *communal* crisis.

The "dreamer religions" that sprang up in several Native American communities in the early and middle nineteenth century provide a poignant illustration of this process. During this time the U.S. government was intensifying its military efforts to push the Native Americans off the lands that white settlers were claiming for their own. The Washini people, who had long dwelled in the forests and mountains of the Pacific northwest, suffered a series of especially devastating defeats at the hands of the much better armed U.S. Cavalry. Smohalla, the Washini chieftain, was forced to flee with his people up the Columbia River in search of a safer place to dwell. As Smohalla and the other Washini abandoned their traditional homeland and hurried to escape the violent attacks of the cavalry, another tragedy struck: Smohalla's daughter suddenly became sick, and in just a matter of days she died. Smohalla had been training his daughter to become his successor as spiritual leader of the tribe, but when she fell ill, none of his medicines or healing rituals could save her.

Stunned by the double blow of his people's forced relocation and his daughter's abrupt death, Smohalla sat at her grave, praying and singing, until he fell asleep and had this dream:

> *He traveled to the spirit world, where the god Nami Piap taught*
> *him a sacred dance and numerous religious songs. Nami Piap said*
> *to him, "Teach the people to be good, do good, and live like Indians.*
> *Give them this song and show them this dance."*

When Smohalla awoke, he immediately gathered all the people of his tribe and spoke to them of his dream. He told the people that Nami Piap had sent him back to earth to teach them these new songs and this new dance and to revive their faith in the old Washini ways and traditions. His tribe's people enthusiastically agreed, and soon other Washini groups in the region were performing the songs and the dance Smohalla learned from Nami Piap. This dream-inspired revival of traditional spirituality gave the Washini people new strength to face a future in which the very survival of their culture was in danger.

In this case the combination of a personal crisis and a communal crisis generated a dream that provided new hope and vitality at *both* levels. Smohalla's dream vision renewed his personal hope for the future, which had been profoundly shaken by the unexpected death of his daughter, and it also helped to renew the spiritual faith of his people, who had become desperate after so many disastrous battles with the U.S. Cavalry. Smohalla was just one of the dozens of tribal leaders who, guided by revelatory dream visions, tried to help the Native American people regain a sense of meaning and value in their lives. U.S. government officials bitterly denounced these new spiritual movements as "dreamer religions," scorning them as dangerously anti-Christian and politically subversive. But the movements continued to spring up and flourish despite the government's efforts to suppress them. The reassurance dreams of Smohalla and other Native American leaders became rallying points for other people in their communities who were also feeling afraid, disoriented, and desperate, helping them to make sense of their painful, confusing present and reviving their hopes for a better, more peaceful future.

The Ultimate Origins of Big Dreams

When Melinda left home to start her freshman year at a small Midwestern college, she had a terrible first few months. She struggled with her schoolwork, she couldn't make any new friends, and her relationship with her hometown boyfriend, who was attending another school, was falling apart. One night while she was at home during Christmas vacation, Melinda had this dream:

> *I'm sitting under a willow tree, on a vast, open field. There are*
> *gentle hills of green grass in the distance. The sky is a beautiful*
> *crystal blue. There are no birds singing, though, and I think about*
> *how strange that is. I'm looking down, playing with a little trinket*
> *in my hands, when Jesus suddenly appears before me. I look up and*
> *smile. I'm not afraid or scared. It's almost as if I was expecting him*
> *to come. I say hello and invite him to sit down next to me. I ask*
> *him to help me, and he says he will. He tells me that things are*
> *never going to be perfect in my life and that the sooner I realize*
> *that, I'll have an easier time. Then he holds my hand, and I feel*
> *a peace wash over me that literally feels like a light rain.*

Melinda's dream responded with a direct and transformative power to her feelings of emotional crisis. "I've never had any sort of encounter with a 'being,' for lack of a better word, from heaven or a power higher than us until that dream," Melinda said afterward. "I remember waking up from the dream happy and with a totally different attitude about my life. I gained an appreciation for life that I didn't have before. Now God has a special place deep in my heart. I think my dream was so phenomenal to me because I could literally feel Jesus in me. It was a great feeling, and in the dream it was very intense."

What are people to make of such dreams? Are people like Melinda *really* encountering Jesus, God, the gods, or other spirit beings in their dreams? Or are those figures in fact nothing more than the neurologically generated fantasies of the dreamers' own unconscious minds?

Instead of choosing sides in this debate, I believe it's best to focus on the well-documented fact that whatever their ultimate origins, whether they come from neurons firing in the brain or divine beings guiding the soul (or, in some mysterious fashion, from *both* these sources), these extraordinary dreams have a powerfully transformative effect on the dreamers. As a direct consequence of these dreams, the dreamers are much better able to face the difficulties confronting them and to move forward with strength and confidence into their future. Again I urge readers to keep an open mind on what kind of language is most appropriate for explaining the nature and the function of big dreams. If you can restrain your rational mind's urge to define and categorize, and if you can concentrate instead on developing a deeper familiarity with the variety of symbols, images, themes, and emotions that appear in people's big dreams, you will find this the best path toward deciding for yourself where you believe your own most extraordinary dreams ultimately originate.

CHAPTER TWO

Dreams of Making Love

All days are nights to see till I see thee
And nights bright days when dreams do show me thee.

—William Shakespeare,
Sonnet 44

One of the most surprising findings of modern laboratory research is that REM sleep always brings with it a high degree of sexual arousal. Every time the brain enters a REM phase, there is a sudden and very large increase in the flow of blood to the genitals, leading to erections in men and clitoral swelling in women. This natural connection between REM sleep and sexual arousal is not related in any way to a person's waking-life sexual activity. Whether you made love right before going to sleep or have been abstinent for several months, your brain and genitals will follow their same basic rhythm of activation and arousal, night after night. This close connection between REM sleep and sexuality has given medical doctors a new tool to use in the diagnosis and treatment of patients suffering from impotence or other types of sexual dysfunction. Doctors now have the option of sending their patients to sleep laboratories for a night or two of observation: If the dysfunction also appears during REM sleep, the cause is probably a physical one; but if there's no change in normal sexual arousal during REM sleep, then the cause is likely to be psychological in nature.

It is interesting that although waking activities do not influence sexual arousal during REM sleep, disruptions to REM sleep *do seem to affect* sexual behavior in waking life. Researchers have found that when certain mammals are experimentally deprived of REM sleep, they experience a dramatic increase in their efforts to find sexual satisfaction. As one researcher described this startling phenomenon, "Cats and rats [that have been REM sleep–deprived] would sometimes have frenzied sexual activity and mount virtually anything, including blocks of wood." Researchers haven't yet observed any such amorous exuberance in their human subjects, although one study did show that REM sleep–deprived people will spend more time gazing at the erotic content of selected famous paintings than will people who have enjoyed a normal amount of REM sleep.

Wet Dreams

In both men and women, the sexual arousal that accompanies REM sleep regularly leads all the way to physical climax. Beginning in adolescence, boys experience seminal emissions, and girls experience orgasms during their sleep. It is obviously difficult to study a phenomenon like this with much precision, but it appears that these nocturnal climaxes initially occur *before* people have had any waking-life sexual experience. Researchers hope that future studies will provide more details about the precise role of wet dreams in the physical and emotional changes that come with the onset of puberty.

The fact that humans regularly experience sexual arousal and climax has posed a serious problem for Christian theologians through the centuries. As far back as Saint Augustine in the fifth century A.D., Christians have worried that wet dreams were sinful violations of God's laws regarding sexual morality. In his autobiography, *The Confessions*, Augustine described his lifelong struggle with sexual desire and said his conversion to Christianity at the age of thirty-two finally gave him the strength to control his lusts and to adopt a life of pure chastity. However, Augustine admitted that, to his surprise and disappointment, even after his conversion he continued to have vividly realistic sexual experiences in his dreams.

Augustine prayed to God to help him make sense of these deeply troubling experiences:

> But in my sleep, . . . there still live images of acts which were fixed there by my sexual habit. These images attack me. While I am awake they have no force, but in sleep they not only arouse pleasure but even elicit consent, and are very like the actual act. The illusory image within the soul has such force upon my flesh that false dreams have an effect on me when asleep, which the reality could not have when I am awake. During this time of sleep surely it is not my true self, Lord my God? Yet how great a difference between myself at the time when I am asleep and myself when I return to the waking state.

Augustine went on to beg God to "extinguish the lascivious impulses of my sleep." Augustine apparently believed that his sexually pleasurable dreams were not a part of his "true self," and if the dreams could be eliminated, his soul would at last be absolutely pure and free of sin.

Other early Christians suffered similar problems with their sexual dreams. The Desert Fathers, the ascetic Christian men whose intense religious yearnings led them to renounce all worldly pleasures and to live a life of solitude in the wilderness, blamed Satan for sending such dreams. A monk named Antiochus Monachus, who lived outside of Jerusalem in the seventh century A.D., preached to his fellow Christians that dreams "are the illusions of evil demons to deceive us. . . . Their enticements [have the] purpose of carrying a man off to pleasure." Monachus warned his followers that all dreams have this potential to deceive people with sinful temptations, and he insisted the safest and most virtuous attitude is to ignore dreams entirely. Unfortunately, many contemporary Christians continue to fear the possibility of demonic influences in dreams, even though the Bible is filled with a number of very positive stories about revelatory dreams sent directly by God to guide and comfort people. About a year ago, a friend of mine who's a spiritual director suggested to the owners of her local religious bookstore that they carry one of my books, *Spiritual Dreaming*, which discusses the role of dreams in the world's religious traditions. The bookstore owners brusquely refused: They told my friend that dreams are too confusing and dangerous to bother with, and a good Christian doesn't need them.

Dreams That Kindle Romantic Passion

Whether or not dreaming is caused by the malicious actions of wicked demons, the connection between REM sleep and sexual arousal is one of the most solid findings of modern laboratory research, and it raises a basic evolutionary question: What adaptive function does this connection serve? Is there any purpose or value to the sexually charged dreaming that all humans are hardwired to experience every night of their adult lives?

The immediate answer is yes, the sexual arousal that naturally accompanies REM sleep has the important evolutionary function of priming the human reproductive system and keeping it in good working order. The ability to reproduce successfully is of course the number one biological aim of any organism. REM sleep evidently promotes that crucial ability in humans by creating the psychophysiological conditions in which they can first experience, and then maintain throughout their lives, the healthy, energetic functioning of sexual desires. Just as REM sleep contributes to the development and maintenance of the brain, it also helps to initiate, support, and fine-tune the workings of the reproductive system. From an evolutionary perspective, the value of REM sleep is very great—by giving people an alert brain and ready-to-go genitals, REM sleep improves their chances of succeeding in the basic biological struggle to survive and reproduce.

But again, as was stated in chapter 1, the functions of REM sleep seem to have nothing to do with dreaming, or at least with any of the dreams people happen to remember. The two-plus hours of sexual arousal all humans experience during a normal night's sleep proceed for the most part without any conscious awareness or recollection. Even when subjects in the sleep lab are awakened in the very middle of a REM-sleep phase (and thus with quite obvious erections or clitoral swellings), the dreams they remember often have no direct sexual content. The implication of this fact is readily apparent: People don't *have* to remember or consciously interpret their dreams for them to serve their basic functions.

Why is it, then, that *some* dreams strike people with a sexual content so strong, so intense, so amazingly *real* that the dreamers literally cannot forget them? Are there any special values in those sexual dreams that people most definitely *do* remember, dreams whose vivid imagery and incredibly stimulating sensations have the power to burn themselves into the dreamer's awareness?

Bobby was a sixteen-year-old high school student who had dated several girls but had not, despite his most gallant efforts at romantic persuasion, slept with any of them. One night he had this dream:

> *I go to this girl's house so we can study together. She's the most beautiful girl I've ever seen, but she has no face, so I can't tell who she is. Instead of studying in her room we become more intimate, to the point where we want to have sex. But her parents are home, so we tell them we're going out for a bite to eat. Then we go to some park and have outrageous sex in my truck; it was the most awesome thing. But later her parents get worried about her, and they find out, and the dad wants to kill me, literally. I wake up right as we come to face her parents.*

Bobby's dream was so memorable to him because of the wonderfully pleasurable erotic feelings he experienced in the dream ("it was the most awesome thing, like nothing I've ever imagined"). Although he had had precious little sexual experience in his waking life, Bobby learned in his dream what it's like to have a wildly enjoyable and deeply fulfilling sexual encounter. It's as if his dream were saying to him, "Here, *this* is what it feels like, *this* is what you should be trying to find and experience in waking life." The value of Bobby's vividly remembered dream is thus to guide his sexual development, to give him a clear and unforgettable idea of how it feels to experience sexual pleasure and satisfaction.

Many people have sexual dreams like Bobby's in which they are making love in a way that's unusually exciting and stimulating. It may be that they are with a special partner, or in a particularly lovely setting, or using an especially arousing position. There is no need to go into graphic details here (I'd prefer that this book not receive an NC-17 rating!), but what can be said is that these dreams almost always have a powerfully stimulating impact on the dreamer. The intensely memorable qualities of such dreams give people new ideas about how they can find sexual fulfillment in their waking lives. As with Bobby's dream, these dreams of passion have the effect of arousing people's desires and aiming them toward their fullest expression and most pleasurable satisfaction in waking life. If the sexual dreams people don't remember keep their reproductive systems in good working order, the sexual dreams they *do* remember teach them how very much fun it can be to *use* that system.

A closer look at Bobby's experience shows that his dream actually goes further and reveals to him a serious obstacle in his waking-life quest for sexual fulfillment. The setting of his dream is perfectly normal—he's with a girl in her family's house, studying in her room, and then driving with her in his truck to a local park. These are ordinary settings and situations that Bobby has been in many times before. This in itself is significant because it suggests that Bobby's desires can be satisfied right where he is. As the dream portrays it, he doesn't have to travel to a distant land or completely change his life—he can find what he wants in the normal, everyday circumstances of his current waking world. That's the good news of the dream. The bad news comes in the symbolic form of the faceless girl. Dreams often have a particular element or image that is absolutely bizarre; everything else in the dream may be normal and true-to-life, but there's one certain detail that stands out as being extremely weird, unusual, or impossible. (This will be discussed at greater length in chapter 5.) The girl with no face in Bobby's dream is such a detail, and it guides his conscious awareness to reflect on an important truth: Impersonal sexual encounters can be enjoyable, but they often have frightening and even dangerous consequences. Many teenage boys like Bobby (and, sadly, many adult men as well) become so obsessively intent on satisfying their sexual urges that they don't care *who* their partner is. In the symbolic language of Bobby's dream, the girl might as well have no face; so long as she's beautiful and willing, it doesn't matter who she is as an individual. But the dream figure of the vengeful father makes Bobby realize that he can get in serious trouble by adopting such an attitude. This is perhaps the deepest level of the dream's meaning for Bobby's young life: Casual sex may be fun, but it can also be very dangerous.

Like most big dreams, Bobby's leaves him with something new to think about. It also leaves him with a new possibility for the future. What if Bobby could learn to see the girl's face? Using this symbolic figure from his dream to reflect on his waking life, what if Bobby learned to form real relationships with the girls he dated and to recognize and respect each of their individual personalities? What new kinds of sexual fulfillment might become possible as a result? The dream leaves Bobby to muse on these questions, with the beautiful but faceless girl as his dream-world companion and guide.

Dreams like Bobby's seem to build on the naturally high degree of sexual arousal that always accompanies REM sleep, with the explicitly sexual content of the dreams having a close connection to the simultaneous physical experiences of the dreamer's body. Other dreams, however, are not quite so graphic and obvious about their sexual intentions. Although these dreams may also be initially stimulated by REM sleep, their symbolic imagery is subtler and more discreet. This is particularly true when the passions being revealed are *taboo*—when a person's desires conflict with or violate the morals and expectations of society.

Miranda was a woman in her midtwenties who was in the midst of a long, painful breakup with her boyfriend, Tim. One night, after a four-hour phone conversation in which they both realized that their relationship could not be saved, Miranda went to sleep and had this dream:

> *I am at the top of a staircase, which is narrow and winding.*
> *It's like the stairway at a school library, but also like the stairs in*
> *my apartment building. I am sitting on a pillow, and my friend*
> *Sara is with me, sitting behind me on the cushion, as if we are*
> *riding a motorcycle. We descend the staircase on this pillow, which*
> *is motorized and moves with great speed. I am experiencing a very*
> *intense feeling of exhilaration and speed. Both of us are laughing*
> *and feeling reckless because of the speed. Then we get to the bottom*

of the staircase, which opens into an empty auditorium. On the
stage, Tim is performing a Shakespearean monologue. It seems to
be Hamlet's "To Be or Not to Be" soliloquy. He is dressed completely
in black and is very pale.

One immediate association Miranda had with the dream was
that in her waking life she had been having troubles with her car
insurance. She had canceled one policy, but the new one had not
yet taken effect; the result was that she was temporarily forbidden
from driving any kind of vehicle. Another association Miranda made
was to her recent reading of Carl Jung's autobiography, *Memories,*
Dreams, Reflections, in which he gives an evocative description of the
"descent" he made into the depths of his unconscious, a journey
that was steep, fast, and uncontrollable.

The key association, however, was to the figure of Sara, one of
Miranda's closest friends. Sara had recently "come out," and she
and Miranda had often talked about homosexuality, different kinds
of intimate relationships, and the effects of a masculine social order
on women's growth and development. Miranda recalled one particular conversation with Sara, when they were sitting together in a
booth at their favorite bar: Miranda admitted how strange it was
that although she had always felt closer to her women friends, she
continued to seek romantic relationships with men.

With these waking-life connections in mind, Miranda saw her
dream as a dramatic and compelling encouragement to continue
questioning her waking-life assumptions about sexuality. The first
half of the dream gave her an extremely vivid sensory experience of
what a romantic relationship with Sara might be like. It would be
intense and exhilarating, joyful and reckless; it would be a wild
journey into the mysterious depths of her unconscious desires.
However, Miranda realized such a relationship would also be a
serious violation of social morality. In waking life, Miranda knew
that if she drove any kind of motor vehicle, she could be arrested,
fined, and even jailed. Her dream made use of this waking concern
to create the bizarre but quite meaningful image of the motorized
pillow: This image symbolically showed Miranda that a sexual relationship with Sara would be "unlawful" and might cause her problems with certain friends and family members, not to mention all

those people in modern society who condemn homosexuality as perverse, immoral, and sinful.

In the second half of her dream, Sara disappears, and Miranda is in the shadows of a large auditorium, watching her boyfriend, Tim. He's standing by himself on a theater stage, pale and dressed all in black, reciting Hamlet's haunting meditation on self-annihilation (see p. 87). In reflecting on the dream, Miranda was struck by the sharp contrast between the somber, despairing tone of this scene with Tim and the happy, almost giddy exuberance of the previous one with Sara. Miranda realized that in waking life Tim was probably very sad and upset about the ending of their relationship; she hadn't really thought of that before. But she also realized that the huge emotional contrast between the dream's two scenes was forcing her to rethink the romantic choices she had made in her life and to question her assumption that she could find sexual fulfillment in a relationship only with a man.

The dream didn't tell Miranda to *do* one thing or another in her love life—dreams are rarely that directive. Rather, the dream gave Miranda something new to think about. The unforgettably wonderful feelings she experienced in that passionate dream ride with Sara opened up new lines of thought, new realms of emotion, and new possibilities for the future expression and satisfaction of her sexual desires.

Miranda's dream raises an interesting set of questions regarding sexual dreams. Why do these dreams so often refer to sexual matters indirectly, in the form of symbols? Why, for example, doesn't Miranda's dream simply show her making love with Sara? Why the strange business about a motorized pillow roaring down a staircase?

As many readers probably know, Freud had a ready answer to these questions. The founder of psychoanalysis said that people are so uncomfortable with their deepest sexual desires, especially taboo desires like having a romantic attraction to a member of the same sex, that they cannot face their wishes as they really are. As a result, dreams devise an elaborate system of duplicitous symbols to protect people from the shocking truth about themselves. Freud believed that people dream of swords and purses instead of penises and vaginas (and rushing down staircases instead of actually having sex) because the shocking reality of their sexual desires is simply too much to bear. In his view, the confusing symbolism of sexual dreams functions to guard the moral sensitivities of waking consciousness.

But Freud's explanation doesn't really work in Miranda's case. It didn't take Miranda long to see that her dream was referring quite directly to unconscious homosexual desires. If the image of riding the motorized pillow with Sara was somehow intended to mask her deepest sexual desires, it did a remarkably poor job of deceiving her. A more likely explanation is that the image symbolically expressed certain meanings that her dreaming imagination could not express in more direct ways. Miranda's dream didn't simply show her having sex with Sara; it showed her having *fun* with Sara— doing something with her that's wild, playful, silly, and exciting. These are precisely the qualities that were missing in Miranda's relationship with Tim and that had been missing with most of her other boyfriends. Her dream created a striking, if bizarre, symbolic image that made clear to her what those qualities are, what they feel like, and where she might turn to find them in her waking life.

The strange symbolism of Miranda's dream did not hide the truth about her sexual desires; on the contrary, it *revealed* the truth and focused her conscious attention on precisely those aspects of her romantic relationships where her deepest desires were not being satisfied.

Sex as a Symbol

Dreams like Miranda's express sexual meanings in the form of strange, unusually creative symbols. Other dreams do the opposite, however, and use sexuality itself as a symbol to express other kinds of meaning. This point was well understood by one of the first dream researchers in Western history, Artemidorus of Daldis. Artemidorus lived near Rome in the second century A.D., during the glorious height of the Roman empire's power and prosperity. He spent many years traveling through the Mediterranean world making a careful study of the dream interpretation practices used by different peoples and different cultures. In his book, *Oneirocrit-ica*, Artemidorus devoted several pages to the symbolic meanings of various sexual images that appear from time to time in people's dreams. Artemidorus's basic method in making his interpretations was to connect the sexual encounter in the dream with a metaphor-ically similar situation in the dreamer's life. Here are two sample passages from *Oneirocritica*:

> To have sexual intercourse with a god or goddess or to be pos-sessed by a god signifies death for a sick man. For the soul pre-dicts meetings and intercourse with the gods when it is about to abandon the body in which it dwells. But for other men, provided they have derived pleasure from the intercourse, it signifies assis-tance from one's superiors. If [the dreamers] did not derive any pleasure from the act, it means fears and confusion.

> The case of one's mother is both complex and manifold and admits of many different interpretations—a thing not all dream interpreters have realized. The fact is that the mere act of inter-course by itself is not enough to show what is portended. Rather, the manner of the embraces and the various positions of the bod-ies indicate different outcomes.

Artemidorus said the same dream image could have many pos-sible meanings, depending on the particular details of the image, the dreamer's emotional experience within the dream, and the outer-world circumstances of the dreamer's waking life (e.g., the dreamer's health, social status, or financial situation). It's true that many of Artemidorus's actual interpretations sound arbitrary or even con-trived, but the basic interpretive principles he used are still valid. Although few people today have dreams of fooling around with Athena or Zeus, the sexual symbolism of their dreams can still pro-vide very specific insights into waking life concerns and conflicts.

Susan, a woman in her thirties who was struggling to balance the competing demands of being a wife, a mother, and a business executive all at the same time, had a strangely frightening dream in which she was enslaved in a small, dark closet. Through a peep-hole in the closet door she could look outside, and to her shock and horror, she could see her company's boss and her husband having homosexual sex with each other. In reflecting on the dream, Susan immediately understood that it wasn't about a "real" homosexual affair between her boss and her husband. Rather, the dream was using that startling sexual image as a symbol to reveal to her the previously unrecognized connection between these two men and the way they were mistreating her. Her boss was always giving her unreasonable deadlines and talking to her as if she was a little girl, and her husband put little time or effort into childrearing and housework, essentially leaving it all to her. Susan's boss and her husband were indeed "joined" in their exploitation of her labor and their enjoyment of selfishly "masculine pleasures." The symbolic sexual imagery of her dream pointed Susan's attention to this frightening similarity between her boss and her husband, and it gave her a new way to focus her emotions. What had before been only a diffuse sense of anger and frustration was now, thanks to her dream, a clearly perceived pattern of mistreatment.

People who are happily married or enjoying a stable monogamous relationship are occasionally startled by dreams in which they commit adultery. Even though the people have no real romantic interest in anyone other than their spouse or partner, their dreams involve them in shockingly passionate sexual liaisons with all sorts of different people. The attention-grabbing quality of these dreams is actually the symbolic point: The dreams use the image and experience of adultery to guide the dreamer's conscious awareness toward some waking-life situation in which there is a serious conflict of commitment. For example, a forty-two-year-old woman named Cathy, married with two children, had a dream in which she was making love to a male friend she hadn't seen in several years. She awoke from the dream feeling strangely disturbed and deeply guilty. But then, as her thoughts moved from the dream to what she had planned to do that morning, the meaning of the dream began to dawn on her. Cathy had always wanted to write fiction, and her children were finally getting old enough that she could have a little quiet time to herself every now and then to pursue her writing. That very morning, Sunday, was supposed to be one of those times because she had persuaded her husband to take the kids out for a few hours. Cathy realized that the aching guilt she felt on awakening from her adulterous dream was identical to the guilt she felt in asking her husband and children to leave the house that morning. And, when she remembered that her male friend was, in waking life, a writer, Cathy understood that the dream was a dramatic commentary on her struggle to balance her love of her family with her long-suppressed desire to write fiction. From the perspective of her family, Cathy's love of writing seems to be adultery, a violation of her marriage vows and a breaking of trust with her husband and children.

Once again, the dream didn't tell the dreamer what to do. Instead, Cathy's dream did something much more valuable: It gave her a new perspective on her situation and deepened her awareness of how serious the struggle is between these two powerful commitments in her life. The sexual imagery of the dream stimulated Cathy to think anew of her passion for writing and how it affects, and does not affect, her relations with her husband and children.

Adultery dreams are often closely related to waking-life creative activities. John, a twenty-seven-year-old who split his work life between computer programming and acting in a local theater, had this dream:

> *I'm in a small store, on a nice sunny day. The clerk in the store is Ann, the director of my current show. I come into the store and walk down the aisle past her. We look into each other's eyes but don't say anything. I turn around and come up next to her. We stare at each other and then I start to kiss her. I kiss her ears and neck while unzipping her uniform shirt. While I am doing this, I look out the window and see my fiancée walking home on the sidewalk across the street. I continue to kiss Ann and she kisses me back. We stumble down the aisle knocking things off the shelves.*

The dream goes on from here, with John and Ann enjoying a frolicking session of what he called "really powerful and physical sex." The experience was so intense that when John woke up he realized he'd had a wet dream. He felt a sudden and intense guilt because he saw his fiancée asleep in bed right next to him; what he had felt in the dream had been so incredibly *real* that, for a moment, he wasn't sure if it was just a dream or something he had actually done. But then, as he thought about it, John saw the connection between his feelings in the dream and his feelings about the beginning of rehearsals for a new play, which Ann was directing. John had never worked with Ann before, and although he had no romantic attraction to her, he was very excited about doing the play with her. He knew that putting on a professional theater production is always a physically demanding but emotionally exhilarating experience, bringing pleasures just as wonderfully satisfying as those he experienced in his dream. By symbolically expressing these pleasures as an adulterous sexual affair, the dream brought to John's conscious attention a crucial question: How do the pleasures of the theater relate to the pleasures he enjoys with his soon-to-be wife? The dream didn't answer this question, which goes right to the heart of who John is and where he wants to go with his life. But in leaving him with that unforgettable experience of lustfully crashing through the small store with Ann, the dream guaranteed that John would continue to think about it and keep reflecting on how best to express and satisfy the different passions in his life.

To interpret sexually explicit dreams like these as symbols of nonsexual desires is not to deny that many other dreams have much more direct and literal meanings. Sometimes dreaming about having an adulterous affair really *is* about a person's romantic attraction to someone other than his or her spouse. But the main point here is that sexual imagery and sensations in dreams can express a wide variety of different meanings by using the deeply arousing nature of sexual experience to focus people's attention on certain situations in their waking lives. When people have dreams of incest, for example, it is not necessarily because they were actually incest victims or are now contemplating incest; in most cases the shocking dream image is aimed at concentrating the dreamers' attention on something going on in their lives—something that may have an "incestuous" or inappropriately close quality to it. Likewise, a dream of being raped may relate to a waking-life situation where the dreamer is feeling violated; a dream of raping may relate to something the dreamer is using great force and violence to obtain; a dream of sadomasochism, to a relationship in which the dreamer feels either dominant or submissive; a dream of masturbation, to a waking activity that gives only the dreamer pleasure. Sometimes a dream has both symbolic *and* literal aspects to it. A dream of molesting a child may relate to an actual past experience of being molested and also to a current waking-life situation in which the dreamer struggles to find a mature romantic relationship. As always, the dreamer is in the best position to say for sure where the primary meanings of his or her dream may lie.

New Perspectives on Relationship Troubles

Freud was once asked to describe, based on his years of psychoanalytic research, what he thought were the ultimate goals of human life. Instead of a grand and elaborate theoretical exposition, Freud said only this: "lieben und arbeiten" ("to love and to work"). Setting aside for the moment the importance of creative work (a topic that will be discussed in chapter 8), most people would probably agree that the experience of love is the single greatest source of meaning and value in their lives. To have intimate, caring, loving relationships is by all counts a supreme good, something as fundamental to our well-being as food, air, and sunlight.

Real love is not always easy to find, however. Most people spend much of their lives struggling with painful difficulties in forming and maintaining romantic relationships. The paradox of modern society is that sexual imagery is everywhere, but romantic fulfillment is perhaps harder to find than ever. Despite the inescapably explicit sexual content of ads, movies, and television shows, and despite the urgent advice of talk show hosts, therapists, and sex doctors, many people in today's society feel a terrible desperation about finding truly fulfilling romantic relationships.

So can dreams help you improve your love life? If only it were that easy! The more modest truth is that some dreams do speak directly to people's romantic concerns, giving them a better understanding of how to express and to satisfy that fundamental human yearning to love and to be loved.

A few of these dreams are remarkably straightforward and unambiguous in their meanings. One night Jimmy, a nineteen-year-old college sophomore, had a dream in which he was at the beach with his girlfriend. In the dream, it is a pleasant day, and they have a decent time talking and lying around on the beach. Jimmy didn't think much of the dream. But the next night he had the same basic dream, with two key differences: Instead of being with his girlfriend he is with another female friend, and instead of having a moderately good time, he has a total blast. Jimmy awoke from the second dream feeling happy and excited, and he realized the two dreams were crystallizing various emotions he had felt in his waking life. He realized his relationship with his girlfriend had grown stale and monotonous for both of them, and he had to admit that he had much more fun spending time with the other young woman. In this case the dreamer did act on his dreams: Jimmy broke up with his girlfriend and started going out with the woman in his second dream.

A dream can of course guide a person in the opposite direction, too. A young woman named Caroline and her boyfriend had a terrible fight one night, and afterward she went to sleep resolved to break up with him the next day. But then she had a dream in which she and her boyfriend were doing all the things they most enjoyed doing together. When she woke up, Caroline understood that the dream was reminding her of everything that was good about her relationship with her boyfriend. She still felt angry and hurt from the previous night, but the positive, hopeful feelings of her dream persuaded Caroline to stay with him and try to work through their problems.

Every once in a while, a dream does more than point out new aspects of a troubled relationship. These rare but fascinating dreams go on to frame the dreamer's romantic situation in a broader context of meaning, often with explicitly religious or existential dimensions. Rose, a twenty-four-year-old married woman with a two-year-old daughter, had this dream:

In the dream I can see myself asleep in bed next to my husband.
It is as if I am looking down from the ceiling watching us sleep.
As I watch myself sleep, an angel or spirit comes to me and takes
me up through the ceiling into the starry sky. I cannot see this
spirit, but I can feel her presence. As we soar through space,

*I feel totally exhilarated. It seems there is some sort of static
electricity surging through my body. The spirit asks me if I want
to see heaven. I ecstatically agree. Just then I look ahead and I can
see where the sky and stars end and heaven begins. It is similar
to the view from the beach where the water ends and the horizon
begins. It is a bright, beautiful, and misty place. I feel an overwhelming sense of peacefulness and happiness. Just as we are about
to cross over into heaven, I feel an urge to share this with my husband. I reach down with my arm and somehow am able to reach
all the way back through the ceiling into our bedroom. I grab hold
of his hand and "telepathically" tell him to come with me to see this
beautiful place. But instead of floating up to meet me, he pulls me
back into our bedroom. The ceiling closes up and I do not get to see
heaven. I am extremely disappointed.*

As readers may have guessed (if only because of the similarity
with Karen's experience in chapter 1), this dream came to Rose at a
time when she and her husband were having serious problems with
their marriage. Their daughter was old enough to go to a neighborhood child care center, and Rose, to her husband's displeasure,
had returned to work and school after two years at home being a
full-time mother. The dream's powerful impact on Rose had several different sources: First was the strange initial perspective of
floating in the air above herself, a point of view that gave the whole
dream a quality of "higher awareness." Second was the female spirit
who guided Rose, a striking otherworldly figure with mysterious
powers far beyond the understanding of ordinary humans. And
third was the nearly indescribable sensation that Rose felt when she
approached heaven—she said later, "I remember feeling elated and
extremely peaceful and happy. These emotions were much more
intense than what I had ever experienced in an 'awake' state."

Rose knew that at one level the dream was referring to the
problems with her husband, that it was symbolically showing his
lack of support for her career. But she knew the dream was also
saying something else, something more fundamental about her life,
her hopes, and her dreams for the future. Rose wanted to "reach
for the stars," and she wanted her husband to join her in striving
for something greater in life; but he wouldn't, or couldn't, and

instead he pulled her back to the ground, back into the conjugal confines of their bedroom. The dream's divine imagery and incredible emotional vitality gave Rose a deep sense of confidence that she was right and that the vitality and mutuality of their marriage was at an end. But even though the dream seemed to support her feeling that her husband was holding her back in life, Rose was honest enough to admit that the dream could also be suggesting a more negative, self-critical explanation for her marital problems: Perhaps by diving back so quickly into her out-of-home activities Rose had been "drifting away" from her family. If that were true, perhaps then her husband was only trying to bring Rose back to earth, to "ground" her once again. This, by the way, is a perfect example of how big dreams prompt people to *think* differently, to consider different perspectives, to imagine new possibilities, and to reflect on possibly unpleasant truths about themselves.

In the end, Rose and her husband agreed to get a divorce. With the powerful dream image of the female spirit a vivid presence in her memory, Rose moved out and settled in a new home where she could focus on raising her daughter and pursuing her professional and educational aspirations.

Dreams of Bill

In the summer of 1992, I started a research project on the nature of political imagery in people's dreams. The project was aimed at bringing together two lines of thinking that had long been running through my mind. One came from reading a famous book called *The Meaning of Dreams* by cognitive psychologist Calvin Hall, in which he asserts that "dreams contain few ideas of a political or economic nature. They have little or nothing to say about current events in the world of affairs." This struck me as far too broad a generalization, for I had heard of many people who had experienced dreams directly relevant to political and/or economic aspects of their waking world. The second line of thinking arose from the writing of *Spiritual Dreaming*, in which I focused on historical and cross-cultural dream practices. In the course of doing research for the book, I found that people in various cultures around the world believe that dreams have the power to reveal valuable truths not only about the dreamer's own individual life but also about the dreamer's community. Throughout history people have relied on dreams to guide them in collective activities such as the building of temples and shrines, the performance of communal rituals and celebrations, the settlement of legal and economic conflicts, and the decision of whether to go to war.

Taken together, these two lines of thinking led me to wonder if, despite the pronouncements of psychologists like Calvin Hall, people today still have dreams that relate to important issues and concerns in their waking-world communities. If so, what would that mean for the understanding of the nature and functions of dreaming?

I figured if there was ever a time to look for evidence of a connection between dreams and current events, the 1992 U.S. presidential election was it. The campaign that year was lively and unpredictable, involving a close, hard-fought race among Arkansas Governor Bill Clinton, billionaire businessman Ross Perot, and the incumbent, President George Bush. Over that summer and fall, I gathered nearly two hundred dream reports from people around the country, and I examined the relationships between the contents of the dreams and the waking-life political attitudes of the dreamers. It turned out that many of the dreams had close, and often quite humorous, ties to the dreamer's views of the presidential campaign. One person, for example, dreamed the night after the first presidential debate that Bush and Clinton got into a huge food fight. Another person, who had a rather negative view of Ross Perot, dreamed that the diminutive Texan appeared in a purple suit and announced he was taking charge of a state mental hospital. And another person, who was happy about the results of the election, dreamed of seeing Clinton and his running mate, Al Gore, standing in a spotlight, their arms around each other, singing "Amazing Grace."

The basic finding of my research to this point was that, yes, at least some people do have dreams directly relating to current events in the world of politics. Dreams are not *only* about the dreamer's own internal worries and concerns. Sometimes the "inner world" of dreams offers direct and meaningful commentaries on the "outer world" of politics and society.

As I continued to collect dream reports in the months following the November election, a certain pattern began to appear in people's dreams of newly elected President Bill Clinton. In some dreams Clinton was dressed in casual clothing; in others he was sharing a meal with the dreamer; and in others he was sitting or standing near the dreamer, having a friendly, intimate conversation. A few of the reports involved women dreamers having romantic or sexual encounters with the president. The remarkable *closeness* to Bill Clinton that several people experienced in their dreams seemed to reflect his waking-world political ability to make voters feel a personal connection with him (many pundits and editorial writers said this ability was the crucial difference that helped him win the election). In most cases the people who dreamed about Bill Clinton had in fact voted for him and supported his political policies. Their dreams gave symbolic expression to the happiness they felt at the election of a president who they believed shared their feelings, values, and ideals.

Beth was one such Clinton supporter who voted for him in 1992 and who felt closely allied with his political goals. Like Clinton, she had come of political age in the 1960s. She had been politically active for most of her life, devoting herself to antiwar candidates and causes and then serving as a Democratic committeewoman in the 1970s. Her joyful happiness at Clinton's election and her feeling that his presidency would lead to the advancement of her most cherished political ideals were clearly expressed in her dreams. The first of these dreams, which came just a few nights after Clinton's election on November 4, is the most overtly sexual:

> We are with Bill and Hillary Clinton, among others. At some
> point, I go to try and repair something at the base of this sofa.
> (This is my house? It doesn't look like it.) The sofa is a boring,
> plaid thing with wood trim, and I'm on the floor at the far end,
> trying to reattach some dowel/rod that has come off. Bill Clinton
> has come over and is helping me, but as we're on the floor together,
> he's also promising to help me with other things, to get me what
> I want or need—it's some kind of work thing, I think. I realize he's
> being seductive, especially as we are lying on the floor and he is at
> my ear.

The dream goes on to portray, in vivid and surprisingly graphic terms, Beth giving him oral sex. When she woke up, Beth laughed aloud at the unusually lascivious nature of the dream. She understood that the dream was comparing the president to other seductive Southern men she had met in her life and was expressing her enthusiastic support for his policies. However, she knew the dream was also referring to the sexual misconduct charges that had dogged Clinton throughout the recently ended campaign. In waking life Beth had dismissed these charges as nothing more than politically motivated slander.

Beth's next dream followed the president's first State of the Union speech in February of 1993, which she had watched on TV with great pleasure. Like the previous dream, this one also used a powerful experience of physical intimacy as a symbol to express her political views and feelings:

> *Bill Clinton is there, and I ask if I can hug him. He opens his arms wide, and we give each other a wonderful, warm, sincere hug— actually, it's more my hugging him and his accepting my love and energy. It's a really nice encounter and hard to put into words.*

A few months later, Beth had a dream in which she was at some kind of college campus, part of a crowd waiting outside a building to hear the school president speak. She noticed that Bill Clinton was there in the crowd. Suddenly there was a commotion, and Beth heard people say it was an attempted assassination:

> *We all go inside the lobby of the building. Maybe I'll get to talk to Bill? Then he comes over to where I'm standing by the fireplace. He asks me something about what's going on but moves his face close to mine, ever so lightly nuzzling in. I realize he wants a whiff of my hair. I'm glad it's clean.*

Like many Clinton supporters, Beth felt that the relentless personal attacks on the president by his political opponents amounted to a kind of character assassination. She saw her dream as a dramatized, highly accurate reflection of her continuing allegiance to Clinton and his political ideals.

Over the next several years Beth had a few other dreams of the president, but it wasn't until late 1997 that one of those dreams really stood out in her memory. The day before the dream, she had read a long article by Gore Vidal in the *New Yorker* about the astonishing sexual misbehavior of John F. Kennedy during his three years in the White House. Beth was shocked by the article, which revealed that a politician she had revered was, underneath it all, an almost dangerously compulsive womanizer. That night she dreamed this:

> *I'm part of the Clinton entourage, staying in a room connected to other rooms—at a hotel in Arkansas, I think. And there's something about playing cards, and later, I'm resting on this bed that's positioned like a sofa under these windows. Clinton is there and he's tired. I get up and tell him, "Here, you're the president of the United States; you're the one who ought to be resting." And he lies down and I cover him up.*
>
> *Then we are in another room—the card room?—and he and I are seated on a sofa. He closes in on me and proposes that we need to get together. It would be very easy to yield, we're close enough for the kiss he's wrangling for, but I resist. I tell him I'm not that kind of girl. He persists in his entreaty, very close and quite appealing. I say honestly, "You're being so seductive and so sexy that I'm going to have to get out of here," and I rise. He reaches for me and says, "But what will we do?" I say, "Let's be friends," perfectly sincerely. He sniffs but I say, "Look, we're the same age and we both have really smart spouses," meaning we have a lot in common and it would be fun to be friends.*

It took Beth a while to fully wake up from the dream; she felt a moment or two of confusion about whether it had really been a dream or not. Once she was completely awake, her first thought was, "Yep, he really *is* a randy s.o.b." The previous day Clinton had given a long press conference in which he had defended himself against the various ethics charges brought against him. Combined with her association to the *New Yorker* article about JFK, Beth felt the dream was an attempt to reconcile her increasingly conflicted feelings about the president. She still believed he was doing an excellent job promoting the social and economic policies she believed were most important; but, like many other Clinton supporters, she was beginning to worry that his powerful charisma and seductive appeal had perhaps led him to cross lines of personal conduct that he should not have crossed.

I'm continuing my project on dreams and politics during the 2000 presidential campaign, and I'll be curious to see if the dreams show any effects of the Clinton-Lewinsky scandal on people's unconscious imagination. Will an intimate dream encounter with the president symbolize not a happy affirmation of shared political ideals, but rather a destructive violation of basic trust and morality?

Was Freud Right?

One of Freud's primary legacies was to remind people that dreams can be a valuable source of insight into their romantic yearnings and sexual desires. Of course Freud was not the first to see this connection between dreams and sexuality (recall the Christian Desert Fathers and their nightly battles against the seductive, lustful temptations of the devil). Freud's distinctive contribution was his careful, focused study of the "polymorphous perversity" of dreaming. He explored the incredibly variegated symbolism that dreams use to express sexual wishes, and he showed that dreams are remarkably informative expressions of people's struggles to satisfy their fundamentally human need to love.

It has become fashionable in some intellectual circles to denounce Freud and his psychoanalytic theories as outdated, misguided, and even fraudulent. On this particular point, however, the evidence shows that Freud was right: Dreams do indeed express unconscious sexual wishes, wishes that sometimes conflict with social morality and the dreamer's own conscious self-image. Where I agree with Freud's critics is in seeing problems with his explanation of the basic function that sexual dreams serve. In Freud's view, dreams have the aim of deceiving the dreamer, of deliberately hiding painful truths from conscious awareness. I don't believe this explanation stands up to close scrutiny. It may be true, as Freud claims, that people often resist confronting unpleasant or embarrassing aspects of themselves. Indeed, I think Freud's skepticism regarding a dreamer's ability to perceive meanings beyond the almost inevitable resistance of consciousness is worth taking to heart. But in my view, such resistance is a product of the unwill-ingness people often feel about changing and revising their self-images. The resistance is *not* the effect of any deliberate intention of the dreams themselves.

I would offer an alternative account of the function of these dreams. The sexual dreams that strike people with an especially powerful sense of realness have the vital and very positive function of stimulating their desires and guiding them toward their fullest waking-life satisfaction. The verisimilitude of these dreams, the intensely memorable feeling that the dream is *really happening*, can be understood as serving an important evolutionary purpose. The more arousing these dreams are, the more vividly they will be remembered. The more they are remembered, the more the dreamers will think about how to find a comparable kind of fulfill-ment in waking life. It's not that the dreamer will necessarily try to do what he or she did in the dream; rather, the dream prompts the dreamer to think about what real romantic fulfillment is like. Whether it's a dream of intense pleasure or one of terrible frustra-tion, the key impact of this type of dream on waking consciousness is to stimulate reflection on the nature of sexual fulfillment, how it feels, and what obstacles block the dreamer from its experience.

Putting it in strictly biological terms, sexual dreams strengthen people's basic ability to reproduce, and thus help to perpetuate the species. In this regard sexual dreams are a kind of self-maintenance program, a built-in feature that ensures all psychophysiological sys-tems will be ready for action whenever the dreamer has a waking-world opportunity for reproduction. I believe this same essential idea can be expressed in a less clinical and more spiritually sensitive fashion. Certain dreams burst onto conscious awareness with a power and vitality so astonishing that the dreamer cannot help but remember them. Some of these dreams focus the dreamer's atten-tion squarely on a romantic relationship, giving the dreamer a new perspective on the relationship and how satisfying, or unsatisfy-ing, it has become. Other dreams reveal previously unrecognized romantic wishes and desires, suggesting new possibilities for sexual experience, exploration, and fulfillment.

In a very basic sense, these dreams teach people what it means to love.

CHAPTER THREE

❦

Nightmares

Keeper: *Why looks your Grace so heavily today?*
Clarence: *O, I have passed a miserable night,*
            So full of fearful dreams, of ugly sights,
            That, as I am a Christian faithful man,
            I would not spend another such night
            Though 'twere to buy a world of happy days,
            So full of dismal terror was the time.

—William Shakespeare, *Richard III*

People's most memorable dreams are, in many cases, their most intense nightmares. There's no mystery as to why these dreams are remembered so clearly for years and even decades later—forgetting them is simply not an option. The dreamers will often say, "How could I ever forget suffering such incredible, unbearable anxiety, or witnessing such horrifying violence, or feeling such a helpless, desperate sense of vulnerability? How can I *not* remember these intensely frightening dreams?"

Nightmares stand out among all other dream experiences in *demanding* conscious attention. Even though the dreamers realize on awakening that the monster chasing them through the forest wasn't real, the heart-stopping fear they felt *was* real, and it doesn't go away as soon as they open their eyes. The true mystery, then, is whether people's nightmares serve any purpose or function. What value could there be in the deep sensations of fear, terror, and dread generated by these horrible dreams? What good could possibly come out of so much darkness?

In recent years researchers have looked closely at the psychophysiological elements of nightmares, and their findings have shown there are at least three distinct types of nightmares. The first is what can be called the *classic nightmare*. Usually occurring in the second half of the night toward the end of a long REM-sleep period, classic nightmares are similar to other dreams in that they have relatively distinct settings and characters and possess a discernible narrative structure. They differ from other dreams in that they are dominated by intense anxiety and/or a host of negative, unpleasant emotions (e.g., confusion, sadness, panic, shame, hopelessness). In some cases the dreamers can't specify what exactly makes their dreams feel so frightening—a seemingly ordinary object or an otherwise normal situation suddenly evokes terror so overwhelming that the dreamers have to wake themselves up to escape it.

Very different from a classic nightmare is a *night terror*. Night terrors usually occur within the first two hours of sleep, in non-REM sleep. The person experiences a strangely agitated and drawn-out arousal from sleep, with an extremely fast heartbeat; uncontrollably twitching muscles; ragged, labored breathing; and a feeling of pressure on the chest. Sometimes a brief bit of imagery comes along with the physical sensations, but many times there is no visual content whatsoever. This is why many researchers regard night terrors as physiological disorders of arousal rather than as true dream experiences. Waking-life stress and fatigue often contribute to the occurrence of night terrors.

The third type are *post-traumatic nightmares*, which are directly caused by a physically and/or emotionally traumatizing experience in waking life. They can occur in both REM sleep and non-REM sleep, and their imagery involves a graphic, hyperrealistic replaying of the horrible incident the dreamer suffered, exactly as it happened, over and over and over again. Along with the almost documentary-quality imagery, post-traumatic nightmares are often accompanied by yelling, crying, and a great deal of thrashing about in bed. Much of the research on post-traumatic nightmares has been done on wartime veterans and victims of the Holocaust, people who night after night dream about their unspeakably horrible experiences with battlefield carnage and concentration camp torture.

Things That Go Bump in the Night

Nightmares are most frequently experienced by young children between the ages of three and six. For many preschoolers the bad dreams come as often as two or three times a week. It could well be that infants have nightmares even more frequently than this; parents often suspect as much when their babies start screaming in the middle of the night for no apparent reason. Researchers will probably never know for sure because children younger than about three cannot verbally report their experiences. We do know, however, that the incidence of nightmares gradually tapers off as people get older. A grade school child may have a bad dream once a week, an adolescent once a month, and an adult once or twice a year.

The remarkably high frequency of nightmares in early childhood seems to be a natural feature of human development. All children, not just those who have suffered a major trauma or catastrophic crisis, experience nightmares on a fairly regular basis. In light of this fact, the question stated earlier in this chapter becomes even more puzzling: What possible adaptive value could there be in afflicting children of this very young age with horribly frightening dreams?

The answer to this question involves first imagining what it's like to be a young child:

You're a very small person in a very, very large world, a world dominated by all-powerful, all-knowing giants. At any moment one of those giants can suddenly snatch you up off the ground, or take a toy away from you, or simply disappear, leaving you all alone. Besides the giants, you also have to be worried about huge, smoking trucks, and roaring buses, and big, barking dogs, and maybe older siblings, too, demigiants every bit as dominating and unpredictable as the grown-up kind. Every day you have experiences that are new and challenging, that stretch your young mind, and that tax your small body. Things are constantly happening to you that are so scary or so painful they make you cry. No matter how stable your family is or how comfortable your home, your life is a continual process of change, struggle, conflict, and growth.

From a child's perspective, the everyday world provides more than enough material for the regular occurrence of bad dreams and nightmares.

Through much of my time as a doctoral student at the University of Chicago, I worked part-time as a teacher's assistant in the Laboratory School, the grammar school affiliated with the university. From that work and from my later experiences as a parent with my own three children, I've developed a deep appreciation for the powerful drive young children have to understand and make sense of the world around them. Children really, really want to figure things out—they want to know how things work, where things go, why things happen the way they do. I remember sitting out in the play yard one day at the Lab School watching a group of pre-schoolers engage in a spirited game of "house." Each child had an assigned role in the family (mother, father, older sister, younger brother, crying baby, and family dog), and the fun of the game clearly lay in the process of exploring what it felt like to play the different roles. The parents talked earnestly about the need for the children to behave well, the older sister said she was going on a date, the younger brother wanted new toys, the baby screamed for a bottle, and the dog barked and dug holes in the ground. The game went on in this way for nearly an hour, and the single-minded exuberance with which the children threw themselves into their parts amazed me. They were doing their very best to *be* the different characters, to figure out how each one fit into the complex pattern of family relationships.

Playing games like this enables children to explore the world around them, to learn how its many different parts fit together, and to figure out what their own role is in that world. This inborn "cognitive imperative" is what gives young children the strength and the vigor they need to meet the challenges that confront them every day of their lives. I believe nightmares are a part of this innate drive to know and understand. To put it in the simplest terms, bad dreams respond to bad experiences in waking life. Nightmares are efforts to process the worst feelings, the most confusing ideas, and the most frightening occurrences that happen to a child.

When Tom was eight years old, his parents began having serious marital problems. They argued continuously, screaming and crying and throwing things at each other. Even though Tom didn't understand their problems, he knew his mother and father were on the verge of getting a divorce. The terrible fights became so frightening that Tom began taking refuge in the basement, hiding with the family dog behind the washing machine. One night, after his parents had a particularly violent fight, Tom dreamed this:

> *I look down the street and see King Kong coming to attack my house. No one else in my family is around. It's just me against King Kong. He's hundreds of feet tall, dwarfing me. He chases me outside, but I get to a hiding place so I can shoot him. The only way I can fight back against him is to make paper airplanes and shoot them out of a BB gun. But it's very frustrating to make each individual paper airplane and insert it in just the right way into the BB gun, and then shoot it. Because it's so hard to make the airplanes, he catches up to me, and I become more and more frightened, and decide I have to run and hide. I go down a steep ravine behind my house and hide in a little gully, covering myself with leaves. As King Kong comes down the hill, I can feel my heart beating heavily. Then he sees where I'm hiding and lets out a roar. I try to make more paper airplanes, but I can't do it fast enough, and he reaches down toward me. . . . I wake up shaking and sweating, too scared to go back to sleep.*

Tom's father was a domineering, controlling man, and he was always the aggressor in the arguments. This particular night, Tom's mother had evidently had enough of his belligerence, and she started arguing back. This enraged Tom's father all the more. From his hiding place down in the basement, huddled with the dog, Tom could hear the fight escalate beyond anything that had happened before—there was screaming, and slamming doors, and the sounds of things being thrown and broken. Then Tom heard heavy footsteps on the floor directly above him, and he realized his father was charging at his mother. Without thinking, Tom jumped up, grabbed a broomstick, and ran upstairs. In the living room, he found his mother in a corner, crying, and his father standing in front of her. Tom could tell he hadn't actually hit her, but for the first time he had clearly come close to venting his anger in physical violence. Despite his own terrible fear, Tom started yelling at his father, telling him in a torrent of words to leave his mother alone and to stop being a bully to everyone. Tom's father said nothing. Instead, he turned around, walked out the door, and went for a drive.

An experience like that is an awful lot for an eight-year-old to deal with. That's precisely why Tom had a bad dream about it. Tom's nightmare was an emergency effort in the process of trying to make sense of what happened that horrible night. The huge, hundred-foot-tall King Kong perfectly expressed Tom's perception of his father as an intimidating and violent creature. The boy's frustrating attempts in the dream to fight King Kong by shooting paper airplanes at him symbolically reflected Tom's terrible dilemma—he wanted to stop his father, but he did *not* want to hurt him. Paper airplanes could never really kill King Kong, just as a broomstick could never really stop Tom's father. Tom's nightmare grappled desperately, and heroically, with the core emotional conflict Tom experienced in the confrontation with his father. He felt helpless and frustrated at being too small to do anything about his father's belligerence, and yet he also felt an urgent determination to try to stop him by whatever means he could. The nightmare did justice to both feelings and thus helped Tom reconcile the full range of emotions he experienced the night of his parents' fight.

It is interesting that even though Tom always remembered the dream with absolute clarity and vividness, it wasn't until he was eighteen that he consciously made the connection between King Kong and his father. And perhaps more interesting is that when Tom made that connection, he also realized the night of that terrible fight was the turning point for his parents' marriage. He remembered that when his father came back from his drive, he seemed to have understood at last how bad things had gotten, and he and Tom's mother found a way to work through their problems without fighting and to restore peace to the family's life.

Extremely memorable nightmares from early childhood often have this quality of reaching beyond the horizon of the child's current conscious abilities to create conceptual frameworks that can give shape, coherence, and comprehensibility to unusually disturbing life experiences. The child may not understand right then what the nightmare means; but later in life, the haunting, unforgettable dream images are recognized as revelations of important truths and insights.

Carl Jung had a nightmare like this when he was around four years old. He wasn't sure how, but he thought the dream was related to a waking-life encounter with a black-robed Jesuit priest whom young Carl had seen walking on a path through the village (Jung's father was a Lutheran pastor, and the boy had overheard many suspicious, fearful conversations about the nefarious activities of the Jesuits). Terrified by actually seeing one of these dreaded creatures so close to his home, Carl "ran helter-skelter into the house, rushed up the stairs, and hid under a beam in the darkest corner of the attic." Then he recalled having this dream:

> The nightmare begins in a meadow, where Carl discovers a stone-lined hole with a stairway in the ground. Curious, he descends along the stairway until he comes to a doorway covered with a heavy green curtain. Pushing aside the curtain, he sees a dim rectangular chamber with a red carpet and a low platform in the middle. On the platform is a beautiful golden throne, and on the throne stands something that looks like a tree trunk—twelve to fifteen feet high, one to two feet thick, and strangely made of skin and naked flesh. At the top it is smooth and rounded, with a single eye gazing upward. Although the thing doesn't move, Carl is paralyzed with terror at the thought that it might crawl off the throne and come after him. Then he hears his mother's voice say, "Yes, just look at him. That is the man-eater!" This makes him even more afraid, and he wakes up in a panic, covered with sweat.

Jung said, "[This was] the earliest dream I can remember, a dream which was to preoccupy me all my life." Only much later did he realize that the "man-eater" was a great phallus, symbolizing all the terrible subterranean powers of the instincts. The religious doctrines Jung had been taught by his father were silent about such powers; the church's nice, comforting image of "dear Lord Jesus" made no room for alien forces of destruction reigning beneath the ground. But even as a very young child, Jung knew that something was missing from the church's view of God, and he sensed that his father's fear of Jesuits was a first clue to those other aspects of the Divine. After having this dream, Jung's whole view of religion changed: "Lord Jesus never became quite real for me, never quite acceptable, never quite lovable, for again and again I would think of his underground counterpart, a frightful revelation which had been accorded me without my seeking it. The Jesuit's 'disguise' cast its shadow over the Christian doctrine I had been taught."

Every once in a while, children will have nightmares that are destined to stay with them their whole lives, remaining a vivid presence in their memories far into adulthood. These dreams seem to reach beyond the children's daily experiences and grasp at deeper, more complex truths about how the world works. It's often a lifelong task for a person to develop a sufficient depth of consciousness to understand and to appreciate those truths.

Trauma and Healing

In the course of normal development, the nightmares of childhood slowly diminish as a growing person gains more and more physical and cognitive competence in dealing with the ordinary demands of daily life. But nightmares often return whenever people are struck by something that violently disrupts the normal course of their lives—something like suddenly getting in a terrible car crash, or being attacked by a mugger, or having their house burn down. People often have nightmares in direct response to such horrible, unexpected events for the same reason that young children have nightmares: Bad dreams are attempts to make sense of bad experiences. A truly traumatic event can overwhelm a person's ordinary means of processing information; emotionally and cognitively, the experience just "doesn't compute." Unable to make sense of what happened, yet unable to forget that it did happen, the person dreams about it again and again and again.

With time, luck, and perhaps the help of a therapist, a person suffering from post-traumatic nightmares will slowly experience a "fading" effect. Instead of an exact replaying of the traumatic event, the dreams begin to change, to become more dreamlike. You're driving along that same stretch of freeway, but the truck in the next lane doesn't hit you like it did in waking life; instead, the pavement suddenly turns to sand, and your car skids into a shallow lake. Or the mugger is still attacking you, but this time it's daytime, not night, the mugger is wearing a clown outfit, and you actually manage to get away from him. Or, you're still caught in a fire, but now it's a hospital, not your house, and the flames turn out to be confined to a small wastebasket, and they're easily extinguished.

This gradual weaving of normal, nontraumatic details from the person's waking life into the recurrent nightmares seems to be part of the process of emotional and cognitive adaptation to the traumatic event. Researchers aren't clear yet on how exactly this experience of fading contributes to the healing process, but it seems that the dreams work to slowly but surely reestablish a sense of stability and balance in the person's world. The more the trauma can be connected to other aspects of daily existence, the more capable the person will feel in going on with life. In short, if you can dream about it, you're on the road to getting over it.

That may not be true for all people, however. In some cases the trauma is so severe and so overwhelming that the only hope is not to dream at all—to suppress the dreaming process itself. A recent study conducted by sleep laboratory researchers in Israel found that among a group of Holocaust survivors, the people who were judged to be psychologically "well-adjusted" remembered far fewer of their dreams than did the "less-adjusted" survivors. Furthermore, the dreams that the well-adjusted people did remember were shorter, less complex, and less emotionally compelling than the dreams recalled by the less-adjusted people. The findings of this study suggest that when a traumatic experience reaches a certain level of intensity, dreams are no longer sufficient to process whatever horrible event happened to the person; in these cases the best, most adaptive option may well be to shut down all dreaming as much as possible.

Warnings

Nightmares do not only react to traumatic experiences; sometimes they anticipate them, warning the dreamer to beware of dangers lurking on the horizon. The Book of Job describes this signaling function of nightmares in theological terms:

> For God speaks in one way, and in two, though man does not perceive it. In a dream, in a vision of the night, when deep sleep falls upon men, while they slumber on their beds, then He opens the ears of men, and terrifies them with warnings, that He may turn man aside from his deed, and cut off pride from man; He keeps back his soul from the Pit, his life from perishing by the sword.

The intense realism of these nightmares has the function of emphasizing the warning, making sure the dreamer pays conscious attention to what's going on in his or her waking life. By dreaming about a threat and experiencing what it would *really be like*, the dreamer is all the more motivated to prevent it from ever happening in waking life.

One night, a nineteen-year-old college student named Kevin had the most vivid nightmare of his life:

> *I'm in my car, catapulting down a twisty mountain road, with my tires screeching as I approach the next turn. Rain is covering my windshield, making it difficult to see. White clouds of fog cover the road, and as I hear the high-pitched whine of the engine, I know I'm driving way too fast and on the verge of being reckless. I can feel the heavy force of acceleration deep in the pit of my stomach. As I continue to race along, my tires barely making contact with the contours of the road, I feel the adrenaline rush. "What an awesome feeling!" I exclaim, when all of a sudden a deer jumps out directly in front of my car. It happens so quickly that I don't*

have much time to think. As I slam on the brakes and try to avoid
the animal, I swerve off the road, roll down an embankment, and
end up flipped upside down. I unbuckle my seat belt and manage
to free myself from the wreck. I am so nervous and terrified I can
barely stand up. Police cars and ambulances arrive, and then my
parents are there, and also, for some strange reason, our family
friend Lee. They rush over to me to make sure that I'm all right,
and I assure them I'm fine. But I'm still in complete shock that
I rolled the car off the road. The overwhelming state of fear con-
tinues to consume me.

When Kevin awoke from this dream, he struggled for several minutes to figure out if the accident really happened or not; he said it felt *so* vivid and lifelike, with such incredibly strong and dramatic physical sensations, that he couldn't believe it was just a dream. But an immediate clue to the dream's meaning lay in the figure of Lee, a close friend of Kevin's mother since childhood. When Lee was nineteen (the same age as Kevin when he had this nightmare), he was a passenger in a tragic car accident; he broke his neck and was confined to a wheelchair for the rest of his life. Kevin's nightmare gave him an unforgettable sense of how easy it would be to experience a car crash like Lee did. One minute he's feeling great, full of energy and exuberance, and the next he's totally out of control, in danger of losing everything. The setting of the dream is a long stretch of mountainous road near Kevin's home where teenagers had always loved racing their cars. The amazingly realistic physical sensations Kevin experienced in the dream, the thrilling feelings of speed and power, were precisely the sensations that made speeding down that road so irresistibly appealing. The nightmare recreated those exhilarating feelings, and then turned them around completely: "It happens so quickly that I don't have much time to think." That was the key moment in the dream, showing Kevin that in the blink of an eye the good feelings could suddenly change to terror, helplessness, and disaster.

In thinking about his nightmare, Kevin recalled that there had been a fatal accident along that road just a few months earlier. Combining that fact with the striking appearance of Lee, the night-mare's warning was clear: *slow down.* The intense memorability of the dream guaranteed that every time Kevin drove along that particular road, he would be a little more cautious than before. He would experience an extra wariness that might give him a few extra seconds of reaction time should he ever face a sudden danger.

The warning Kevin's nightmare offered him was remarkably literal because the dream imagery of driving was directly connected to his waking-life experiences with driving. More often than not, nightmares express their warnings in a much more symbolic or metaphorical fashion. (It's possible that Kevin's dream had additional levels of symbolic meaning beyond the direct connection to waking-life driving, but if so he didn't share them with me.) For many people in modern society, driving in cars, riding on trains, flying in airplanes, and traveling by various other mechanical means of transportation are regular features of daily life. The threat of crashing while engaged in these forms of travel is a real concern, and the dreaming imagination often uses this waking-life fear as a symbol to focus a person's conscious attention on other threats he or she does not fully appreciate.

Curtis, age twenty-seven, had just left his job, and he hadn't yet found a new one. He wasn't too worried, though, because he had some money saved up, and anyway he was too busy having a great time going out every night with his friends. After one evening of carousing, he had this dream:

> I'm on a plane flight going somewhere. I don't know where we're headed, but that doesn't matter. Everyone on the flight looks almost the same. They're all wearing black and all of them have a very serious look. I'm enjoying the flight, but it's not long before I look out of my window and notice the ground is too close. The plane's about to crash. Everyone else has suddenly disappeared.

When Curtis woke up, he felt a strange uneasiness, like he was about to get in trouble for something. Even stranger, he didn't know where the feeling was coming from. Not knowing what else to make of the dream, he got out of bed, put on his clothes, and went about his business. All through the day, the dream kept coming back to his mind, and Curtis realized that there must be something more going on. As he reflected on it, he began identifying various connections between the dream and his waking life, and a potent warning gradually emerged. Just as in his dream Curtis didn't know where the plane was going, in waking reality he didn't know where his life was going—in both situations he essentially had no direction or goal. The serious, black-clad people in the plane offered a sharp contrast to the carefree joviality of his current companions in waking life. Curtis took the plane's imminent crashing to be a serious warning that he needed to step back, to look more carefully at his life, and to figure out what he wanted to do with himself.

The dream doesn't necessarily condemn Curtis for enjoying his vacation between jobs. Indeed, the image of the stern passengers on the plane may well suggest that he should avoid moving toward the opposite extreme of a life without any color, fun, or animation. But the fundamental message of the dream was crystal clear: You don't know where you're going, and you're in danger of crashing. The overall impact of the dream was to focus Curtis's mind on the current aimlessness of his life and to stimulate fresh thinking about how he could better balance his various needs, desires, and aspirations.

Deeply disturbing warning dreams may not be pleasant to experience, but like all scare tactics they have a definite effect on a person's attitudes and behavior. By creating a vividly realistic sense of danger, these nightmares make sure the dreamer will become more aware of something in his or her waking life that has not received enough conscious attention. William Dement, the sleep laboratory researcher who coined the term *REM sleep*, once had a powerful warning nightmare of his own, and he said the nightmare perfectly illustrated the problem-solving function of dreaming:

> *Some years ago, I was a heavy cigarette smoker—up to two packs a day. Then one night I had an exceptionally vivid and realistic dream in which I had inoperable cancer of the lung. I remember as though it were yesterday looking at the ominous shadow in my chest X ray and realizing that the entire right lung was infiltrated. The subsequent physical examination in which a colleague detected widespread metastases in my auxiliary and inguinal lymph nodes*

was equally vivid. Finally, I experienced the incredible anguish of knowing my life was soon to end, that I would never see my children grow up, and that none of this would have happened if I had quit cigarettes when I first learned of their carcinogenic potential. I will never forget the surprise, joy, and exquisite relief of waking up. I felt I was reborn. Needless to say, the experience was sufficient to induce an immediate cessation of my cigarette habit.

This dream had both anticipated the problem and solved it in a way that may be a dream's unique privilege. "Only the dream can allow us to experience a future alternative as if it were real, and thereby to provide a supremely enlightened motivation to act upon this knowledge."

Frightening Encounters with the Other

Many people's most memorable dreams are horrible chasing nightmares in which they are relentlessly pursued by monstrous, violent antagonists: a bloodthirsty vampire, a crazed murderer, a massive shark, a tribe of cannibals. These dreams are not obvious reactions to a waking-life trauma, nor are they specific warnings. Rather, they simply confront the dreamer with the undeniable, inescapable *reality* of some force or power that is radically alien to the dreamer's normal sense of self. Monsters, zombies, savages, werewolves, madmen, space aliens, wild beasts, criminals—these and the countless other malevolent beings who chase people through their nightmares share a quality of fundamental *otherness*. They appear in manifold ways as the absolute opposite of a normal, civilized human being—they are "not-humans," and they almost always arouse a terrible fear and desperation in the dreamer.

My own interest in dreams originated in a long series of chasing nightmares during adolescence. In the dreams, I would run and run, dodge and feint, and use every bit of subterfuge I could, but I was never able to escape my terrifying pursuers. For example:

I am being chased around an office building by the Incredible Hulk. I run this way and that, up and down stairs, but every time he sees me and keeps chasing me.

I am in a house, and I see a murder occur. I grab the hand of the killer as it reaches back through a hole in the wall. I now see the murderers, and we throw things at one another. I begin running, trying to get out of the house, with a man in pursuit.

The most striking antagonist of all my nightmares was Darth Vader, the huge, black-robed archvillain of the *Star Wars* movies (I was a teenager when these movies first came out):

I have just come down onto a beach with a steeply sloping hill on the right as I face the water, dense vegetation to the rear, and a long strip of beach backed by cliffs to the left. I am with three other people. Very soon our opponents are on the beach. Their leader is Darth Vader, and he says that because we have messed up his plans somehow, he is going to take his vengeance and anger out on me. I drop all my other things, grab a pack that seems to have my essential things in it, and flee back into the little valley between the hill and the cliffs. I climb a couple of flights of stairs, dash through a house, through doors and windows, all the while thinking that Darth might be right on my trail. Right before I wake up I know that he was not right behind me, but I understand with great anxiety that I had not escaped him, and that no matter how far I ran or how well I hid, he could still get me.

The persistence of these extremely unpleasant nightmares left me no choice but to try to understand what they were all about. I don't remember as a child being taught anything one way or the other about dreams. So when I began trying to interpret my recurrent nightmares, I had absolutely no idea what to expect. Being something of a nerd, the first thing I did was read as many books on the subject as I could find. One book that immediately caught my interest was Carl Jung's *Man and His Symbols*. In Jung's view, the totality of the human psyche extends far, far beyond the sphere of ordinary awareness—"the ego is only a bit of consciousness which floats upon the ocean of the dark things." Outside the realm of consciousness lies a vast array of unconscious desires, instincts, forces, and energies, some of which conflict with the narrower attitudes and aims of the conscious self. Jung said that if the conscious self tried to distance itself too far from those unconscious desires, the result would be a violent internal battle. One clear indicator of such an internal battle was the experience of recurrent chasing nightmares in which the repressed unconscious desires take the dream form of monstrous creatures who violently oppose the conscious self. The more the conscious self resists the reality of the unconscious desires, the more *evil* the nightmare antagonist appears, and the more violent the fighting between the dreamer and the antagonist becomes.

In these ideas of Jung's, I found my first real help in understanding my recurrent nightmares. The antagonists in my dreams symbolized "other" parts of myself, parts that I did not like, parts that conflicted with the public image of myself that I had always tried to maintain. My conscious self had no room for such desires or instincts, but the recurrent nightmares forced me to acknowledge their reality—*I could not run away from them.* It's hard to describe the feeling of revelation I experienced in thinking about my nightmares from this perspective, and it's even harder to describe my surprise when the nightmares responded to me—when my acknowledgment was acknowledged:

> *I am with, or am a captive of, Darth Vader. He is in his black cape, but I realize his helmet is off, revealing an aged, lined face and a head of beautiful golden blond hair, about shoulder length. He also wears some soft leather boots, tan. As we walk through his ship, he says to me, "You have some of the best guerrilla fighters in known space—but you don't have me."*

I had this dream about two years after the earlier Darth Vader nightmare, and I felt it was an affirmation of my efforts to better appreciate the value, beauty, and wisdom of the "darker" sides of myself. I had consciously responded to the chasing nightmares, and now the dreams were responding back to me. Instead of being chased by Darth Vader, my relationship with him had changed; I was now either his captive or his companion, an ambiguity that seemed to suggest I could be *both*. Darth had changed, too. His frightening black mask and helmet were gone, and to my great surprise he actually looked noble and lordly. With his parting words, he seemed to acknowledge and to respect what I had accomplished, and yet he also seemed to be challenging me to continue to grow and develop in the future. The dream was a reminder that the process of self-integration was by no means over; the sense of revelation I had experienced was just the beginning of something that would take the rest of my life to accomplish.

As the previous sections of this chapter indicate, not all nightmares have the function of revealing unconscious conflicts within the dreamer. But many nightmares do, and the stimulation such dreams give to the process of self-reflection can be truly remarkable. They compel people to expand and to deepen their sphere of consciousness, welcoming into their awareness parts of themselves that have been neglected, rejected, or demonized (what Jung called "the shadow" elements of the psyche). Creating a relationship with these other parts of the self can be extremely difficult and painful; in the symbolic language of the nightmares, it feels like the dreamer's conscious self is in danger of dying, of being destroyed or devoured by some huge, horrible, alien *thing*. But if the dreamer can move beyond the fear and can avoid being trapped in the primal fight-or-flight pattern of response to such mortal dangers, the possibilities for discovery, insight, and growth are astonishing.

Steve was a twenty-year-old college junior who had suffered recurrent chasing nightmares for as long as he could remember. They always began as normal dreams in which he had pleasant, unremarkable interactions with other people in a variety of ordinary settings. Suddenly, the scene would freeze, and with a jolt of terror he would become aware of the presence of his pursuer. At that point everything else in the dream disappeared, and the same basic nightmare narrative took over:

> *In the midst of darkness, I turn the corner carefully. My eyes dart around the hallway searching for any signs of danger. My heart begins to thump rapidly, while sweat trickles down the sides of my face. I hear a noise that frightens the hell out of me. The noise reminds me of an electrical arc, or a stun gun. I turn around to see the source of the noise and come face to face with my fears. The shadowy figure has found me again, and this time it may finish the job. I try to scream as the figure reaches for me, but I can't. I wake up covered in sweat and quite a bit shook up.*

Sometimes Steve dreamed that the shadowy figure was actually in his room waiting for him to wake up. On these occasions when he did finally awaken, he experienced a few terrifying moments of believing the malevolent figure was really and truly there, right in his room. Even though Steve had experienced these nightmares two or three times a week for at least five years, he had no idea what they meant, and he felt stupid for being so afraid of them.

One of Steve's good friends suggested that he go to the student health center at their university to see if anyone could help him with the painful moodiness he was always complaining about. Steve agreed this was probably a good idea, and he made an appointment to see a psychiatrist. He soon began a regular series of therapy sessions with the psychiatrist, and he also began taking an antidepressant medication. Soon, his emotional balance was restored. The agonizing mood swings stopped, and his general energy level rose dramatically. Steve realized he felt better than he had in years. And almost immediately he noticed a total change in his dreams—the dark antagonist was gone, and the plague of recurrent nightmares had ended. Steve understood then that the shadowy figure of his chasing nightmares was that part of himself that he didn't want to show other people and that, thanks to the therapy and medication, he was just now starting to fully accept. "I could not face the 'real' me," he said, "because it would eliminate the 'me' that I portray, causing the protective barriers I built to come crashing down."

Steve was amazed at the direct connection between the imagery of his nightmares and the self-esteem problems he had quietly suffered for so long. He felt his dreams were giving him a clear and very positive inner response to the beginning of his therapy and his use of the medication. When Steve acknowledged and accepted the otherness within himself, the shadowy figure stopped pursuing him—it didn't have to chase him any more because he had stopped running from it.

Nightmares Leading to Lucid Awareness

Some nightmares become so unbearably intense that the dreamer will suddenly realize, "This is just a dream. I can wake up and make all of this stop!" The terror is so great, the pursuer is so close, and

the physical sensations are so intense that, as a last act of utter desperation, the dreamer "awakens" within the dream and tries to
assert some distance from the frightening experiences of the nightmare—"It's not real, I'm not going to die, this isn't actually happening, I don't have to be so scared, *it's just a dream.*"

In the research I've done on the dreams of young children, I've
found that many of them have spontaneously developed the ability
to become lucid in their dreams specifically as a means of fending
off recurrent nightmares. For example, seven-year-old Zoe had
always been afflicted with horrible nightmares of a man chasing her
with a gun, trying to kill her. One night Zoe somehow realized she
could "wake herself up" in her dreams, and this knowledge that she
was dreaming gave her the self-confidence to stop running from
the man and to turn around, look him in the eye, and tell him to go
ahead and shoot her. The first time Zoe tried this, the man killed
her with one shot; but the next time she had the nightmare and
became lucid, it took him longer to kill her. After a few weeks, the
nightmares ended with the man shaking his head, saying he was
impressed with her courage and leaving her alone for good.

A similar process happened to Trey, who also suffered recurrent chasing nightmares throughout his childhood. Now an adult,
Trey says that when he was eight, his bad dreams became so severe
that he started having trouble falling asleep at night because he
knew the ghosts and monsters were waiting for him as soon as he
closed his eyes. He became very frightened of the dark and insisted
that he never be left alone. Finally, out of desperation, Trey told his
parents about the nightmares. His mother told him that the dreams
were in his own imagination and that if he really tried he could put
an end to them. She had him repeat this phrase to himself each
night before going to sleep—"I have the power to stop the nightmares, I have the power to stop the nightmares, I have the power
to stop the nightmares." Four nights after first talking with his parents, Trey had this dream:

*I'm in a small, narrow corridor that resembles the corridors of the
USS Enterprise in Star Trek. As soon as I find myself there, a
black and slimy creature starts chasing me for no apparent reason.*

I scream at the top of my lungs as I run for dear life through the never-ending corridors. As the creature is gaining on me, it suddenly occurs to me that I'm dreaming. I start screaming inside my head to wake up, and immediately I do.

A sudden feeling of elation and triumph filled Trey when he awoke—he had actually made the nightmare stop! His fears of the dark and of being alone immediately disappeared, and he found he could go to sleep each night in peace, confident in his newfound power over his dream antagonists.

For the next several nights Trey successfully managed to wake himself whenever he perceived danger in his dreams. Although pleased by this achievement, he was also puzzled by the continuing recurrence of the nightmarish chasing theme. So one week after initially learning to become lucid in his dreams, Trey tried something different:

I find myself in the same corridor as in my first lucid dream. The same black and slimy monster is chasing me while I try my best to run away from it. This time, however, instead of waking up immediately on sensing danger, my mind freezes the chasing image as if I was pressing a pause button on a VCR. I think about whether I should end the dream now or let it go on. I decide to allow it to continue, and I turn around to face my approaching nemesis. As the sound of its footsteps grow louder, so does its moaning sound. I wait while the horrifying sounds reach their peak, and then all of a sudden there's complete silence. There's no monster in sight; it seems to have vanished completely.

With that, Trey's chasing nightmares ended for good.

As with Zoe, no conscious interpretation is involved in Trey's experience. The confrontation with the shadowy "other" occurs entirely within the dream, and yet it has a powerful impact on the dreamer's waking life—eliminating the fears, boosting self-confidence, and expanding the dreamer's own sense of power and ability. This is an important point that emerges most clearly in children's dreams, but it applies to many adult dreams as well: Sometimes the integration of conscious and unconscious parts of the self can occur *without* a rational, verbalized interpretation. Children like Zoe and Trey did not yet have the cognitive abilities to systematically analyze their dreams, but their experiences suggest that such analyses are not necessary for the integration process to be successful. What's necessary is simple courage, a willingness to face one's fears and to trust in one's own power to overcome those fears. For adults, rational analysis and interpretation can provide valuable assistance, as Steve found in the therapy sessions with his psychiatrist. But in some cases, too much analysis can actually block the integration process by creating new barriers between the conscious self and the repressed instincts and desires of the unconscious. In the end, there's no substitute for that basic courage.

The achievement of lucidity in a dream can be a powerful means of confronting the "otherness" that so often threatens people in their nightmares. But the joyful sense of power that comes with lucidity can itself, in possibly the most frightening nightmares of all, become an experiential foil for a new kind of dream terror:

I'm in my bedroom when I suddenly feel sick and start suffering from allergies. I start wheezing and experience difficulty in breathing. I realize I need some medicine, and I go to my dad for help. We speed through the dark, silent night to a drugstore and then look frantically through the aisles for my medicine. Suddenly I notice footsteps, which seem to be following us on the other side of the shelves. We finally find the medicine when suddenly our pursuer, who is dressed in a long black robe like a witch, starts chasing us. We run out of the store as fast as we can into the dark, deserted streets.

Suddenly I find myself falling into a large pit, while my dad and our pursuer vanish into thin air. I realize that I am in a dark, murky pit full of snakes slithering around. My heart is pounding, and I am afraid to move even an inch, when suddenly I open my eyes and I can see the ceiling of my room. My younger sister is asleep in the next bed. Shaken and terrified, I get up to go to my parents' bedroom—but I'm suddenly horrified to see snakes all over my bedroom floor! Despite the fact that I'm wide-awake, all I am

*able to see are snakes everywhere. After blinking my eyes, testing
the reality of the situation, I finally muster up enough courage to
get out of my bed. I then run to my parents' bedroom, hoping to
escape from this horrible nightmare and seeking comfort. To my
astonishment, when I enter the room, I find the same thing—the
floor is covered with black hissing snakes. My parents try to comfort
me, but they cannot do anything to soothe me. In my mind I am
still surrounded by venomous snakes.*

Winnie was eight years old when she had this dream, and it
made an indelible impression on her young mind. From that night
on, she never quite thought of the "real" world in the same way.
The nightmare confronted her with the possibility that she could
not always trust her sense of "being awake," and she was left to
ponder the frightening idea that what she was experiencing at any
given moment might be a dream.

Winnie's nightmare-within-a-nightmare was not a sign of mental illness because, on the whole, she was a very intelligent and
well-adjusted child. Her remarkable experience is better understood as an early discovery of an age-old piece of philosophical wisdom. In Hindu mythology there are numerous stories in which
people find themselves unsure of whether they are awake or
dreaming. The ancient collection of folktales called the *Yogava-
sistha* includes the story of an Indian king who dreamed he was
a lowly Untouchable and then awoke to find that he really was
an Untouchable. It also includes a story of a wise Brahmin who
dreamed he was an Untouchable who then dreamed he was a King,
who wondered who he really was or where he actually came from.
The characters in these marvelous and philosophically profound
stories discover that although you can prove you're dreaming by
waking up, you can't ever prove you're really awake—it's always
possible that what you're experiencing right now is actually a
dream, and you're going to wake up from it in just a moment.
Winnie's nightmare reveals the same philosophical truth that's
expressed in these myths—that being "lucid" is not an ultimate or
absolute state of consciousness. On the contrary, dreaming and
waking exist in a dynamic and unpredictable relationship, and the
great existential challenge people face is that they must live their
lives never knowing for certain which is which.

Those Annoying Exam Dreams

Extremely vivid nightmares of being late for class or unprepared for an exam occur to people long after they are finished with formal schooling. The dreams bring them back to their student days and create a situation of terrible anxiety, shame, and embarrassment. Many people react to these nightmares with annoyance— Why do I keep having highly realistic dreams of being back in my high school algebra class and suddenly realizing I'm not ready for the test the teacher is passing out to all the other students? That was *years* ago, so what good is it to relive the worries and anxieties I suffered way back then?

Exam dreams are one instance of a broader type of nightmare in which the dreamers realize, with a horrible shock of anxiety, that they have failed or are about to fail at something: missing a train, forgetting an appointment, not completing an application on time, not knowing how to work a machine, being in front of a crowd but not having a speech prepared, not being able to find the church on your wedding day, and so forth. The uncanny power of these nightmares derives from their remarkably realistic portrayal of actual situations from the dreamer's waking life. These dreams don't involve werewolves, space aliens, or otherworldly journeys; they tend to have normal, ordinary settings, and the dreamer is most often engaged in some kind of common activity from his or her daily life. It's this very normality of the dream's setting that sparks the intense feelings of anxiety—the dreamer suddenly thinks, *"This is really happening!"* and the immediate reaction to that thought is an eruption of fear so strong the dreamer usually wakes up right away.

One way to look at exam nightmares is to regard them as symbolic expressions of a current waking-life situation that unconsciously reminds the dreamer of a similarly anxiety-provoking situation from the past. Thus, a dream of being unprepared for a high school algebra test might symbolically reflect the dreamer's present worries about an important project at work; a dream of being late to a class could relate to the dreamer's present concern about filing a late tax return.

I've found that many of these nightmares are best understood by considering them in connection to what the dreamer feels on awakening, at that startling moment when the dreamer sits up in bed and gasps, "Thank God it was only a dream!" This grateful realization brings with it a flood of relief as the dreamer understands that he or she is not *really* late for class or unprepared for the test. The sharp experiential contrast between the fear in the dream and the relief on awakening gives the dreamer a positive new perspective on what's going on in current life. In this way, certain exam nightmares are transformed into reassurance dreams because the joyful awakening from the nightmare shows the dreamer that however bad and worrisome things in waking-life may seem to be, they're not *that* bad—you're *not* in your high school algebra class unprepared for the test. This new perspective can be especially valuable in waking-life situations where the stress and the pressure have become so great that people feel utterly trapped by their anxieties. The dreams not only remind people that they've faced similar (if not worse) situations in the past and survived, but also give them a shot of positive emotional energy at a time when they can really use it.

Hyperrealistic Sensations of Falling and Paralysis

A certain class of nightmares is most remarkable because of the powerful physical sensations that accompany them. These dreams may or may not contain other characters, and their settings can be either completely familiar or utterly strange. What really stands out about them, and what gives them such extraordinary memorability, is the feeling that something is *really happening* to the dreamer's body. Here are a few examples:

> *I'm being chased through the desert by a group of gangsterlike people. They are older men with tommy guns and such, straight out of the twenties and thirties. I run as they shoot at me, and I try to hide, but it's useless; they always find me. When they get close, I keep running and look over my shoulder to see where they are. When I look back, I fall off a cliff and feel a sense of terror as I fall. I'm not screaming, but I am overwhelmed with fear. Then I wake up short of breath.*

I lie in bed, and feel helpless and insignificant. I feel as if I am the size of an ant, and I can barely lift my arms and legs. Then fear sets in, and everything in my room moves. Then out of nowhere, a shadow enters at the center of my room. The black shadow, which I cannot describe exactly, slowly extends his hand toward me, and as the hand moves closer it grows larger. Out of panic and fear, I try to pull the sheets over myself, but I can't.

"Last night, Mother, I saw a dream. There was a star in the heavens. Like a shooting star of Anu it fell on me. I tried to lift it; too much for me. I tried to move it; I could not move it."

The first two examples come from male college students in the present day, and the third from the ancient Sumerian epic *Gilgamesh*, written more than three thousand years ago. Falling and paralysis nightmares like these can be found in any culture around the world, in any period of history. Current research suggests that these frightening experiences have a definite basis in the physiological processes of sleep and dreaming. When people enter a REM-sleep phase, the major muscle groups of their bodies become *atonic* (unresponsive) and relax completely. In a very literal sense, their bodies are paralyzed for the excellent reason of keeping the people from getting out of bed and physically acting out whatever it is they're experiencing in their dreams. Furthermore, this natural experience of atonia during sleep can at certain points generate an acute sensation of falling—if this kind of total muscular relaxation happened while you were awake, you would instantly fall to the ground. Indeed, it could even be that a tendency to experience highly realistic falling nightmares evolved for the specific adaptive purpose of keeping our tree-dwelling primate ancestors alert to the serious possibility of falling off their branches while sleeping. Being hard-wired to experience a falling nightmare every once in a while would serve the valuable function of reminding our ancestors to be careful about finding a stable and secure perch for each night's sleep.

The strong physiological influence on the occurrence of dreams of falling and paralysis raises the question of how different kinds of stimuli can shape and even instigate dream contents. Researchers have found that external stimuli can sometimes have an effect on what a person is dreaming (e.g., a sleeping subject whose arm is squeezed by a blood pressure balloon gauge might dream of being caught in a vise). Most people have some familiarity with this phenomenon—as they have had dreams that took an external sound like a siren or someone talking outside their bedroom and incorporated it into the ongoing narrative of their dream. The most interesting question raised by this research is *how* exactly the external stimulus is used by the dreaming imagination. The same bell might be rung next to the ears of four sleeping people, but it would have very different effects on each of their dreams: The first person might dream of church bells ringing on Sunday morning, the second of the siren of a police car, and the third of an alarm clock. The fourth person might not dream of any sounds at all. What psychological or physiological factors can account for these differences?

To the despair of experimental psychologists, no obvious natural laws have yet been found to explain the particular ways in which external stimuli are incorporated into people's dreams. The same is true of the incorporation of internal stimuli. Why is it that the muscular atonia that all humans experience every night while they sleep appears in some dreams as a feeling of running in slow motion, in other dreams as an inability to yell or cry out, and in other dreams as a sickening fall? And if these internal physiological changes occur every night, why are they incorporated into only a few dreams, with the vast majority having nothing to do with the muscular conditions of the dreamer's body?

I don't have a simple answer to these questions, but I do have an idea of what is happening in those rare but particularly memorable nightmares that include strong physical sensations of falling or being paralyzed. I believe that in these cases the experientially vivid narrative being created by the dreaming imagination deliberately aims toward a particular, internally generated, physical sensation as the climax of the plot. The intensely realistic bodily experience comes as the culmination of the dream's narrative trajectory, completing the dream story and symbolically emphasizing the emotional importance of its meanings.

Jim had a recurrent chasing dream throughout his childhood that always started with him running frantically through a dense rain forest:

I'm being chased, but I'm still not sure by what. All I know is, if I stop, I'll surely be killed. I realize while I'm running that there is nothing I can do about the situation. I feel so helpless and scared. The path starts to wind up a small rolling hill. In my dream I am surprised at how easily I can run and how effortless it feels. All of a sudden, I see to my left a fairly modern looking shack. A moment later, a rather large black woman is headed for me swinging a huge broom. She looks like a grandmother who is doing the housecleaning, but I feel that she is going to rip my head off. Another second later, I see a figure coming up the path. I realize this is the man I was running from. Frozen from fear, I hesitate just long enough to see that he is holding a shiny, black, nine-millimeter pistol and wearing a loud red Hawaiian shirt. I break into a run, but this time I feel as if I'm running in slow motion. A few seconds later, I'm looking straight off a cliff into the deep blue tropical ocean. Then I see the hundreds of sharks that are thrashing around waiting to devour me. With only a split second to make up my mind, I realize I must jump. I take the plunge with confidence, and always wake up right before I hit the water.

Jim said the sensations of this recurrent nightmare were so intensely realistic that he would awaken each time with his heart racing and his muscles tensed. The whole dream was filled with a terrible helplessness and confusion, right up to the point where he decides to jump off the cliff. Paradoxically, as Jim falls down toward the hungry, thrashing sharks he feels a sudden sense of hope or possibility, a strangely reassuring confidence that he's made the right decision, that he still has the power to choose what to do.

In reflecting on the dream, Jim recognized that the waking-life context of the recurrent nightmare was his parents' divorce, which resulted in his father's moving out of the house. Jim now felt he had the emotional responsibility of caring for his mother and younger siblings. He understood that the nightmares were vivid reflections of how deeply the divorce had upset and frightened him (with the gun-wielding man symbolizing, at one level, his father, and the woman with the broom symbolizing his mother). But Jim also understood that the nightmares were revealing a deep strength within him, a determination to make the best choices he could in a horrible situation. The primary meaning he took from the dreams was that the only way he could be defeated would be if he gave up trying to think, to decide, and to act on his own.

Jim's nightmares had elements of both paralysis and falling— but significantly in my view, these elements came at the *end* of the dreams. A long narrative preceded the sensations of not being able to run anymore and then jumping off the cliff, and this suggests that the dream was not *instigated* by the physiological changes that naturally accompany REM sleep. Rather, Jim's dreams made dramatic use of those sensations to further the overall narrative direction of the plot: At first he can run surprisingly fast; but then he's been slowed down, and sheer flight is no longer an option. His best hope is to jump, a choice that seems suicidal but that in fact fills him with new energy and confidence. In Jim's nightmares (and in the extremely memorable nightmares of many other people), the intense bodily sensations serve the narrative demands of the dreams by adding an experiential power to the dream's primary meanings.

Falling and paralysis nightmares like Jim's offer important insights into the origins of unusually memorable dreams. One of the leading theories of modern scientific research is that dreams originate in the autonomous activities of the brain during REM sleep. The extremely energetic neural firings that occur in REM sleep stimulate a random variety of memories, ideas, images, and emotions in the sleeping person's mind. Bombarded with so much chaotic input, the sleep-impaired mind vainly tries to create some kind of meaning out of the intrinsically meaning*less* material. The product of this doomed effort is a dream. Because the REM sleep–generated input is so incredibly chaotic and because the mind's reasoning abilities are so severely reduced in sleep, the dreams that result from this process are usually disjointed, nonsensical, and almost immediately forgotten. This theory proposes, in short, that the neurological activities of REM sleep come first and the contents of the dream second—the brain activates, and then the mind vainly tries to synthesize. But in dreams like Jim's, the initiative seems to switch—the narrative demands of the dream come first, and the neural firings leading to the production of high states of physiological arousal come second. Rather than the linear, brain-to-mind process that produces most dreams, a vastly more complex two-way relationship between the brain and the mind appears to be the source of certain falling and paralysis nightmares (and, more generally, of all unusually memorable dreams). In ways that researchers are only just beginning to understand, the dreaming imagination evidently has the power to control the dreamer's body and to stimulate intense physiological sensations that enhance the experiential impact of dreams' primary meanings. In these dreams the imagination creates, and then the body enacts.

The Otherworldly Experience
of Titanic Dreams

In Greek mythology, the Titans were "the Elder Gods," the primordial deities who were born of heaven (Ouranos) and earth (Gaia) and who, for untold ages, ruled over the cosmos. Here is classicist Edith Hamilton's description of the Titans:

> They had the shattering, overwhelming strength of earthquake and hurricane and volcano. In the tales about them they do not seem really alive, but rather to belong to a world where as yet there was no life, only tremendous movements of irresistible forces lifting up the mountains and scooping out the seas. The Greeks evidently had some such feeling because in their stories, although they represent these creatures as living beings, they make them unlike any form of life known to man.

Over the years I have heard several people describe dreams that, for lack of a better term, have a "titanic" feeling to them. These dreams are unusually abstract and disembodied, and they're filled with tremendous force and power. The dreamer is usually the only character present, and the setting tends to be dark, empty, and utterly devoid of organic life. From a detached, floating perspective, the dreamer perceives strange forces and movements that seem to have a mysterious intentionality to them. It's hard to generalize about these dreams in any more detail, so here are a few examples:

Jeannie: *My most memorable dream contains no characters. It starts off looking like a crumpled sheet of paper, with areas of light and dark. The areas of light and dark move away, revealing many more points of light and areas of dark. It becomes almost like a television screen of static, only there isn't movement on an individual level, but the entire area begins to move and roll. A big ball appears and rolls over the area, and I start to fall back into the area until it feels as though I reach the atomic level. I wake up with an unpleasant feeling.*

Meg: *I start to dream about this dark abyss—very dark. It is like I am at the bottom of a hill I cannot see. The only thing I can distinguish is a sound of something big and destructive rolling down the hill. Its noise is constant and gains momentum. It rolls down the hill making a louder and louder noise until I force myself to open my eyes. It is always dark, and I never see the object. But the noise and impending danger always force me out of sleep and cause anxiety.*

Kirk: *I am in a space-type of setting, devoid of any matter and shedding little light. I see two gigantic metal/steel ball bearings hurtling toward each other with the speed of a comet. The scary part is I know these objects are going to collide in a massive, almost nuclear explosion. After the objects collide, I dream on to the next catastrophic scene, elevated about one thousand feet above the earth. The feature objects this time are two huge, powerful, bullet-train locomotives, set on the same railroad track heading right for each other. Again, I know these two locomotives are headed for each other, and I am present to see the tremendous collision.*

Phil: *I would say that I'm flying . . . or not necessarily flying, but viewing things from a perspective other than the ground. I can't recall ever having a dream in which I view things in an unworldly way like that. I believe I'm in outer space, looking down at the world. The scene is very much like the scene in the movie* Deep Impact, *in which they depict an outer-space view of the meteor colliding with earth. And that is just what I see—only it is more dramatic, and there is actual emotion to the vision—unlike that passiveness I feel whenever I see the commercials for the movie.*

Delia: *I'm in bed, trying to fall asleep, when all of a sudden, the scenery all turns dark, pitch black, as the sky appears on a cloudless night. No moon to reflect the sun's light, no stars. I see a winding path suspended in midair. On the path, there rolls an immense sphere, which I fear will collapse if a tiny little stone obstructs its path. I wait for the collapse to occur, but at the same time my mind does not wish for or against the stumbling of the sphere. I do not think of what might happen, I just do not want it to fall—there is a need to keep that structure intact. I have a feeling there is going to be a very loud noise, unbearable perhaps. Then I hear the sound, like a bowling ball rolling down an alley, and the sound is so massive I know that the sphere has to be gigantic.*

All of these titanic dreams have a disturbing, vaguely frightening effect on the dreamer. They don't, however, evoke the visceral kind of terror of a classic chasing nightmare, probably because the dreamers don't really have bodies in these experiences—their thoughts are somehow detached from ordinary physical existence, and they seem to have no ability to act or to move of their own volition. They are simply present to witness the movement and the interaction of mysterious forces that have no apparent connection to ordinary human life. Not surprisingly, the dreamers often have great difficulty putting their otherworldly experiences into words. Delia, for example, said that even though she could give a basic summary of her dream—"a sphere rolls on a path through outer space"—she couldn't begin to describe the *power* she had felt, seen, and experienced in the dream.

The people who have had titanic dreams are generally at a loss to provide any waking-life associations to them. The dreams do not clearly symbolize any particular aspect of the dreamers' work, romantic relationships, personal health, or financial affairs. Rather, the dreams seem to reflect a different order of reality entirely, an order of almost pure physics: mass, energy, speed, momentum, gravity. It is as if the dreams were somehow giving the dreamers a glimpse of what it's like to *be* an atom or to *be* a star. Jeannie said that in her dream, she felt as though she had "reached the atomic level." I can't help wondering if maybe Jeannie is being more than metaphorical. Could it be that in certain dreams people have the ability to extend the range of their awareness so far that they actually leave the realm of organic existence entirely? Could it be that in these extremely rare but absolutely unforgettable dreams people have a direct experiential encounter with the mighty cosmological forces that create and sustain the basic physical structure of the universe?

I admit the questions sound fantastic, and I don't know how any method of investigation currently available could answer them. But for those people who have had such dreams, I would suggest they at least keep their minds open to those possibilities. The limitations of current scientific knowledge should not be mistaken for the limits of the dreaming imagination.

CHAPTER FOUR

Dreams of Death

To die, to sleep—
No more—and by a sleep to say we end
The heartache, and the thousand natural shocks
That flesh is heir to. 'Tis a consummation
Devoutly to be wished. To die, to sleep—
To sleep—perchance to dream: ay, there's the rub,
For in that sleep of death what dreams may come
When we have shuffled off this mortal coil,
Must give us pause. There's the respect
That makes calamity of so long life.

—William Shakespeare, *Hamlet*

The historical roots of the connection between sleep, dreams, and death go back in Western culture at least as far as Hesiod, the Greek poet from the eighth century B.C. In *Theogony*, his lyrically rendered myth of creation, Hesiod described the birth of all the gods and goddesses of the Greek cosmos, including the terrible children of Night: "And Night bore frightful Doom and the black Ker [a spirit of destruction], and Death, and Sleep, and the whole tribe of Dreams." In cultures all over the world, sleep has been regarded as a close kin to death. According to one very widespread religious belief, when people go to sleep at night, their souls are released from the confines of their bodies, and they are free to

87

travel through the spirit world. When their souls come back, the people wake up, and they remember the experience as being a dream. When their souls don't come back, the people's bodies die, and their souls remain for eternity in those mysterious, supernatural realms.

Modern scientific research has yet to find any definitive proof of the continued existence of a "soul" or any other part of a human being following physical death. But there is a convergence of views between religious traditions and current science on one important point. Medical statistics have shown that the peak time for people to die from a disease-related cause is from 6 to 8 A.M.—right in the middle of the longest REM phase of an average night's sleep. Not only are people more vulnerable to external attack while sleeping, they're also more vulnerable to the mortal thrust of a stroke or a heart attack and to the last lethal push of a degenerative disease. Researchers are not clear yet on the precise role REM sleep plays in the physiological events immediately preceding death, but the evidence is strong that REM sleep can have a significant impact on the exact time of death. According to one medical researcher, "REM sleep, particularly in people with cardiovascular and pulmonary disease, is a time of increased risk for cardiac arrhythmias, respiratory insufficiency, and susceptibility to the toxic effects of sedative drugs and alcohol."

The teachings of world religions and the discoveries of modern science thus find a small piece of common ground regarding the close relationship between sleep and death. Whether the cause is believed to be the final departure of the soul or a sudden seizure of the heart, the shared recognition is that sleeping is the time when people come closer than ever to the perilous boundary separating the living from the dead.

Nana Comes Back

Manuel's grandmother died when he was thirteen years old. His "Nana" was originally from a small village in the desert hills of Mexico, and Manuel always remembered her as being the center of emotional power in their large, close-knit family. Whenever Manuel got sick, his mother would take him to Nana, and she would perform a traditional ritual to restore his health, whispering prayers in Spanish and rubbing a potion made of herbs, oils, egg, and ash all over his body. Everyone in the family treated Nana with the greatest of respect, out of awe for her deep wisdom and also, Manuel knew, out of fear of Nana's anger when she was crossed. The terrible sense of loss Manuel felt when Nana died was only made worse when his older relatives got into a bitter argument over Nana's money and possessions. The family split into several angry factions, and for years afterward Manuel was deeply saddened by haunting memories of the old family parties and holiday gatherings that were so much fun when Nana was still alive.

When Manuel got older, he went to a first-rate university on the East Coast. He was the first member of his family to go to college, and as graduation approached he thought of how very, very much he wished Nana could come back and be a part of the ceremony.

One night during his senior year at school, Manuel had this dream:

It's my college graduation, but the ceremony is in the hall where my high school baseball banquets were held, so it feels like home. A big crowd of people are there conversing, and I see a few family members, but I hear nothing. I see people's mouths moving and realize that people are understanding each other, but no words can be heard.

Next, I look toward the entrance of the hall and see some of my great-uncles entering the hall. Following them is my Nana, who is followed by my great-aunt. They are all walking directly toward my family and me. Suddenly, I am overcome with good feelings. I feel no worries, no tension at all. Everybody is just happy. My eyes lock with my Nana's eyes, and I experience extreme feelings of joy and happiness. Everything is still mute, but she is communicating to me that she is very proud.

All of a sudden I see my Nana with her back to the floor. I am on my knees right beside her with my arm supporting her neck and my left hand caressing one of her hands. I have a weird feeling, and I look up and sense that everyone is in a state of pandemonium.

*I see complete panic on my family's faces. I hear nothing, but I can
tell by their faces that they are thinking that they need an ambulance and that they are fearing for Nana's life. But I just keep
thinking that everything is all good. I look back at Nana's face,
and I see in her eyes that she is telling me not to worry, that everything is fine. I know I don't have anything to worry about, and I
communicate to her that, yes, I understand. Everyone else is still
panicking. Inside I feel nothing but complete bliss, and as I look at
my Nana, I am one hundred percent sure that she is at peace with
herself. Everybody needs to relax! I continue to caress her hand, and
with each moment I become more and more overwhelmed with
feelings of complete bliss and ecstasy.*

At this point Manuel suddenly woke up, filled with those same
incredible feelings of joy and contentment. He smiled, and then
burst into several moments of uncontrollable laughter. He said that
as he lay in bed, he felt an "absolute happiness flowing throughout
all parts of [his] body." The feelings were so vivid that they stayed
with him for the rest of the day.

At a rational level, Manuel did not have a simple explanation for
what he had experienced. He remembered that Nana had always
said that when she died, she would come back to people in their
dreams to make sure they continued behaving well. Maybe his
dream showed that Nana's soul was indeed still alive and had actually come back to him, just as she had said she would, to guide him
in a time of need. Or maybe his dream simply reflected his own deep
unconscious desire to have Nana back in his life, a desire so strong
that it generated this remarkable dream experience. Manuel wasn't
sure, and he couldn't with certainty rule out either possibility.

Whatever its final explanation, Manuel's dream became a valuable source of emotional strength in his ongoing efforts to bring
his fractured family back together. At the beginning of the dream,
Manuel's family is part of the friendly but anonymous crowd, talking in a way that Manuel is not able to hear. He can't follow what
they're talking about because he's evidently tuned in to an entirely
different mode of perception. Suddenly his Nana and several other
deceased relatives come into the auditorium. Manuel and Nana
"lock eyes," and silently, without using words, they begin sharing

their thoughts and feelings with each other. Then there's an abrupt shift in the scene, and Nana is suddenly on the floor, with Manuel holding her. The rest of the family panics, fearing that Nana is dying and needs an ambulance; but the special connection Manuel has with his Nana remains strong and clear. He knows that Nana is fine and that everyone in the family should just calm down and try to relax.

There's no cowardly denial of Nana's dying in this dream, no wish-fulfilling fantasy of her getting off the floor and returning to normal life. What Manuel discovers in the dream is a profound confidence that even though Nana is leaving him, *they will still be together.* The rest of the family can't see beyond Nana's dying; they can't perceive anything other than the painful sadness they feel about her leaving them. Manuel now understands what the rest of his family does not—that even after Nana has died, a mysterious but incredibly powerful emotional connection will remain. Manuel's dream reveals to him the deeply paradoxical truth of this living connection beyond Nana's physical death. Even though he couldn't explain exactly what had happened in his dream, he now *knew*, with an absolute and unshakeable certainty, that he had to continue following Nana's guidance and do his best to remind his family of her continuing influence on all of them.

I call dreams like Manuel's "visitation dreams" because they involve a vivid and extremely memorable encounter between the dreamer and a deceased loved one. These dreams are quite different from other dreams in which the person who has died appears once again as a living character. In a visitation dream the dead person is more *alive*, more animated and self-possessed than in other dreams. "It felt like the dead person was *really* there" is a common reaction people have to such dreams. As in Manuel's case, the dreamer is often the only character able to see or to communicate with the dead person, who has returned to provide the dreamer with guidance, reassurance, and perhaps an important warning. Visitation dreams have a tremendous experiential impact on people, an impact so great that the images, sensations, and emotions of the dream remain clear and distinct in their memories for years afterward.

Last Embraces

Many visitation dreams culminate in the dreamer enjoying one last hug with the person who has died. In the midst of the embrace the dreamer focuses special attention on the quality of the dead person's body and the physical sensations of their touching each other. Manuel's dream is a good example because his description distinctly emphasized the physical sensations of holding Nana as she lay on the floor of the banquet hall—"I am on my knees right beside her with my arm supporting her neck and my left hand caressing one of her hands."

Another good example of this comes from a thirty-four-year-old woman named Ruth, whose mother was unexpectedly diagnosed with brain cancer. Her doctors did everything they could, but the cancer spread too quickly to be stopped. In just a matter of weeks, she died. Ruth and her family were devastated by the horribly sudden loss of the woman who had always been the emotional center of the family. Three months after her mother's death, Ruth had this dream:

> I'm at my family's house, and I hear some noise upstairs, the wind blowing a door open and shut. I call, "Mother, is that you?" and I hear the door open and shut twice, as if in response. Then I'm in the kitchen, and I see Mother's slippers on the floor, moving toward me. Mother slowly materializes up from her slippers and reaches out to me. Her eyes are closed at first, and she slowly struggles to open them. I'm terrified, but I don't run. I let Mother hug me, and her body feels strange, thin and kind of soft. I ask her how she's doing, and she says, "It's good, it's good," over and over. I want to ask more questions, but I realize Mother won't give me any more answers. Finally she says she must go and tells me she can come back one more time. Mother hugs me, and I wake up hugging myself.

Ruth called this "one of the 'realest' experiences of my life, a dream unlike any of the others I've had of Mom since she died." When Ruth awoke from the dream she found herself tightly hugging her own body. She couldn't help thinking that her mother had *really been there*—the physical power of the dream was so different from any other she had experienced. And, yet, Ruth knew that the paradoxical meaning of the dream was that her mother was really gone, too: "I realize Mother won't give me any more answers."

In some visitation dreams the physicality of the encounter takes on an almost clinical quality. Thirty-two-year-old Kim went with a group of friends to visit their old college roommate Keith, who had been stricken with cancer and was near death. Kim was overwhelmed by the horrifying sight of her good friend lying in the hospital's intensive care unit, heavily sedated and hooked up to a variety of life-support machines. From his hospital bed, Keith was able to hear Kim and the others when they spoke to him, but he could respond to them only through a machine that beeped at each reaction. After they left the hospital, Kim realized with a stab of regret that she had forgotten to hold Keith's hand one last time—she had been so overcome with emotion that she never physically touched him. A week later Keith died, and that night Kim had a dream:

> *I am lying in my bed when I see Keith at my bedside and feel the warmth of his skin as he slowly reaches for my hand. He stands close to me and holds my hand gently yet firmly for a long time. This feeling of his hand against mine is so real, too real to be a dream. In addition to the warmth of his flesh, I feel the firmness and thickness of his hand and the wrinkles that form on his palm and fingers as he holds my hand. [I almost opened my eyes to see if Keith were in fact standing by me for I had never experienced in dreams feelings that felt so real.] Neither of us speak nor is there any sound in the dream, and the atmosphere is that of tranquillity.*

When Kim awoke, the touch of Keith was still in her hand. She couldn't believe she could have such an intensely realistic physical sensation without actually having held another person's hand in her own. Kim was generally a skeptic regarding supernatural phenomena, and her work as a high school biology teacher gave her a strong appreciation for reason, logic, and science. Although she didn't think her dream proved that ghosts or spirits really exist, she admitted that she had never had such an experience before, and she even hesitated to call it a dream because it was so uniquely realistic. She felt that somehow or other Keith had really come back, and he was trying to help ease her regrets about that last sad visit in the hospital. In the dream, their positions are reversed—now Kim is the one lying motionless in bed, and Keith is standing beside her. Then he does what Kim wished *she* had done: He reaches for her hand and takes it in his own for a final, wordless goodbye.

When Kim woke up, she saw that Keith was gone. Slowly, she remembered that yesterday he had died, but Keith's touch still lingered in her hand. As Kim lay in bed, she knew she would never forget this feeling of having *really* been with him one last time.

The saddest, most poignant visitation dreams are those in which the dreamer desperately tries to touch or to hug the dead person but can't. One of the earliest historical descriptions of such a dream comes toward the end of Homer's epic poem *The Iliad*. In Book 23 of *The Iliad*, the great warrior Achilles prepares a funeral pyre for his fallen friend Patroclus, who had died in battle defending Achilles' honor. Achilles goes to sleep and has a dream of his recently deceased friend:

> The ghost [Patroclus] came and stood over his head and spoke a word to him: "You sleep, Achilles; you have forgotten me; but you were not careless of me when I lived, but only in death. Bury me as quickly as may be, let me pass through the gates of Hades. . . ." [Achilles replied,] "I shall do as you tell me. But stand closer to me, and let us, if only for a little, embrace, and take full satisfaction from the dirge of sorrow." So he spoke, and with his own arms reached for him, but could not take him, but the spirit went underground, like a vapor, with a thin cry, and Achilles started awake, staring.

Dreams like this, in which the dreamer is unable to make physical contact with the dead person, have the effect of emphasizing the permanence of death and the radical difference between the living and the dead. Particularly when people are having trouble accepting the painful reality of a loved one's death, dreams such as Achilles' come to make it absolutely clear that the person is gone and that the time has come for the mourning to be completed and the loved one allowed to depart.

A Murderer's Confession

On April 29, 1997, the Norristown, Pennsylvania, police received a frantic phone call from thirty-two-year-old Craig Rabinowitz, who screamed that his wife had just been murdered. When the police arrived at the suburban Philadelphia home, they found Rabinowitz's wife, Stephanie, naked in the bathtub, strangled to death. Holding his crying one-year-old daughter in his arms, Rabinowitz told the first officers who arrived on the scene that while he was asleep, his twenty-nine-year-old wife had gone to take a bath, and then someone must have broken into their house and killed her. The police became suspicious, however, when the autopsy showed a high level of sleeping medicine in the dead woman's bloodstream, an amount that would have made it almost impossible for her to get herself into a bathtub. When the police made the further discovery that Rabinowitz stood to receive $1.8 million in insurance money following his wife's death, they began a formal investigation of his role in the murder. What emerged in the police investigation was a lurid story of deceit and betrayal that became a local tabloid sensation.

It turned out that Rabinowitz did not have a job as a latex salesman, as he had led his wife and everyone else to believe. In fact he had been cheating several friends in a pyramid scheme, selling them $233,000 worth of phony shares in a fake company. The police also discovered that Rabinowitz currently owed over $100,000 to several credit card companies. The biggest scandal was that his huge personal debt was due in large part to his payments to numerous prostitutes. Rabinowitz was particularly obsessed with an exotic dancer who used the stage name "Summer" and who worked at Delilah's Den, one of the notorious "gentlemen's clubs" that lined the Delaware River area of Philadelphia. The police found that in the four months preceding Stephanie Rabinowitz's death, while she went to her job each day as an attorney with a small law firm in the city, Craig Rabinowitz visited Delilah's Den more than forty times and tipped Summer thousands of dollars each week. The police investigation also yielded a secret ledger Rabinowitz had written two weeks before his wife's murder. In the ledger Rabinowitz detailed his $671,000 in total debt, and the $2.1 million he expected to receive from the insurance policy, his wife's stock holdings, and the sale of their house.

Just days after the funeral for his wife, Craig Rabinowitz was arrested and charged with first-degree murder, theft by deception, and deceptive business practices. The prosecutor said Rabinowitz had slipped sleeping pills into his wife's drink so she couldn't defend herself, then choked her to death and left her in the bathtub.

Rabinowitz's friends and neighbors were shocked that he could cold-bloodedly murder his summer-camp sweetheart and the mother of his one-year-old daughter. Even after his arrest, Rabinowitz insisted that he was innocent, and he continued to say his wife had been killed by an intruder while he slept. But then on Friday, October 31, the morning his trial was to begin, Rabinowitz stunned the packed courtroom by changing his plea and admitting he was guilty of killing his wife. Crying so hard his whole body shook, Rabinowitz told the court he decided to confess because two days before he'd had a dream. In the dream he was visited by three people who were dead—his wife, Stephanie, her father, and his own father. As Rabinowitz described it:

> They put their hands on my hand and said, "Craig, it's time for you to do what's right. It's time for you to do the right thing."

As his mother and Stephanie's mother wept in their seats behind him, Rabinowitz said he was sorry for what he'd done, and he didn't want to put his family and daughter through a long, painful trial: "My life had become such a sham and a fake and a fraud, and the hole that I had been digging for myself became so deep, and it became deeper and deeper. Right became wrong, and wrong became right. My life was on a slippery slope. There were no excuses. I offer none."

The sad story of Craig Rabinowitz illustrates the darker side of visitation dreams. Those who have died sometimes come back to the living in dreams to deliver warnings and moral condemnations, chastising the dreamers for what they've done wrong and rebuking them for what they haven't done right. In Achilles' dream, his dead friend Patroclus returns to condemn him for failing to perform the proper funeral rites; and in Rabinowitz's dream, his deceased wife, father, and father-in-law come to him to speak for his conscience and persuade him that he must "do the right thing" and confess his crimes. The stern message delivered to Rabinowitz in his dream was emphasized by the presence not just of his dead wife but also of her father and his father, adding extra moral authority to the admonition to confess. The dream's message was further intensified by the sensation of physical contact between Rabinowitz and the three dead people: "They put their hands on my hand." To be touched by someone who has died, to feel their body pressing against your own, is to feel the realness of their presence and the inescapable truth of their words.

The Montgomery County prosecutor's case against Craig Rabinowitz was very strong, so it's likely he would have been convicted whether or not he confessed. Indeed, Rabinowitz may well have fabricated his dream to make himself appear more sympathetic and to cut a better deal with the prosecutor (by pleading guilty, Rabinowitz avoided the death penalty and was sentenced instead to life in prison without the possibility of parole). It's hard to trust anything said by a man whose entire life had become a sickening tangle of lies and deceptions. But the dream Rabinowitz says he had certainly does correspond to the basic features of other visitation dreams reported by people in various times and places all over the world. The dead people who return in these dreams come for the specific purpose of pressuring the dreamers through spoken admonitions, physical threats, and silent glares to do what they *know* at a certain level is the right thing to do.

The Soul and the Superego

As mentioned at the beginning of this chapter, many of the world's religions have understood visitation dreams to be real encounters with the souls of people who have died. This notion is so widely shared by traditions all across the globe that some scholars have gone so far as to argue that religion itself actually originated in dream experience and that prehistoric people first got the ideas of a

soul, an afterlife, and a whole mysterious realm of spiritual existence from the experiences they had each night in their dreams.
According to this theory, when prehistoric people woke up in their
caves or out on the savanna each morning, they talked with each
other to puzzle over what they had seen and felt while sleeping; and
over time a set of beliefs developed to explain the apparent realness
of the people and the places they had encountered. These beliefs
then became the basis for all religions, mythologies, and theologies.

Most researchers agree that whether dreams are the ultimate
origin of religion or not, dream experiences have certainly helped
to sustain, support, and renew people's religious beliefs. Visitation
dreams in particular have given people a deeply felt confirmation of
the continued existence of their loved ones in a nonphysical form
of existence.

But there is a different way of explaining visitation dreams, a
way that does not rely on religious or theological notions. The psychoanalytic concept of the superego provides a more naturalistic
account of how these dreams arise and what functions they serve in
people's lives. Freud introduced the term *superego* in his 1923 work,
The Ego and the Id, to describe the part of the mind that stands in
critical, judgmental opposition to the ego (the German word *Uber-
ich* could also be translated as "the over-I"). The superego is built
up in childhood out of parental prohibitions and demands; Freud
said in effect that all the dos and don'ts your parents beat into your
head as a kid are psychologically internalized until they form a distinct, autonomous part of your mind. Thus formed, the superego
has three different functions: first, to serve as the voice of conscience, judging your thoughts and behavior as right or wrong; second, to observe the ego and to provide a sense of self-awareness;
and third, to promote the basic ideals, values, and goals that guide
the ego through life. Although the words and actions of a child's parents are the immediate source of superego formation, Freud said
that a child's mother and father are actually involved in a process of
teaching a collective moral code that reaches far back into the history of their culture: "thus a child's superego is in fact constructed
on the model not of its parents but of its parents' superego; the
contents which fill it are judgments of value which have propagated
themselves in this manner from generation to generation."

The concept of the superego can be used to clarify many important aspects of people's visitation dreams. Particularly when the dead person who returns is a parent or a grandparent, these dreams have a powerful moral impact on people. They remind the dreamers of the love and the respect they *still feel* for the person who has died. Even though the loved one is physically gone, the ideals and the values that that person taught the dreamer remain a living, active presence in the dreamer's mind. In this view, the feeling of reassurance that people often experience in visitation dreams comes from a positive relationship between their ego and their superego, whereas feelings of fear or alienation would symbolize a conflict between the two parts of the mind. From a psychoanalytic perspective, the religious aura that surrounds so many visitation dreams makes perfect sense because religion is a tremendously powerful force in teaching, perpetuating, and enforcing a community's basic moral code. Whether or not visitation dreams involve an actual encounter with the soul of a deceased loved one, in psychological terms the dreams can be understood as self-generated symbolic expressions of how well the dreamers are, or are not, living up to the moral standards of their parents, their family, and the broader community.

Forebodings

As much as the preceding psychoanalytic theory explains, I hesitate to say it accounts equally well for other dreams involving death, dying, and encounters with the dead. Indeed, a few of these dreams defy explanation by *any* theory based on conventional psychological knowledge. Before going on, let me repeat what I believe is a crucial methodological principle in the study of dreams: *If we want to make an honest and thorough examination of the full range of extraordinary dream phenomena, we must not be scared off by theoretical assumptions about what is or isn't possible.*

With that said, here is a set of dream reports that raise particularly thought-provoking questions about the relationship between dreaming, dying, and death.

1. In early April of 1865, Abraham Lincoln told his wife, Mary, and Ward Lamon, an old Illinois attorney friend, that "just the

other night" he'd had a dream "which has haunted me ever since." Lincoln said that after awakening from the strange dream he opened the Bible, and suddenly found dreams, visions, and supernatural visitations everywhere he looked. Mary, who took matters of the spirit very seriously, became terribly worried, and Lincoln admitted that perhaps he shouldn't have mentioned his ominous dream to her. "But somehow the thing has got possession of me," he said and went on to describe the dream:

> About ten days ago, I retired very late. I had been up waiting for important dispatches from the front. I could not have been long in bed when I fell into a slumber, for I was weary. I soon began to dream. There seemed to be a deathlike stillness about me. Then I heard subdued sobs, as if a number of people were weeping. I thought I left my bed and wandered downstairs. There the silence was broken by the same painful sobbing, but the mourners were invisible. I went from room to room; no living person was in sight, but the same sounds of distress met me as I passed along. It was light in all the rooms; every object was familiar to me; but where were all the people who were grieving as if their hearts would break? I was puzzled and alarmed. What could be the meaning of all this? Determined to find the cause of a state of things so mysterious and shocking, I kept on until I arrived at the East Room, which I entered. There I met with a sickening surprise. Before me was a catafalque, on which rested a corpse wrapped in funeral vestments. Around it were stationed soldiers who were acting as guards; and there was a throng of people, some gazing mournfully upon the corpse, whose face was covered, others weeping pitifully. "Who is dead in the White House?" I demanded of one of the soldiers. "The President," was his answer; "he was killed by an assassin!" Then came a louder burst of grief from the crowd.

Mary and Lamon were both terribly alarmed by the dream, but Lincoln tried to reassure them by saying the dream portrayed not him, but someone else falling to an assassin.

A few days later, on Good Friday, April 14, 1865, Lincoln was shot while attending a play at Ford's Theater, and he died early in the morning of April 15. On April 19 his body lay in the East Room of the White House in a coffin atop a flower-covered catafalque, while hundreds of weeping mourners gathered around him to pay their last respects.

2. Gregg was a seventeen-year-old high school junior who lived in New York City and took the subway to and from school each day. One night he had three dreams right in a row that were so extremely intense and frightening that he got out of bed and ran to his brother's room, unable to sleep by himself for the rest of the night. In the first dream, Gregg is walking from the street down the stairs to the subway, when someone suddenly jumps out and stabs him. In the second dream, Gregg is sitting in a subway car and sees a woman dressed in black sitting across from him; he looks at her more closely, and to his horror he sees that the woman's face is a death's-head. The imagery of the third dream was more vague than the first two, but Gregg remembered being on the subway again and being stabbed with a knife.

Two weeks later Gregg was riding the subway back home from a party. He asked another passenger for a cigarette, and as the man gave him one, the train suddenly lurched and pitched sideways. Gregg and the man both lost their balance, and they awkwardly fell into each other's arms. The man suddenly became enraged, and he and his companion pulled out knives and began chasing Gregg through the train. Terrified, Gregg ran to the end of the car and tried to pry the door open, but it was stuck. Before Gregg could defend himself, the man stabbed him in the chest. Despite the blood pouring from his wound Gregg managed to fight off the two men and escape; he got out of the train at the next station and collapsed at the feet of a police officer. An ambulance rushed him to the hospital, where the doctors were just barely able to save his life—the deep knife thrust had punctured Gregg's left lung, but fortunately it had missed his heart by an inch.

3. Carol was a fifty-two-year-old Franciscan nun living in the United States. One night, she had a dream of her close friend Michael, a priest she had last seen several years earlier in Ireland. In her dream Michael is dressed in a khaki coat, wearing a hat and gloves, and carrying a small briefcase in his hand. Three times he says the same sentence to Carol: "All I wanted was fifteen minutes of your time to say goodbye to you." That was the end of

the dream. When Carol woke up, she felt puzzled and more than a little worried about Michael's well-being. Two days later she received a letter from a mutual friend in Ireland telling her that Michael's mother had died. Carol figured this was what her dream had been about; so she wrote a letter to Michael saying how sorry she felt and how much she missed his companionship. But the next day Carol received the shocking news that Michael had suddenly died of an unexpected heart attack. Her dream wasn't about Michael's mother, Carol thought to herself with a mixture of wonder and sadness; it was about Michael himself.

The next week Carol received a letter from another mutual friend. This friend said she felt the need to tell Carol of a very strange experience she had the morning of Michael's funeral. She dreamed that Michael comes to her, dressed in a khaki coat. In the dream the friend asks Michael if he is going to the funeral, and Michael says, "No, I don't like big events like that, and anyway I have something else to do: I have to go and say goodbye to Carol."

4. Judith was a thirty-four-year-old single mother from Guam who, because of serious health and financial problems, had to give her son Chris to her sister for legal adoption when the boy was born. Judith lived with Chris and her sister for the first few years of his life, and when the boy reached school age Judith moved to the United States to find better-paying work. One night at the end of the summer of 1990, when Chris was just about to start his first year of high school, Judith sprang awake in her bed—she'd just had a dream in which Chris is in his room at her sister's house when a huge earthquake hits. Judith quickly got on the telephone and tried to call Chris, but the line was busy. She tried to get the operator to cut in, but the operator said all lines to Guam were temporarily out of order because a major earthquake, measuring 8.2 on the Richter scale, had just struck the island.

It was two days before Judith finally reached Chris and found to her relief that he was fine. Yes, he said in answer to her hesitant question, he had been in his room when the earthquake hit.

5. Twelve-year-old Janet came home from school one day and asked her mother if it would be okay for her to help her best friend Sandra baby-sit Sandra's younger sister on Friday night. Janet's mother said that was fine, so the next day Janet told her friend San-

dra they were all set. But a strangely frightened Sandra said she suddenly didn't think it was a good idea. She told Janet that the previous night she'd had a terrifying nightmare. In the dream she and Janet are baby-sitting. Sandra and her sister are upstairs in a room playing, and Janet goes downstairs to get a glass of water. She runs into a burglar who had snuck into the house. He takes out a knife and slices her throat. Sandra and her sister hear the commotion downstairs and hide together in a closet. At that point Sandra woke up from the dream, crying and trembling with fear.

Later that day Janet mentioned Sandra's dream to her mother. Her mother was a deeply religious and superstitious woman, and she immediately changed her mind and forbade Janet from babysitting at Sandra's house. Janet became very upset and angry, shouting, "But, Mom, it was just a dream!" Her mother was adamant, however, and she said her decision was final.

When Janet came home from school on Monday, she ran to her mother's side and hugged her. Through her tears Janet said that while Sandra had been baby-sitting Friday night, a man had broken into the house. Luckily, Sandra and her younger sister were upstairs playing, and when they heard noises coming from below, they had quietly gone to hide in a closet. They stayed in the closet, crying and holding each other, for two hours until their parents came home.

6. Sixteen-year-old Vicky had a dream one night about being at a coffee shop with three friends, one of whom had moved to Oregon the previous year. The four of them are chatting and laughing when all of a sudden the friend who had moved to Oregon stands up and leaves. He walks out into the street, gets hit by a car, and dies.

Later the next day Vicky got a frantic phone call from one of her friends, telling her that their Oregon friend had been driving home last night when he got into a fatal car crash. Vicky was horrified, and she couldn't help feeling that their friend had really come to her in her dream and that somehow she had missed an opportunity to prevent his death.

The quickest and most dismissive explanation of dream reports like these is that the people are simply making them up. That's always a possibility, and one that may well account for a significant percentage of such reports. But it's hard to believe that *all* reports of what I call "dreams of foreboding" are pure fabrications, total and complete lies with absolutely no connection to any actual dreams the people experienced. The reports come from too many different people in too many different circumstances, and none of the people have any obvious motivation to lie about what they've dreamed. Look back at the first example: If you can't trust Abraham Lincoln to honestly and faithfully report what he's experienced, whom can you trust?

The second quickest explanation of these reports is to grant that, yes, the people are honestly describing their dreams, but they're wrong in connecting the dreams to a particular waking-life event. The dreams may *appear* to accurately predict something that later happens in waking life, but *in fact* there is no real connection, and the dreamer is incorrect to infer any such causal relationship between the dream and the event. It's just a coincidence.

This explanation is supported by two powerful arguments. First, there's no apparent reason why these few dreams come true while many others just like them don't. Every time someone dreams of an earthquake, there isn't an actual earthquake; people have car crash dreams all the time, but in only a fraction of these cases do the people subsequently get into a waking-life auto accident. Indeed, there's a good probability that over a long enough period of time *someone* will dream about an earthquake at the same time a real earthquake strikes somewhere nearby and *someone* will dream of a car crash the night before he or she really has an accident. This isn't prophecy; it's just the law of averages.

The second argument supporting the "it's just a coincidence" explanation is that current psychological knowledge cannot specify exactly how a dreaming person's mind could accurately foresee an event. Several decades of careful scientific inquiry have proven that the human mind operates according to basic physical laws that govern perception, memory, reasoning, and even emotion. These laws can be clearly identified, rationally understood, and experimentally verified; and the problem with the six dream reports is that they show scant evidence of obeying such laws. The details are too fuzzy and inconsistent (e.g., why does Vicky dream about her

Oregon friend being hit by a car when in waking life he was the driver?), and the time factor is often confused (e.g., why do some people dream of future events a few weeks before the given event, while others dream about the event the very night before?). If the dreaming mind does have the power to foresee the future, it employs that power more obscurely and arbitrarily than any other mental faculty known to current science. It's all the more likely, then, that seemingly prophetic dreams are in fact just very unusual coincidences.

The force of this explanation is strong, although it rests almost entirely on theoretical grounds. Good, solid, scientific research on these kinds of extraordinary dreams is notoriously difficult to conduct. How could you generate empirical data on this phenomenon—bring a group of subjects into a sleep laboratory and measure their dream reactions as you go, without their knowledge, to a distant city and violently threaten their friends or family members there? No Human Subjects Committee is going to approve that project! The difficulty for researchers is that the circumstances in which dreams of foreboding naturally occur cannot be easily controlled, replicated, or measured. As a result, the only empirical data on such dreams come from isolated personal reports like the six presented earlier, and these reports are always vulnerable to the charges of fabrication or coincidence.

I don't have a quick and easy answer to the question of how to explain dreams of foreboding. But I do believe, very strongly, that someday researchers *will* be able to explain these dreams according to basic physical laws that can be clearly identified, rationally understood, and experimentally verified. Right now, the best data available are several good pieces of evidence that may not add up to a complete explanation but that do point researchers in potentially fruitful directions of investigation.

One of these pieces of evidence is the unusual intensity of these dreams: Perhaps the difference between nonpredictive car crash dreams and the rare few that actually do anticipate an accident in waking life is the extreme vividness and experiential power of the latter. Perhaps genuine dreams of foreboding carry with them an extra charge of neurochemical energy, an energy that could be measured and analyzed by currently available research technology.

106   TRANSFORMING DREAMS

Another important piece of evidence is the subject of the dreams: In most cases these dreams involve a sudden threat of often violent death to the dreamer or to an especially close friend or family member. People don't have dreams of foreboding about trivial, emotionally insignificant events; rather, their dreams deal with immediate and unexpected threats to the very survival of either the dreamers or people the dreamers care deeply about. This suggests that dreams of foreboding are somehow tied in with basic instincts for self-preservation. The capacity to have such dreams may therefore have evolved according to the same principles of adaptation and natural selection that have shaped the rest of the human mind.

Yet another piece of evidence comes from research on the role of dreams in helping people anticipate and prepare for future activities in their waking lives (e.g., a basketball player dreaming about how the next game will be, a teacher dreaming about the lesson plan for the next day's class). As one researcher put it, dreams "enable us to revise our pictures of our present selves and to rehearse our responses to future challenges." If dreams are already known to have the ability to look toward the future and to prepare the dreamer for different probabilities, perhaps dreams of foreboding like those described earlier involve a special extension of that prospective ability to anticipate coming events and experiences.

The last piece of evidence is the fact that, at least in modern Western society, dreams of foreboding are most frequently reported by children and adolescents. Admittedly, one possibility is that children and adolescents have weaker powers of reasoning than adults and thus are more likely to confuse fact with fantasy. But another possibility is that humans are born with certain dreaming abilities that, with the passage of time, are lost, outgrown, or socialized into disuse.

Here is one final report to support that latter possibility:

Wanda was a thirteen-year-old girl who was being raised in a fundamentalist Christian family. A few weeks before her eighth-grade prom, she dreamed that her mother would be in a car accident the very night of the prom. In her dream Wanda saw that, for some unknown reason, her prom dress was in the car, as was her mother's collection of record albums. Wanda told her best friend about the dream, and they were both stunned when on the night of the prom Wanda's mother did indeed have a car crash. Without telling Wanda, she had taken her daughter's prom dress to be hand-tailored, and on the way to the tailor she was taking her stereo and albums to loan to a friend. When Wanda and her friend told her mother about the dream, and about other dreams Wanda felt had accurately foreseen future events, her mother became frightened and angry. "I'm not going to be the mother of a *witch!*" she shouted. Realizing how upset her mother was and how inconsistent her dreams were with the family's religious beliefs, Wanda simply stopped having such dreams. "To this day," she said some years later, "I believe I somehow chose to shun that ability, but I do not know how I might turn it 'on' again if I wanted."

Death as a Symbol

Even if the possibility is left open that a few dreams do accurately foresee the death of the dreamer or of someone emotionally close to the dreamer, it remains true that the vast majority of death dreams has a symbolic rather than a literal meaning. The supreme existential importance of death makes it a perfect symbol for the dreaming imagination to use in conveying a variety of meanings. When people suffer especially dire losses or find themselves going through painful periods of change, dreams of death often emerge to bring to the people's full awareness their deepest feelings about what they're experiencing. Just like dreams in which sexuality serves as a symbol to express nonsexual meanings, these dreams use dramatic, attention-grabbing images of death and dying to symbolize other kinds of serious waking-life concern.

One night during her sophomore year in college Rita had a terribly frightening dream that her father had died. The dream's setting jumped from place to place, but what Rita remembered most clearly was being at her high school football field where in waking life she and her classmates had gathered for graduation:

She is there for her father's funeral. Rita is supposed to give a speech for him, with hundreds of people sitting in white chairs on the field before her. She starts talking, but midway through her talk the people in the chairs start filing off the field row by row. She keeps going with the speech anyway, and when she is finished, Rita's mother pulls her aside and says, "It was only supposed to be a penny!" Although this phrase doesn't seem to fit the situation, Rita knows that her mom means she was only supposed to talk for one minute.

Then Rita is pounding on the kitchen floor of her boyfriend's home, screaming "It's not fair!" over and over again.

When she woke up, Rita was in tears, and she couldn't sleep for the rest of the night. First thing in the morning, she called her dad to make sure he was all right—she feared her dream might mean he was really going to die. She learned that her father was fine, and after their conversation Rita was left to ponder the meaning of her deeply affecting but evidently *not* prophetic dream. As she thought about the dream, she realized that in addition to feeling sad, she also felt angry and frustrated because there was nothing she could do to change or to fix the situation—the recurrent cry "It's not fair!" echoed in her mind as a poignant expression of deep, raw emotion. Another thing she noticed was that in all the various scenes she was the only person grieving; no one else seemed to be expressing any real feelings. And Rita was especially struck by the coldness of her mother's criticism for exceeding the proper time in her funeral speech. The strange words her mother used—"It was only supposed to be a penny!"—had a demeaning and hurtful tone.

Several friends and family members in the dream asked Rita how her father had died, and to her intense frustration she didn't know how to answer them. The fact that in her dream her father's cause of death was unknown led Rita to try to think of a more symbolic or metaphorical way of understanding the experience. She found herself thinking about how in waking life she missed seeing her father on a regular basis. As Rita focused on these feelings of sadness and loss, the various elements of the dream began to make sense. Her parents had separated two years earlier, during the summer following her high school graduation. As a result, Rita's father had moved to a different town, and he and Rita could not see each other as much as they had in the past. The night before the dream, Rita and her mother had argued about the separation, which seemed to be the basis for their strange interaction about the funeral speech. Although Rita had struggled over the preceding two years to hide her grief, in the dream she finally let loose with her real emotions, despite the crowd's inattention and her mother's dismissive words. Rita's high school graduation was the last time she remembered her family being together and happy, in stark contrast to the atmosphere of tragic sadness in the dream. She took this contrast to be the key to the dream's meaning: "I believe the dream was telling me that I need to find a balance in my life, in which I let go of what I can't change and make the best out of what I have." Although she did not lose her dad physically, she realized that she had lost him in other ways, that he had symbolically "died." She now knew the time had come for her to accept that fact and to move on with her life.

The understanding that Rita gradually reached about her dream highlights an important element in dreams of death: Death is always the beginning of new life. This element is often lost amid the overwhelming feelings of sadness and loss; but if people reflect carefully enough, they almost always find amid all the desolation a ray of hope in the dream, a reason to continue having faith in the future. The eternal cycle of life, death, and rebirth that governs Nature also governs people's emotional lives; and dreams like Rita's illustrate how any experience of loss, no matter how tragic or devastating, creates the opportunity for new life and new growth. After her high school graduation Rita had gone on to college, where she had met new friends, done very well academically, and learned how to live on her own. Although her dream made her more aware of how deeply hurt she is at the loss of her father (that is, it did not wishfully deny or repress her negative feelings), the dream also encouraged Rita to move forward in her life, just as she did when she left high school and went to college. The mysterious paradox of this cycle of life, death, and rebirth is that only by fully accepting the reality of a terrible emotional loss can new life begin to take form and to grow into the future.

When the Dreamer Dies

One of the pieces of folk belief I picked up as a child was the idea that if you died in a dream you would really die. This bit of playground wisdom sounded perfectly plausible to me because my chasing nightmares usually ended right at the point when the monster was about to catch me. I knew I was going to be killed, there was no hope of escaping, the monster was *right there*—but I never actually died in the dream. However, I could readily imagine all the horribly painful things the monster would do to me if I didn't wake up at just that moment; so I was always grateful that I could break back into consciousness before actually dying in the dream and possibly dying in waking life, too.

As mentioned at the beginning of this chapter, medical statistics show that a high percentage of disease-related deaths occur during sleep. It may well be that at the moment people die in their sleep, they are also dreaming of dying. If so, the mentally experienced dreams would be caused by the physically experienced process of dying. But what I heard as a kid from my friends was that the reverse was possible, too: If you died in a dream, you might suddenly die for real, even though you were otherwise healthy and sickness-free.

As a researcher I've always had a special interest in hearing dream reports in which the dreamer does have an experience of dying. Such dreams are quite rare, but they definitely do occur. Beyond satisfying my personal curiosity about the folk beliefs of my childhood, these dream reports are worth studying because they add a new dimension to the understanding of the dreaming imagination.

Betsy was a teenager whose most memorable dream involved such an experience:

> *I am in a bedroom, but strangely I can't remember whose bedroom it is. I notice the room is furnished mostly in pink, with pink sheets, pink pillows, and a pink comforter. The walls are pink, too. I am lying on a bed, and my mom and a friend of hers are also in the room. My mom asks me to pass a hair dryer (or maybe hair rollers), and for some reason my mom suddenly gets mad and starts yelling at me. I think maybe I have been too slow, but I am really not sure why my mom is so mad. Then my mother reaches back and grabs a gun and shoots me in the head. I could vividly feel the blood rushing through my body, especially my head.*

After a few moments of this very disturbing and weird sensation, Betsy woke up.

Betsy knew that the dream symbolized the troubled nature of her relationship with her mother. The two of them were not close, and Betsy was aware that her mother felt very angry that they didn't spend more time together. At the time of the dream, they had been fighting over what Betsy should choose as her major in college. Her mother wanted her to study computer science. Because Betsy had no real interest in the subject, she vigorously resisted her mother's pressure to conform to her expectations of what her daughter should do and be. The dream image of being shot in the head perfectly expressed Betsy's terrible feeling that she could never please her mother. In symbolic terms, her mother's demands were threatening to kill her.

What most struck Betsy, though, was the extreme realism of the experience of being shot. She had never actually been shot before, but in the dream the sensation of blood rushing out of her head was remarkably clear and disturbingly lifelike.

The question arises, then, of why the dreaming imagination would go to the trouble of creating, without any prior experience on which to build, such a uniquely horrible feeling. Why would a person's mind make up a dream of actually dying? The answer, at least in Betsy's case, seems to be that the dream created these intense physiological sensations in order to emphasize the vital importance of its symbolic meanings. When Betsy woke up, she couldn't help but think about what her mother had done to her in the dream. This in turn forced her to reflect more directly on what was going on in her waking-life relationship with her mother, and specifically on their disagreement about her college major. The vividly felt experience of being shot in the head gave unforgettable emphasis to the dream's basic message that her mother's demands posed a genuine threat to Betsy's survival—not literally to the life of her body, but more symbolically to the life of her mind. Betsy's dream made sure she was fully aware that in these arguments with her mother, nothing less than her future was at stake.

Phillip was another adolescent who was struggling in his relationship with his parents. To the outside world his family looked perfectly tranquil and trouble-free, but Phillip had increasingly begun to doubt the sincerity and depth of their love for him. When he was twelve years old, he had the following dream:

> *I'm swimming in my backyard pool by myself on a normal summer day. My father is barbecuing over the fire pit, wearing a chef's hat and a plain white apron over his golf attire. He is whistling some tune, but to me it sounds very distant and indistinguishable. My mother comes outside holding a tray of glasses. She asks repeatedly in a monotonous voice, "Would anyone like some lemonade?" That is all she says, over and over again. I don't answer her but continue to swim. I turn on my back so that I can just float in the water. Then I notice a tiger, pacing back and forth on the plant platform that hangs over our pool. This terrifies me, and I am frozen stiff with fear and can't move. The tiger begins to pounce; and just as he does, I hear from behind me, "No need to worry, sir, I'll take care of that." I turn around and see a nineteenth-century hunter, one who looks as if he would hunt an elephant for nothing more than the prize of his ivory tusks. Complete with baggy khaki pants and hard hat, his rifle is already pointed and he fires. At this moment the dreamtime goes into slow motion. I see the bullet traveling straight for me. I see the tiger just hanging in the air, claws out and teeth in a snarl. I see my parents kissing in the corner, unaware of what is happening to me. I see the hunter with his curly mustache wink at me. I see all these things, but I am immobile. The bullet strikes me right in the chest, and I feel my heart explode. I know I am dead. I feel my body float on top of the water, and my vision turns red. Everything I see is through a shade of dark red. Then I feel my body being pulled upward as I begin to float. I hear very demonic drums pounding all around me, and that's where the dream ends.*

The first connection Phillip noticed between the deeply disturbing dream and his waking life was the behavior of his parents. The dream's picture of them as a stereotypical suburban couple, blissfully ignorant in their little backyard utopia, accurately expressed Phillip's view that they had always cared more about their social image than about him, or about anything else. Phillip initially thought the tiger was a force of evil trying to kill him, and he assumed the hunter had appeared to rescue him from the tiger. But closer reflection made Phillip question that first reading of the dream. Perhaps, he wondered, it wasn't an accident that the hunter's shot missed the tiger and fatally struck him instead. Perhaps the hunter's cryptic words, "No need to worry, sir, I'll take care of that," were referring to the problem of *Phillip*, not of the tiger. Maybe the savage power of the tiger was actually his savior, rescuing him from the highly civilized but ultimately lifeless world of his parents—a life in which he was passively floating in a pool of suburban self-satisfaction. The more Phillip thought about the hunter and his negative associations with the rich, aristocratic men who slaughtered noble animals for no other reason than to increase their own material wealth, the more Phillip began to reevaluate who was good and who was evil in his dream.

In the dream's final scene the hunter's bullet strikes Phillip in the chest and he feels his heart explode. His vision turns to red, his body is being drawn upward by an unseen power, and he hears demonic drumming pounding all around him. The physical sensation of upward movement was very strong in the dream. It made Phillip think of the biblical story of Jacob's dream of the heavenly ladder and also of Sunday school teachers telling him that when good people die they ascend to heaven and that when bad people die they descend to hell. More broadly, the experience of dying in his dream made Phillip think about religion in general and about the difference between his parents' religious beliefs (they were devout Catholics who went to Mass every Sunday without fail) and his own uncertain ideas: God does exist, but the Catholic religion is not 100 percent right about everything.

As Phillip grew older, he came to believe that the dream symbolized "the death of an innocence of always believing in what my parents told me as being the definitive truth." What died in his dream, he felt, was his parents' view of religion. Phillip's upward ascension following this death marked the beginning of a journey to discover his *own* beliefs about the reality and the truth of religion. He understood that this would be a difficult quest—Phillip felt that the demonic drumming was a warning about the dangerous temptations that can arise when a person strays from organized religion. But Phillip drew confidence from the fact that a mysterious *something* existed in his dream that was pulling him through the ominous drumming and up into the heavens. His dream gave him faith that as he grew up he would find new energies and new possibilities, even if those discoveries meant the painful "death" of his identity as the dutiful son of successful suburban parents.

Mourning, Secularization, and the Creation of Meaning

As the dreams described in the previous two sections suggest, symbolic deaths can be just as emotionally devastating as literal deaths. Rita's loss of her relationship with her father following her parents' separation and the ending of Phillip's "age of innocence" within the religious and social world of his family both set in motion the same emotional dynamics that would have accompanied the actual physical death of a loved one. Any experience of deep loss tears a hole in a person's life, a hole that can destabilize everything else in the person's world and call into question the basic meanings that had always given order and security to one's existence.

Phillip's story has a special significance because it displays in microcosmic form a kind of emotional loss that afflicts modern society as a whole. In sociological terms this type of loss is called *secularization*, and there are two basic views of what it involves: From one perspective, *secularization* is the historical process by which modern science has defeated religion as the preeminent way of ordering and understanding reality. The defeat of religion and the triumph of modern science is seen in this view as a forward advance in the development of human civilization. Religion was spawned by ignorance, fear, and weakness, but science now enables people to do without religion's comforting illusions and to adopt a more mature, realistic view of the world. Some people may initially feel sad that religion is gone, but with time they will learn that they can actually be happier and more fulfilled without religion's mind-stunting dogmas and morally restrictive rules of conduct.

Scholars who take the second perspective reverse this argument and claim that secularization involves the process of religion adapting to, rather than being destroyed by, modern science. Religion hasn't been defeated; it has just taken new and improved forms. In this view of secularization, humans have an inherent and indestructible *need* for religion; and as traditional religious institutions have declined in influence, new forms of religious expression have arisen to take their place and to satisfy that basic human need. Psychology is perhaps the most important new arena in which modern people explore fundamentally religious concerns. Psychology performs many of the basic functions that religions have traditionally served—it reveals deep truths about human nature, offers advice on how to live a fulfilling life, and provides therapeutic treatments to cure people's suffering. Although people in modern society are right to feel sad about the loss of traditional religion, they are fortunate that their religious needs can be satisfied just as well by psychology and by various other new forms of religious expression.

The sharp contrast between these two views of secularization corresponds exactly to a contrast in the dream theories of Freud and Jung. Many people are unaware that for several years, beginning in 1908, Freud and Jung were extremely close colleagues and very intimate friends. Jung was Freud's heir apparent as leader of the budding psychoanalytic movement, and the two men worked vigorously together on editing publications, organizing conferences, establishing training institutes, and generally promoting each other's ideas. You might say that Jung was one of the earliest Freudians, and Freud one of the first Jungians. But in 1912 they had a bitter falling out. Although many factors contributed to the rupture in their friendship, one such factor was their differing ideas about the relationship between dreams, religion, and science. Freud held a "decline" view of secularization: He believed religion originated in the frightening helplessness that humans feel in childhood, and he saw scientific rationality as a force that could help modern Westerners overcome their infantile anxieties and achieve true maturity. Freud believed psychoanalysis had rescued dreams from the realm of superstition and ignorance, and he used dream interpretation as a tool to build up ever greater rational control and mastery over the unconscious. Jung, however, held a "transposition" view of secularization: For him, the scientific and technological achievements of the modern West have been won at the terrible cost of destroying traditional religious symbols and values and creating a painful disunity within each person. He believed that psychology was essentially a new religion that could satisfy those basic needs for existential truth, moral guidance, and relief from suffering. Dreams for Jung were a vital means of helping "disunited" people reintegrate themselves and find within themselves the religious fulfillment they could not find from modern science.

Looking back at Phillip's dream of being shot and killed by the hunter, I think that neither Freud's nor Jung's view of secularization adequately accounts for what he experienced. Phillip saw his dream as expressing the death of his life within the world of his family—a world that was governed by both religion *and* science. His parents were devout Catholics, and they were also affluent members of a highly rationalized and thoroughly materialistic society. The challenge for Phillip wasn't choosing one or the other way of life; rather, it was trying to find a *new* source of meaning and value that would enable him to transcend the stifling dogmas of religion and the lifeless materialism of science.

In this way, Phillip's dream reflects what I believe is a fundamental challenge facing many, many people in contemporary society. Traditional religious teachings are no longer truly satisfying, but neither is a purely rational, scientific worldview that values nothing other than material gain. The various psychologies and New Age movements that have arisen in recent years do not provide any real fulfillment or guidance either.

Freud's and Jung's views of secularization, first formulated at the beginning of the twentieth century, fail to appreciate the terrible complexity of the existential dilemma confronting people who are living through the end of that century and looking into the beginning of the next: What does a person do when God is dead and Science is dead, too? Where does a person find the ultimate meanings and values to orient his or her life?

The interest that many modern people have in dreams is motivated by a growing belief that in these mysterious expressions of the unconscious imagination, they may find a resolution to that painful existential dilemma. The dreams of death discussed in this chapter show why that belief is justified: *Dreams mourn our losses and begin the process of creating new meanings*. Dreams of death respond to experiences of loss by helping people face the inescapable, irreversible reality of death (whether literal or symbolic); the dreams guide people toward the creation of new values, new ideals, and new ways of understanding life. The intense memorability of these dreams is key, because it's only when the dreams become *conscious* that the losses are finally accepted and the new meanings can truly begin to take shape.

In a world of unprecedented historical change and social transformation, the highest value of dreaming may be to provide each individual with a direct personal resource to help in the process of mourning the losses of the past and of striving to create new meanings for the future.

PART TWO

Pathways

CHAPTER FIVE

Reflecting on Your Dreams

Romeo: *If I may trust the flattering truth of sleep,*
My dreams presage some joyful news at hand.
　　　　　—William Shakespeare, *Romeo and Juliet*

The first four chapters of this book have focused on the deep experiential impact that dreams can have on people's lives. By means of strikingly vivid imagery, haunting, multilayered symbolism, and hyperrealistic physical and emotional sensations, certain dreams have the power to change people's whole outlook on life, expanding their self-awareness and enriching their sensitivity to and their understanding of the world around them. The stories narrated in the preceding chapters testify to the mysteriously potent force of dreams in human life, a force that neither religion nor science has ever adequately explained.

The next four chapters shift from tales to pathways, from narrative descriptions of people's most powerful dream experiences to the practical exploration of the many dimensions of meaning to be discovered in those experiences. The coming chapters offer readers a clear and systematic approach to the interpretation of especially memorable dreams. The methods and techniques presented in the following chapters are intended to provide practical guidance to anyone—and I do mean *anyone*—who wants to explore these types of dreams in greater detail. Therapists; counselors; members of the clergy; academic researchers from the humanities, social sciences, and natural sciences; artists; teachers; health care providers; social workers; and just ordinary people who simply want to learn more about their own dreams—*all* are invited to try the approach I offer and to see if it doesn't lead to a better understanding of the nature and the meaning of their big dreams.

Shapes in the Clouds

Before going any further, I'd like to address an issue that goes to the heart of all efforts to interpret dreams. This is an issue that dates back at least as far as Aristotle, the Greek philosopher from the fourth century B.C. who composed, among his many writings, two short treatises on the subject of dreams. Aristotle was, of course, quite familiar with the religious and mythological traditions of his culture, and he knew that many of his contemporaries believed dreams were revelatory messages from the gods. But Aristotle thought the phenomena of the natural world were better explained by science than by religion; regarding dreams, he suggested that any meanings they might have were most likely the result of humans reading messages *into* them. Aristotle compared dream interpretation to the pastime of trying to discern shapes in passing cloud formations—dreams "possess verisimilitude after the manner of cloud-shapes, which in their rapid metamorphoses one compares now to human beings and a moment afterward to centaurs."

Putting Aristotle's point in modern terms, dreams could be compared to the Rorschach ink blots that are widely used in personality testing and research. There is no intrinsic meaning to the Rorschach ink blots; they are random, purposeless shapes. However, when people look at the ink blots, they usually imagine they see faces, or animals, or a variety of other objects, all of which seem to be part of an intentional design. But, in fact, that apparent design is entirely of the person's own creation, a projection of subjective meaning onto an objectively meaningless context. Just so, interpreting dreams could be regarded as nothing more than a process of subjective projection, the fanciful imposition of personal wishes onto what is essentially a nonintentional, noncommunicative, purposeless phenomenon of the mammalian brain.

I have two responses to this skeptical line of thinking about dream interpretation. The first is a pragmatic one, the "even if" response. *Even if* dreams are intrinsically random products of the brain's autonomous activities during REM sleep, the process of interpreting them can still provide people with extremely valuable insights into their deepest conflicts, concerns, hopes, and desires. The many psychologists who administer Rorschach tests do so because the distinctive projections a person makes onto the different ink blots are tremendously helpful in revealing that person's fundamental personality dynamics. The fact that the ink blots are intrinsically meaningless by no means invalidates the important knowledge that can come from analyzing and reflecting on the shapes and the forms that people imagine they see in the blots. The same is true, I would argue, of interpreting dreams: Whether the dreams are meaningful or meaningless in themselves, the process of interpreting them can provide great personal insight and a significant expansion of self-awareness.

From a strictly practical point of view, then, the skepticism of Aristotle does not undermine the methods and the techniques of dream interpretation to be outlined in the following four chapters. Dreams are certainly no less useful than cloud formations or Rorschach ink blots for eliciting subjective projections that can provide valuable insights into the most important concerns of a person's life.

Having said that, I have a second and much stronger response to this general question about the legitimacy of dream interpretation. This response goes beyond the purely pragmatic perspective to focus on the extraordinary qualities of big dreams, qualities that have been discussed in great detail in the first four chapters of this book. Taken as a whole, I believe these qualities point to the following conclusion: *Big dreams are not random.* Unlike clouds and ink blots, highly memorable dreams do indeed have intrinsic meanings that relate in specific, discernible ways to the dreamer's waking life. In some cases the connections between the dream and the person's life are immediately obvious, and the dreamer sees them right away. In other cases the meanings appear more gradually, after a process of patient analysis and reflection. Whether the interpretation comes quickly or slowly, the key point is that the meanings of big dreams are *not* random—they emerge directly out of the imagery and the symbolism of the dreams themselves and are not simply the product of the dreamer's personal projections.

John Keats and the Negative Capability

When people begin the process of trying to interpret a big dream, they often have one of two different reactions. The first is an uncomfortable and vaguely threatening sense of confusion and emptiness: "Geez, I have absolutely *no* idea what this dream could possibly mean." The second reaction is the opposite: an overwhelming urge to *talk*, to instantly give voice to all the different ideas and insights that come rushing into one's mind. Both of these reactions are understandable and even natural responses to big dreams. The feeling of confusion is an accurate expression of the vast distance that separates the conscious mind from that shadowy unconscious realm from which such dreams originate. The powerful urge to talk reflects a legitimate eagerness to bridge that gap and to bring the energies of the dream into connection with conscious self-awareness.

But as understandable as these two reactions may be, they both have an unfortunate tendency to impede the process of interpretation. The first reaction exaggerates the difficulty of discerning a big dream's meanings, and the second exaggerates the speed and the simplicity of grasping those meanings. In both cases the interpretive process is short-circuited before it even begins.

My counsel to someone who is seeking to interpret a big dream is to begin by adopting what the poet John Keats called "the negative capability." Keats said that this was the mental condition in which a person "is capable of being in uncertainties, mysteries, doubts, without any irritable reaching after fact and reason." The frame of mind Keats is describing is one that is calm and loose, fully engaged in the matter at hand and yet completely open to the emergence of new and unexpected possibilities. The best synonym I can think of for this mental state is *playful*—a readiness to play, to explore, to experiment, to learn, and to create. Keats said the negative capability is the essential precondition for the writing of poetry, and I believe it's also the best starting point for the interpretation of especially memorable dreams.

One must admit that entering into this frame of mind is no easy matter. If a person is feeling tired or stressed, or hurried or distracted, if he or she is suffering from heartburn or a headache, it can be pretty difficult to get into a spirit of Keatsian playfulness. Many people find that the practice of some kind of relaxation exercise like deep-breathing, yoga, or meditation is an essential preliminary to the interpretation of dreams. Other people need nothing more than a quiet room in which they can be alone, without interruption, for a half hour or so. Whatever it takes, the closer they can come to an attitude of relaxed, playful openness, the better.

As an aside, I believe this explains why it's so difficult to interpret dreams in a public setting, particularly in performative contexts such as radio talk shows, television interviews, and classroom or general audience lectures. Settings like these bring with them a variety of extrinsic pressures and anxieties (e.g., worries about social conformity, desires for status enhancement, rigid time constraints) that make it almost impossible to achieve that calm, playful attitude from which the fullest and most satisfying interpretations emerge. This doesn't mean valid work can't be done in such settings—I make public presentations on dreams all the time, and I'm pretty confident the people in attendance walk away with a genuinely better sense of what their dreams mean. But I'm always acutely aware of how much *more* people can learn in other settings that are free from such pressures and limitations. In the end there's no substitute for a quiet, relaxed, unpressured frame of mind, whatever the methods one uses to achieve it.

Asking Questions of Specification

If you can generate a mental state that somewhat approximates the negative capability, I suggest that you first ask questions of *specification* of a big dream. These questions take their point of departure from the fact that dreams have infinite creativity at their disposal—dreams can set you in any place, with anyone, doing anything. *Why, out of all the infinite possibilities available, does your dream portray* these *particular details?* Take as an example a dream of driving a red sports car. Questions of specification for that dream could be: Why does the dream have you in this particular vehicle rather than in a station wagon, a public transit bus, or a horse-drawn carriage? What makes a red sports car a distinctive kind of transportation? Have you ever seen, been in, or owned such a vehicle? How would a red sports car be different from a green one, or a brown one, or any other color it could have been? How would you describe a red sports car to a friendly alien from another planet who had no idea what a car was? What do cars *do?* How are they made? What role do they play in people's lives?

Take as another example a dream of seeing your best friend from third grade. You could ask such questions as: What are the most distinctive qualities and characteristics of that friend? How is she different from any other person you've known? What did she look like, where did she live, how did she dress? How would the feel of the dream change if, instead of your third-grade friend, you saw your high school sweetheart, or your supervisor from work, or your next-door neighbor? How would you describe your friend to that alien from another planet—what are friends, anyway? How are they different from other kinds of people? How are friendships formed, and how do they end?

If you ask these questions of specification of each element of the dream, the answers will come in the form of a stream of memories, associations, and connections between the dream and various waking-life thoughts and experiences. At the beginning of a dream interpretation, it's best to allow this stream of ideas to flow as freely as possible, without prematurely settling on one or another association as "the meaning" of the dream. Identifying as many of these connections as you can is what initiates the full process of delving into the deeper lying meanings of the dream.

Other Questions

It's easy to stop reflecting on a dream at this point, after some initial connections have been made between elements of the dream and waking-life memories—"Oh, so *that's* what the dream is about. Now I understand." With big dreams, however, questions of specification are only the beginning of the interpretive process. Although such questions can reveal a great deal of helpful information about where the dream has come from, they don't give much direct insight into where the dream is *going*. To learn more about where the dream might be pointing you and to discover what new directions for growth and development are being revealed in your life, a different set of questions is needed. I've found that the following four questions can be especially helpful in stimulating further reflection on big dreams, pointing the dreamer toward a deeper appreciation of the dream's meanings for his or her waking life:

1. What is the most vivid element, the point of greatest energy, intensity, and vitality in the dream?
2. Are there any abrupt, unexpected changes in the settings, in the behavior or appearance of various characters, or in the progress of the narrative flow of events?
3. Why, given the dreaming imagination's preference for images from ordinary life, do these dreams go to the trouble of creating such strikingly unusual and unrealistic elements?
4. Are there any notable patterns of symmetry and contrast in the dream?

FOCUS ON: THE MOST VIVID ELEMENTS

The first of these questions is: *What is the most vivid element, the point of greatest energy, intensity, and vitality in the dream?* This element may be an especially vivid and radiant character, a surprisingly strong physical sensation, a brightly colored object, or a strikingly beautiful setting. Whatever it is, focusing your conscious attention on this point (or points—there may, of course, be more than one area of heightened vitality) is important because this is a place where the dreaming imagination has generated something special and unusual, something that stands out from everything else in the dream. By inviting this extraordinary dream element into your conscious awareness and playfully pondering its unique qualities and attributes, a wealth of new insights into the dream as a whole can be discovered.

Nina was in her early forties when she was involved in a terrible auto accident. She broke both legs and several ribs, and she suffered a severe head wound that left her with permanent brain damage. After many years of physical therapy, she finally got enough strength back to walk unaided by anything but a cane, and she regained enough of her mental faculties to speak, read, write, and remember almost everything that happened to her. Although she still experienced blackouts and memory losses on a regular basis, Nina knew she was fortunate compared to most other people with injuries like hers. For this reason she volunteered much of her spare time at the hospital at which she had been treated, helping to organize support groups for people who had suffered severe brain traumas. Nina became very good at this work, and with the encouragement of several members of the hospital staff, she decided to make a presentation at a major health care conference. In the weeks leading up to her presentation, as Nina became increasingly anxious about what would be her first real public appearance since her accident, she twice had the same very powerful dream:

> I'm leading a group of children, or miniature adults, toward a grassy clearing, trying to find the road that will take us home. We're all very tired, and the sun is very bright and hot, but my fear and anxiety make me want to push on. I signal the children to come fast. I quickly glance around the clearing, determine that it's safe, and motion the children to be quiet and fall in line behind me.
>
> We start across the clearing, and I see a vegetable crate. I'm apprehensive, but curious, too. It is clean and new looking, and I can almost smell its cleanness and freshness. As we get closer, I see that there is a decal on the end of the crate showing an artichoke outlined in red, then yellow, then white. There's no lettering, and I find this remarkable. As we get even with the crate, I slow us down a bit. I motion the children to stay where they are. I start to slowly walk toward the crate, somewhat fearful. It seems to move. I stop, then take a step closer. A green tiger with dark purple stripes comes straight out of the box. I scream, and tell the children to stay back. I look the tiger in the eye and see the red and yellow fire there. He grows larger and larger, and the crate falls away

from him. He looks poised for attack, and I wake up just as he springs.

The most vivid element in Nina's dream wasn't hard for her to find. The green-and-purple-striped tiger in the crate literally "jumped out" at her as soon as she began consciously reflecting on her experience (the first time she had the dream, Nina woke up screaming and shaking, with muscular spasms and tics all over her body). The tiger's strange coloring, blazing eyes, ever-increasing size, and dynamic, tensed energy all came together to burn an unforgettable image in Nina's memory.

The clue that revealed the tiger's significance for Nina's life was the vegetable crate from which the creature sprang. As she thought about the different possible meanings of the crate she noticed a pun—a visual play on the word *vegetable* for a person who is brain dead. Nina, like anyone who has suffered brain damage, lived in constant fear that she would become a vegetable, that some day her mind would finally go for good. Although she had made a surprisingly strong recovery, Nina knew that a downturn could happen at any moment and that if that occurred, her doctors would have no choice but to confine her in the permanent "crate" of a psychiatric institute.

In the dream Nina is afraid of the vegetable crate, but she's also curious. It strikes her as odd that the crate doesn't have any lettering on it; the feeling grows on her that this is no ordinary box. When Nina comes up to it, she's startled to find that bursting out of the box is a magnificent creature of astonishing life and vitality. The ferocious tiger that springs forth has an external similarity to an artichoke, with its strange green and purple coloring. But the "heart" of this animal is powerful and passionate; he is brilliantly alive and ferociously ready for action.

As Nina reflected on the vivid figure of the tiger, she realized that *he was in her.* Nina suddenly understood that out of the fear of becoming a vegetable, she had found a surprising reservoir of energy and determination by devoting herself to helping people with worse injuries than her own (represented in the dream by the children/miniature adults). Nina's dream gave her a stirring affirmation of the great power she still had within her, reassuring her that despite the blackouts and occasional memory lapses, she could rely on the irrepressible vitality of the fiery-eyed, green-and-purple-striped tiger.

FOCUS ON: SHIFTS AND TRANSFORMATIONS

The second question I suggest people ask in reflecting on big dreams is: *Are there any abrupt, unexpected changes in the settings, in the behavior or appearance of different characters, or in the progress of the narrative flow of events?* These changes are usually signaled by the word *suddenly:* "I dreamed I was walking down the beach, when *suddenly* a bunch of cannibals rushed at me." or "I was talking with my uncle, but *suddenly* he turned into a dog and ran away." Sometimes the changes are not particularly abrupt, but they're very noticeable nevertheless: "I dreamed a group of friends and I were having a party, but when I walked out of the room, I somehow found myself alone in a desert."

It's helpful to focus special attention on these shifts and transformations because in most cases these are points at which the dreaming imagination is bringing something *new* into the dream. A moment of sudden change in a dream is a moment when novel possibilities are coming into the dreamer's awareness, when new connections are being made across different aspects of daily life, when the dreamer is confronting aspects of reality that he or she may never have consciously noticed or thought about before.

Brad was a twenty-nine-year-old freelance graphic designer who had contracted HIV when he was a teenager, at the time when AIDS was just beginning to be recognized as a major public health problem. Knowing how many thousands of people were dying of the disease, and knowing that there was no cure in sight, Brad forced himself to accept the fact that at most he had only a few years to live. He formed a close relationship with a slightly older man named Bill, and together they made a plan for caring for Brad once he started getting sick. But surprisingly, Brad didn't get sick. Indeed, he stayed healthy year after year, taking good physical care of himself, working hard at a job he increasingly enjoyed, and living a relatively normal, AIDS-free life. As his thirtieth birthday approached Brad thought of how he had been so sure that he would never reach twenty-five, let alone thirty. One night, a few months before his birthday, he had this dream:

A good childhood friend of mine and I are traveling in London. We are on our final day there and have a couple of hours before we have to head to the airport. We are both feeling a little sad about having to leave, yet happy to be there and generally just enjoying each other's company. We decide to take a walk through the streets and enjoy the city one last time before we head out. As we are walking through the streets, we come across a path that leads down a little hill with an overpass above it. Carved into the side of the overpass is LONDON ZOO. *There are many plants and lush greenery all around it, and it is a very enticing entrance. The day is overcast, and a damp moisture fills the air. We decide to take the path and see where it leads. As we walk down the hill under the overpass, and out the other side, the scenery suddenly changes. There are many little grassy hills with oak trees growing about. The path is paved and meanders through the little hills and valleys. It is like a park. There are no other people around and no animal cages or anything. As we continue walking, we come upon some koala bears (they are actually the size of panda bears). They are large, cuddly, and very playful. A couple of them are playing and rolling about. My friend and I stop and watch them for a while. A feeling of joy and happiness envelops me as I watch them play and frolic. The word* innocent *comes to mind to best describe the experience. In the distance, I notice two wolves approaching. They seem to be totally disinterested in the koala bears and us, and we do not feel any sense of fear or danger in their presence.*

As they approach the koalas, one of the koalas goes running off to the top of a knoll out of fear, or instinct, or being generally uncomfortable with the presence of the wolves. The other koala does not seem to be aware of the approaching wolves. My friend and I stand silently and watch. The wolves nonchalantly come up to the lone koala bear, one in front and one behind. They still do not seem interested in it, they are merely passing by it, so it seems. Suddenly and without any warning, the wolf behind the koala lunges out and grabs the hind leg of the bear. Just as quickly, the one in front

*lunges forward and grabs the koala bear by the neck. They pull vio-
lently and tear the koala in half in one violent and horrific motion,
throwing it up in the air and tossing it about. I can't believe what
I have just seen. I begin screaming wildly at what has just happened. I just stand there hysterically screaming and crying.*

*This feeling from deep within me seems to be taking over. I am
just screaming and crying and feeling more and more that I am
going crazy. I know I am going crazy, and there is nothing I can
do. I am slowly losing control of myself, and I am unable to stop.
I slowly drop to my knees and collapse on the ground. I am terrified
over what I have just witnessed, and now even more terrified that
I am totally out of control of my body, unable to stop the uncontrollable crying. Slowly, my screaming and crying take on a howling
quality. I begin howling and howling, still very mentally aware of
what I am doing, yet unable to stop. My howling seems to be calling
other wolves in the distance over to the kill. I don't want them to
come, I don't want to endanger more bears, yet I can't stop myself.
I look up at my friend, who is kneeling beside me. She wants desperately to help me, yet she can't do anything. I know she can't do
anything. I have gone too far into my madness and there is no
return.*

Brad woke up from this dream with a start—short of breath,
gasping, and feeling emotionally drained by the experience. He felt
as if he'd been crying, yet his eyes were dry. "It felt as if I had actually *lived* this experience," he said later.

Brad's dream has two shifts that are specifically described as
"sudden" and one shift that occurs more gradually. The first abrupt
change comes when Brad and his childhood friend walk under the
overpass—"the scenery suddenly changes." Instead of the urban
environment of London, they now find themselves in a beautiful,
peaceful park. Brad felt it wasn't a shift from something he didn't
like to something he did like; rather, the change was from something enjoyable to something *very* enjoyable. This seemed to echo
in a symbolic fashion what Brad had experienced with his continuing good health. Not only was he surviving with HIV, a feat in
itself, but he was actually flourishing, able to work hard, go to parties, go hiking in the mountains, take fun vacations, and do pretty

much anything he liked. This first sudden change in the dream reflects and amplifies Brad's surprising discovery that unexpected turns in one's life path are sometimes turns for the good. He had told himself for so many years that he was about to die that he could no longer believe any other future was possible.

The second sudden change brings into the dream an entirely different kind of energy, a violent, hungry aggression that shatters the idyllic peacefulness of the park. Brad is horrified at the sight of the two wolves shredding the unsuspecting koala bear to bloody pieces. In the dream's third major change, Brad's screaming and crying is slowly transformed into a mad, out-of-control howling that calls more wolves to the kill. These two changes turn the dream into a true nightmare, leaving Brad with a sickening sensation of revulsion and terror when he woke up.

But as he later reflected on the dream, Brad had to admit that these horribly frightening elements did have an important connection with his waking life. He and Bill had gone to London together earlier in the year, and during the trip Brad began to feel something was wrong between the two of them. Brad was in better physical health than he ever had been, and he suddenly realized he was trapped in a relationship that was based on *dying* rather than on *living*. Brad's dream revealed the emergence of a powerful new vitality within him, a vitality that was strong, wild, and aggressive, demanding *freedom*. There was no room for such energies to express themselves in his relationship with Bill (whose gentle personality and friendly appearance could accurately be described as "bearlike"). Life with Bill had been very safe and comfortable, but also very passive and childlike; Brad realized that that was just the way he felt in the idyllic park scene with his childhood friend. Now something *new* was happening to Brad—new powers were growing within him, powers that were ferociously overwhelming his customary, cautious sense of who he was and how he should live his life.

After several months of deep emotional struggle, Brad finally admitted to himself that however much he feared those powers welling up inside him, he could no longer fight them. He went to Bill, and in one big rush he told him what he felt was wrong with their relationship. The conversation was painful, and it took a long time for them to reach any sort of mutual understanding. But they did, and they decided that even though they would stay close, now was a good time for Brad to move to a new apartment and try living on his own for a while.

A dream like Brad's has many, many dimensions of meaning, and the analysis I've just presented falls far short of a total and complete interpretation. But in discussing Brad's experience, I hope to have met a more modest goal, namely to illustrate how a focus on sudden shifts and transformations can lead relatively quickly to a dream's most important realms of meaning.

The frequent occurrence of extremely abrupt shifts and transformations in dreams has attracted a great deal of attention among sleep laboratory researchers who explain such sudden changes as the product of intense bursts of neurochemical activity during REM sleep (the technical term for such a burst is a "PGO spike"). In the view of many researchers, when a neurochemical burst occurs in the midst of an ongoing dream, a person's mind becomes flooded with so much new stimulation that the whole dream is *forced* to make a sudden and arbitrary change. Some researchers argue that the close connection between these brain activities and abrupt thematic shifts in dream content is further evidence of the essentially meaningless origins of dreaming.

Here again I would make a distinction between different types of dreams and suggest that in especially memorable dreams the occurrence of sudden shifts and transformations is *not* an arbitrary response to the neurochemical activities of the brain. I believe a close analysis of big dreams shows that these abrupt changes have a direct and deeply meaningful relationship to the overall narrative thrust of the dream. The sudden shifts come at particularly significant moments in the dream's plot, and they introduce vital new elements that are crucial to the dream's impact on the dreamer. In Brad's case the changes and transformations were unexpected *precisely because* they signaled issues in his waking life that he had never consciously recognized or understood before. I suspect that what's happening in these dreams is that regularly occurring neurochemical bursts are being deliberately employed by the ongoing dream narrative to enhance and to intensify the experiential power of the dream and thereby to emblazon the dream's basic meanings ever more deeply into the dreamer's memory.

FOCUS ON: THE STRANGEST ELEMENTS

One of the more counterintuitive findings of modern dream research is that most dreams are *not* especially weird or bizarre. Contrary to what psychological theorists have long assumed, much of what happens in dreams is pretty normal and mundane. People tend to dream of people, places, and situations that correspond quite closely to the ordinary circumstances of their daily lives. Several studies have shown that most dreams portray events that either have actually happened or could conceivably happen in the regular, expectable course of the world in which the dreamers live.

Thus, another distinguishing feature of big dreams is that they almost always include elements that are utterly strange and bizarre, elements that could not possibly be found in normal, everyday life. The third question I suggest people ask of their big dreams is: *Why, given the dreaming imagination's preference for images from ordinary life, do these dreams go to the trouble of creating such strikingly unusual and unrealistic elements?* If some part of the dream is a "counterfactual," a sharp deviation from the normal realities of the dreamer's world, what might that remarkably strange element be conveying to the dreamer's conscious awareness?

Many of the dreams described in this book have a particularly weird, counterfactual element in it—Bobby's beautiful girl without a face, Tom's hundred-foot tall King Kong, Nina's green-and-purple-striped tiger. The following example illustrates as well as any of those dreams how such elements of strangeness can express with impressive clarity and precision the core meanings of a dream.

Maggie was an advertising executive in her late twenties who had been steadily climbing her way up the ladder of her company's management hierarchy. She enjoyed the financial independence and the feeling of personal success that her job provided her, but she was also aware of a deep sense of dissatisfaction lurking within her, a sense that *this* was not the life she should be leading. As Maggie began thinking about the pros and cons of quitting her job and trying to start a new career, she had this dream:

> *My mother drops me off at a high school athletic facility for some kind of competition or test, maybe a licensing exam. I feel both fear and dread as I enter the noisy, chaotic foyer and try to figure out what event to enter. My mother then reenters with a change of clothes for me so I can get ready to compete.*
>
> *I see some rooms off to my left. One of the rooms is like an animal hall at a county fair, with lots of dogs running around. I hear a man say to his wife, "Honey, come here; she's having her puppies." The atmosphere is one of care and love.*
>
> *I am then led (by whom I don't know) into another room to the right, which is similar to a medical examiner's room. On the examination table lies a very large woman, maybe eight feet tall. She is simply dressed and coiffed—a plain Jane. She appears either dead or unconscious. I am not afraid and set out to revive her. I try to move her, to sit her up, which is not easy given her size. Then a flesh-colored, slushy liquid begins to flow from her mouth, and I become hopeful, as I know that if it covers her nose she will fight to breathe, to stay alive. The next thing I know, the woman is revived in my arms. There is a feeling of happiness, fulfillment, mutual gratification, and inner peace.*

The dream's initial atmosphere of frantic competition immediately reminded Maggie of two things. The first was her job at the advertising agency. The agency was relentless in its efforts to promote greater esprit de corps among the employees, and Maggie had always felt uncomfortable with the year-round intramural sports contests and tournaments the agency sponsored. Her second immediate association was to her high school, which was also highly competitive and strictly governed by a standard code of appearance and behavior. She remembered that her mother had prodded her into going out for her school's cheerleading squad. In reflecting on this vividly memorable dream, Maggie realized that in many ways her mother was also behind her decision to work at the ad agency—she recalled her mother insisting it was the best job

Maggie could get, a job that would make for a respectable career and would always help her pay the bills.

As Maggie stands in the dream amid an unpleasantly competitive crowd, not sure what to do or where to go, the dream changes, and something new comes into her view. To her left Maggie sees several dogs playfully romping around, and she hears a man call out to his wife that puppies are being born. In waking life Maggie was a great animal lover, and seeing the frolicsome dogs and hearing about the puppies being born suddenly transforms the dream's atmosphere from dread to love. The term "caring ward" came into Maggie's mind as the best way to describe this new scene.

Then an unseen, unidentified force guides Maggie into a room to the right, which looks like a medical examiner's room (continuing the "caring ward" theme). In this room Maggie sees a woman lying on the examination table.

Up to this moment, everything that has happened in her dream either once did happen to Maggie or could conceivably happen in her daily life. But now something enters the dream that could *not* happen in Maggie's regular waking world: she sees a *huge* woman lying on a table, a woman much bigger than Maggie has ever seen before, much bigger in fact than any woman in recorded history.

Why is the dream deviating from ordinary reality at this point and creating something that has no factual basis in Maggie's waking life? The answer comes from closer reflection on the specific characteristics of this extremely large woman. In the dream Maggie notices two things about her: her simple clothing and hair style, and her being either dead or unconscious. When Maggie thought more carefully about the woman's appearance, she suddenly saw a clear and direct connection with her waking-life worries that if she quit her current job and started a different career, she would probably not make as much money as she did now, which meant she would have to adopt a much simpler, more frugal lifestyle and give up many of the material possessions she had grown accustomed to having. She would have to accept being more of a "plain Jane" herself. But Maggie felt that was *exactly* what the dream was calling her to do. She realized with a rush of insight that the extremely large woman was a symbol of the powerful desire within herself to change her life and to try something new, something that satisfied her yearning to nurture and care for others.

The second notable detail about the woman, her being dead or unconscious, accurately expressed how the powerful desire symbolized by the large woman was not being fulfilled in Maggie's current waking life. Maggie felt sure the dream indicated that it was not too late to change herself. If she could let go of her fears and do what was necessary to revive the large woman, welcoming her energies into conscious awareness (no matter how messy or "slushy" the process might be), Maggie still had time to create a more satisfying and meaningful life for herself.

A few months later, Maggie did leave her job at the ad agency, and despite her mother's anxious disapproval she decided to enroll as a student in a cooking academy.

FOCUS ON: PATTERNS OF SYMMETRY AND CONTRAST

The fourth question I suggest people ask of their big dreams is somewhat more abstract than the first three: *Are there any notable patterns of symmetry and contrast in the dream?*

Cognitive psychologists have found that at a very deep level the human mind operates by making either/or types of distinction. It seems that whenever people confront an array of phenomena, their first mental action is to construct a binary opposition, using a two-part classification to categorize what they're seeing or experiencing. Some researchers have called this "the dyadic instinct," and they point to the fact that in societies all over the world people make the same fundamental distinctions between male and female, child and adult, kin and nonkin, sacred and profane, good and evil, hot and cold, wet and dry, day and night, up and down, front and back, right and left, black and white, alive and dead, light and dark, one and many, and so on. The universality of this dyadic instinct in human thinking has been confirmed by the field research of structural anthropologists who have gathered countless examples from cultures all over the world of people using these same binary oppositions in their myths, religious rituals, kinship patterns, and social institutions. At a very deep level, all humans, from the most savage dwellers of a tropical rain forest to the most civilized residents of a twentieth-century metropolis, make sense of the world by initially dividing things up into categorizations of *this* or *that*.

These same basic binary oppositions regularly appear in people's dreams. Close analysis of a big dream usually shows that it has been formed out of a surprisingly complex pattern of symmetries and contrasts between a variety of dyadic elements. Identifying this intricate pattern can help the dreamer recognize unexpected connections between the dream and waking life. Perhaps most important, reflecting on the dream's structural elements can open up new possibilities for overcoming painful conflicts and seemingly insoluble difficulties in the dreamer's waking life.

The most intense dream Kip, a twenty-one-year-old college senior from Jamaica, could ever remember occurred when he was around six years old. "Though I had quite vivid and elaborate dreams in my early years," Kip said, "this one dream stood out distinctly from the rest":

> *The setting is a vast, prairielike field, the likes of which could not be found on the tropical island where I was growing up. In the field is Jesus and a bunch of kids my age. They—all ten or so of them—are swarming around Jesus, playing with him, walking with him. Though I am in the field with them, I am not a part of this group of kids. I want to join them, of course, because this is Jesus after all. How great would it be to be in the company of Jesus! But for some reason, I'm not a part of them and can't be a part of them. The reason is that something is holding me back. What it is exactly I don't know, but I assume it's one of two things. First, there's a physical barrier that I see between myself and them. It's a transparent force-field-type barrier stretching between us in the form of a thick fuzzy beam. That in itself is enough to keep me from them, but another thing keeping me away is the look Jesus gives me. From what I was taught in school and by my parents, Jesus is supposed to be a figure who unconditionally loves all people. But for some reason, in my case that is apparently not true. Jesus sees that I want to join the rest of the kids, but he shows no empathy. He's been mostly ignoring me, and now he and the swarm of kids start moving away from me. But then he*

does look at me, and it's a look of rejection. In his face, I read, "No, not you."

Kip said this dream had a strong and immediate impact on his life. Simply put, the dream shattered his childhood view of religion. Whereas before he had obediently accepted the Bible stories he'd been taught in church, in school, and at home, Kip now started asking the grown-ups pointed, skeptical questions about what the Bible was really saying. "How come I haven't seen anything magical like that happen?" Kip remembered asking after he had the dream, "How come miracles don't happen anymore? Why are *those* the Chosen People? Why can't we all be the Chosen People? Why should we believe in God if we aren't from the same place those Chosen People are?"

Needless to say, these questions did not endear Kip to his parents or teachers. Despite their discouraging and dismissive responses to his questions, Kip always remembered his devastating dream of being rejected by Jesus, and throughout his childhood and adolescence he struggled to understand what, if anything, religion could mean for him.

The remarkable power of Kip's dream is generated in large part by the simple pattern of binary oppositions structuring the events of the dream. These oppositions are all variants on the same basic theme of "inside versus outside." The dream is set on a vast, open field that Kip immediately contrasts with his small tropical island home—wherever this dream is taking place, it's far outside the realm of Kip's day-to-day experience. On the field he sees Jesus surrounded by a swarm of children, and Kip understands that he is not a part of them. In recognizing this contrast, Kip sees what his true place is in relation to the Biblical religion he'd been taught: he's an outsider to the group of insiders who have been accepted by Jesus.

There are two different (indeed, diametrically opposed) obstacles that keep Kip apart from Jesus and the group of children. First is the "force-field-type barrier" that establishes an impassible physical wall between Kip and the others. Second is the withering look Jesus gives Kip at the end of the dream, a look that forms a kind of spiritual barrier that Kip realizes is just as absolute and impassible as the force field. The combination of these two different barriers reinforces the dream's basic structural theme of "inside versus outside" and emphasizes how radically different the two are in Kip's life. Kip isn't sure why, but he now knows more certainly than he's ever known anything in his young life that he's on the *outside* of religion—everyone else is inside the loving circle of Jesus' care, everyone except for him.

A number of big dreams have this quality of emphasizing an especially important, conflict-laden binary opposition in the dreamer's life. These dreams portray all the different ways the conflict plays out in the dreamer's daily existence, repeating the same theme over and over again like the rhythmic booming of a bass drum. "Look at this pattern in your life, look at this pattern in your life, look at this pattern in your life, look at this pattern in your life. . . ." For Kip, the pattern involved being a religious insider versus a religious outsider. For other people, their big dreams might express conflicts between masculine energies and feminine energies in their lives, or tensions between childhood desires and adult responsibilities, or a clash between caring for others and caring for oneself. In some cases every single element of the dream—the setting, the characters, the colors, the sequence of events—is a variant on one basic opposition between two powerfully conflicting forces in the dreamer's life.

I believe the intense memorability of these dreams serves a valuable purpose by motivating the dreamer to make a conscious, deliberate effort to overcome the opposition in his or her waking life. The dreams may not offer solutions to the conflict; but they certainly give the dreamers a much better understanding of the nature and the significance of the conflict, and they prompt the dreamers to try different ways of bridging the gap between the two opposing forces. In Kip's case, his waking-life response to the painful opposition revealed in his dream was to *ask questions*—to critically examine the Bible stories he had been taught as a child and later to carefully explore the new religious teachings he began studying in college, all the while trying to find a personally meaningful understanding of religion that could overcome the split in his life between gullible, nonthinking insiders and rational, lonely outsiders. Kip's momentous childhood dream initiated him into a lifelong quest of that most elusive of goals: a spiritual faith that both warms the heart and satisfies the mind.

Facing and Overcoming Resistance

Once these four questions have been asked of a big dream—What is the most vivid point? Are there any sudden changes or shifts? What's the strangest element? Are there any symmetries and contrasts?—it is worthwhile to stop and reflect on what has come up so far. This moment of pause can be thought of as a time to "interpret the interpretation." How well has the questioning gone? Have any ideas or insights about the dream come with surprising quickness? Have some meanings emerged only after a long, frustrating period of confusion and uncertainty? Are there any elements in the dream that haven't been touched on yet?

The single greatest obstacle to understanding big dreams comes in the form of *resistance*—the discomfort and reluctance the dreamer feels when alien energies from the dream enter into waking consciousness, pushing the dreamer to change, to grow, and to develop. Everyone should be honest about how difficult it is to change his or her customary ways of thinking and behaving. It is nothing to be embarrassed about; people's innate cautiousness is a valuable trait that has helped the species to survive and to flourish over the long course of natural evolution. But at certain times in people's lives, the only way they can truly flourish is by setting their inherent caution aside and *changing*. Big dreams often come at such moments to propel people down the path of change, guiding them along an unknown road that can be terribly frightening and disorienting even as it leads to a better life.

People who want to interpret one of their big dreams need to do everything possible to be aware of their unconscious resistance to the meanings that may be emerging in the dream. One common sign of resistance is a feeling that the dream doesn't even need interpreting because the meaning is so clear and obvious already. Although some dreams really *are* quite plain and simple in their meanings, most big dreams are surprisingly subtle, complex, and multilayered. An interpretation that stops with the very first insight may well be a sign of resistance, indicating a fearful defense against the deeper, more troubling meanings threatening to arise from the dream.

Another common indication of resistance is a feeling of being "stuck" in the interpretation—no matter how hard you try, you just can't make any sense of the dream's feelings or images. In most cases this frustration comes at an especially significant point in the dream, and it's best to pause for a moment and try to regain something of that Keatsian "negative capability" that dream interpretation requires—relaxing one's body, clearing one's mind, and opening one's imagination. Sometimes an excessively strenuous effort to *figure the damn thing out* can itself be a covert defense against allowing the dream's energies to enter into the realm of conscious awareness.

One little trick to use in testing a dream interpretation for resistance is trying what I call a "surprise reverse." In football a reverse is a play in which the ball is handed to a player running in one direction who then hands it off to a teammate going in the opposite direction; the goal is to lure the defense into overcommitting itself in the first direction, allowing the second runner to get around them by quickly going the other way. The same basic strategy can be used in dream interpretation. If you've come up with a good, confident sense of what a particular dream means, try quickly thinking of the *opposite* interpretation, just as an experiment. For instance, if you've been thinking the dream is about how much your parents have hassled you through life, stop and ask yourself if the dream might be about all the *good things* in your relationship with your parents—just try that as a possible way of looking at the dream, and see if any new ideas or feelings come up. Maybe you were right about the dream the first time, and the surprise reverse comes to nothing. But maybe your first interpretation was only partly correct; if so, you might find that the larger truth of the dream includes these seemingly "opposite" meanings, too.

Having said all this, I freely grant that vigilance against resistance can be taken to laughably paranoid lengths. One of my favorite stories from Freud's *The Interpretation of Dreams* is his account of a patient who questioned Freud's theory that dreams are wish-fulfillments. This patient came to Freud's office one day and described to him a dream in which she took a vacation with her mother-in-law. In the patient's waking life, as she had told Freud during their previous session, she had been dreading this vacation; and just a couple of days earlier she had to her great relief found a way to change the trip so she wouldn't have to spend so much time with her unpleasant mother-in-law. But the patient's dream completely unravels this happy resolution of her problem and, in fact, presents her with the exact opposite of what she truly wishes for. How, Freud's patient demanded, could such a dream be interpreted as a wish-fulfillment?

Freud's response was that her dream did indeed fulfill a wish— *the wish to prove him wrong*. Earlier in their sessions together, Freud had made a comment about a traumatic event that he suspected had occurred in the patient's childhood; the patient had initially denied Freud's suggestion, but later events proved that he was right. The patient's dream, Freud said, transferred her resistance against his comment to a resistance against his theory of dreams: By fulfilling the wish that Freud's dream theory is wrong, the patient's dream fulfills the deeper wish that he be wrong about that forgotten traumatic event from childhood.

This Alice-in-Wonderland logic has baffled and outraged Freud's many critics—so any time a dream doesn't fulfill an obvious wish, it must be a "counterwish" dream motivated by a resistance to Freud's theories? How can you ever know if you're *not* resisting Freud? What makes Freud think he's not suffering from resistance himself and refusing to acknowledge the truths and insights expressed by the people he's psychoanalyzing?

I fully share the suspicion that Freud's notion of counterwish dreams is a logically perverse defense against any attempt to challenge his interpretations. However, I also fully share Freud's deep respect for the strength of people's resistance to unpleasant truths about themselves and their lives. Freud wasn't wrong about resistance; he was just wrong in thinking he or anyone else could ever *escape* the human propensity to resistance. There's no fail-safe test, no scientifically objective method, for proving that a person has found the "true" meaning of a big dream. There's no way ever to be sure that the person is not resisting an even deeper meaning buried somewhere within the dream. In the end, all dreamers have is their personal judgment, their own individual sense of when it is that they have found the most important meanings of their dreams.

It should be said that a vital part of such judgment is the ability to know when a point of resistance is best left *alone*. The battering-ram approach to emotional defenses is usually counterproductive. I always remind people that if there are truly important meanings they didn't consciously understand in one dream, other dreams will undoubtedly find a different way to bring those meanings to awareness. Indeed, those future dreams will likely offer an easier, more effective means of relieving the fears behind the resistance and of opening the way to new growth. (This leads into the topic of how to interpret series of dreams, which will be discussed in chapter 7.)

Going beyond Resistance

The quotation given at the beginning of this chapter comes at a key moment in *Romeo and Juliet*. Romeo has been exiled from Verona for his accidental murder of Tybalt, and now he's waiting in the nearby town of Mantua for Juliet to come join him so they can be together at last. As Romeo walks through the streets of town, he marvels at the strange dream he experienced the previous night:

> If I may trust the flattering truth of sleep,
> My dreams presage some joyful news at hand.
> My bosom's lord sits lightly in his throne,
> And all this day an unaccustomed spirit
> Lifts me above the ground with cheerful thoughts.
> I dreamt my lady came and found me dead
> (Strange dream that gives a dead man leave to think!)
> And breathed such life with kisses in my lips
> That I revived and was an emperor.
> Ah me! how sweet is love itself possessed,
> When but love's shadows are so rich in joy!

Romeo's happy reveries are cut short when his servant Balthasar comes to tell him the shocking news from Verona—Juliet has died. Romeo can't believe it, but Balthasar says it's true, he himself saw Juliet's lifeless body being laid in the Capulet family tomb. Devastated and distraught, Romeo cries out, "I defy you, stars!"

He buys a vial of poison from an apothecary and hurries back to Verona to join his beloved in death. But in his haste, Romeo leaves Mantua before the letter from Friar Laurence can reach him. Friar Laurence, who secretly married the two lovers, has written to Romeo to say that Juliet is not really dead but only asleep; it's part of a secret plan to help her escape Verona and join him in Mantua.

At one level, the level of his waking thoughts and feelings, Romeo's dream seems to foreshadow good fortune for him and Juliet. But at another level, somewhere beyond Romeo's conscious awareness, the dream portends the exact opposite of what he thinks it does—he will soon come into the Capulet tomb to see the (seemingly) dead figure of Juliet, and after he kisses her they will both die. Is Romeo somehow resisting this deeper truth in his dream? Is he wishfully denying the painful waking-world reality that his relationship with Juliet can only end in tragedy? Perhaps. It's true that he's already made one major mistake in interpreting his own feelings, when at the beginning of the play he thought he was in love with Rosaline. Only after he met Juliet did Romeo realize that he was wrong, that *this* is what true love feels like. So maybe Romeo is wrong in the same way about his dream; perhaps he should *not* trust the flattering truth of sleep, perhaps he should be skeptical about these happy feelings and ask if they might not be clouding his perception of what's really going on.

I believe the dream's meaning goes one level deeper than that, to a level *beyond* resistance. Romeo's feeling of lighthearted joy is not misplaced, and his dream is not a cruelly ironic deception portraying the reverse of what is about to happen. When Juliet awakens in the tomb and finds Romeo lying dead beside her she kisses him, just as his dream had foreseen. Then, by plunging a dagger into her breast, she joins Romeo in a new kind of life, beyond the bitter and violent feuding of their families, in a realm where they can forever be together and free. Again, this is just as Romeo's dream had foreseen. The ultimate romantic fulfillment these "star-crossed lovers" could never find in the world of the living, they find in dying. Romeo's dream is thus a true dream, a tragic prophecy pointing beyond the bounds of present resistance and awareness. It is a mysterious revelation of his future, heralding the satisfaction of his most heartfelt desire, to enjoy eternal union with his beloved Juliet.

CHAPTER SIX

❧

Sharing Your Dreams

Gloucester: *My troublous dreams this night doth make me sad.*
Duchess: *What dreamed my lord? Tell me, and I'll requite it*
              With sweet rehearsal of my morning's dream.
            —William Shakespeare, *Henry VI, Part II*

The methods and the techniques outlined in chapter 5 are designed for people to use on their own, in private, individual reflection. I've found that dream interpretation is most effective when private reflection comes at both the beginning and the end of the process. At the beginning, it is important for the dreamer to pay attention to the very first thoughts and intuitions that arise in consciousness in response to the dream. At the end, the dreamer, and only the dreamer, has the responsibility of deciding what the dream means and what relevance it has for his or her waking life.

Between these two periods of individual reflection, it can be very helpful to share the dream with other people. No matter how vigilant one is against resistance, no matter how many surprise reverses one tries on oneself, a big dream always has meanings that lie just beyond the dreamer's reach. Big dreams have a forward-looking, teleological thrust to them, pushing the dreamer into the future, revealing what lies ahead on the path of growth and development. For this very reason it can be difficult for people to fully interpret and understand their own big dreams—it's hard for

147

consciousness to grasp what lies just beyond its present sphere of awareness.

This is where sharing dreams with other people can play an extremely valuable role. Other people are often able to see meanings that the dreamer can't quite perceive or recognize. By hearing the thoughts, suggestions, insights, and questions that come up for other people in response to hearing the dream, the dreamer gains a broader sense of where the dream's meanings lie and a much clearer understanding of how exactly the dream relates to waking life.

Dreamsharing between Parents and Children

Sharing dreams in a family context is a practice anthropologists have found in different cultures all over the world. In our culture, the sharing of dreams between parents and children occurs most frequently in middle-of-the-night consolation sessions, when a child goes running to a parent to describe a terribly frightening nightmare. Another common time for dreamsharing in our culture comes at the breakfast table each morning, when parents and children talk about dreams in which other family members appeared ("Mommy, you were in my dream last night!") and dreams containing especially funny or bizarre elements ("I dreamed our house was suddenly in a jungle. Isn't that weird?").

My two older children, Dylan (nine years old) and Maya (seven years old), are naturally aware of what their father writes about in his books, so they've always felt free to tell me their dreams and nightmares. While I was writing this book, I asked if they could describe for me the most memorable dreams they'd ever had. Maya, after scolding me for asking a question to which I already knew the answer ("Duh, Daddy!"), recounted once again her "Treasure Dream":

The children and teachers from Maya's preschool go to a park. They immediately notice an unusually big treasure chest in the middle of a sandbox, and the children all assume it's not a real treasure chest but just a fake one for kids to play on. But then one of the boys finds a key, and he gives it to Joan (Maya's favorite teacher at the school). Joan puts the key into the chest's lock, and it fits. They open the chest, and to everyone's surprise there is real treasure inside—gold, diamonds, and sparkling jewels of all differ-ent colors. There's a moment of confusion about what to do because all the children start clamoring about wanting this jewel or that jewel. Then Maya makes the suggestion that they divide the trea-sure up equally, so each kid gets his or her own pile. She also says they should save a few extra piles for the children from school who didn't come to the park that day.

The dream ends on that cheerful note, and as Maya was telling it, she was energetically bouncing on her seat, with a big smile on her face. I asked her what she thought made this dream so memo-rable, and she answered, "Because it was such a happy dream." Unlike the nightmares she periodically has of monsters, wolves, and bad guys, this dream made Maya feel really *good*. Not only do she and her schoolmates discover a huge treasure, but Maya herself comes up with the idea that helps everyone share the treasure fairly, so everyone can be happy. I asked her if she would draw me a picture of the dream, and she got right to work on a drawing that focused on the large treasure chest and its wonderfully colorful contents.

When it was his turn, Dylan said the dream that had always stuck in his head was the one about the pirate ship and the magic lamp (like Maya's, this was a dream we'd talked about many times before). The dream came to him several years earlier, when he was four, but in the dream he was older, maybe seven or eight years old:

Dylan and a girl leave a town at night in a motorboat. Pirates have just stolen an extremely valuable magic lamp, which contains a genie so powerful that bad guys could destroy the whole world if they got their hands on it. The other people in the town are too scared of the pirates, though, so it's up to Dylan and the girl to get the lamp back. They drive their boat up to the pirate's ship, turn off their lights (their boat is kind of like a car), tie a rope to the ship to keep the boat in place, and sneak on board. The pirates are having a meeting, so Dylan and the girl are able to slip into the ship's treasure room without being seen. [My kids clearly have a

*thing about treasure!] In the room, amid all the gold and jewels,
Dylan and the girl see a huge red curtain with a skull and cross-
bones on it; and above the red curtain, sitting on a square platform,
is the magic lamp. The two of them start climbing up the curtain,
but they inadvertently make a noise, and the pirate captain suddenly bursts into the room. Then a cloud that's been covering the
full moon moves away, and the captain turns into a werewolf.
The other pirates come, and they turn into werewolves, too.*

That's when Dylan woke up. As I did with Maya, I asked Dylan
if he could draw me a picture of the dream. He sketched out several
versions of what happened, including a number of versions that
elaborated different possible conclusions to the encounter among
the girl, the pirate captain, and him. In one of these alternative versions, the captain hurls gold pieces at the two children; in another,
they shoot lasers back down at him. I asked Dylan what the girl
looked like, and he said she resembled a character on one of his
favorite TV shows, which made sense to him because the girl on
the show was smart and adventurous, just like the girl in his dream.
I also asked him what the pirate captain looked like, and (as I suspected) Dylan said he looked somewhat like me, his dad. The captain was dressed in a classic pirate's outfit, and even though he had
a dark beard and a big black hat, his face reminded Dylan of me.
We both smiled at this, each of us silently thinking about the
amusing yet frightening image of the dadlike pirate captain. Dylan
didn't say anything more after this, and I felt it best to respect his
sense of when he wanted to stop talking about the dream.

The dreamsharing in our family goes in both directions. Dylan
and Maya tell my wife, Hilary, and me about their dreams, and we
in turn periodically share our dreams with them. I've always felt
it important in teaching children about dreams that the conversations be mutual, so that dreamsharing doesn't inadvertently become
another experience reinforcing the false idea that grown-ups have
all the knowledge and children should passively absorb whatever
they say.

A few years ago I had a conversation with Dylan about a short
but powerful dream of mine that I thought he would like to hear.

In the dream I'm going with a group of scientists to one of Jupiter's moons where a skull from an alien species has been found, and I'm very excited at the chance to join such a history-making exploration. Dylan and I had been reading a lot of children's books on space, and we had talked several times about what it would be like to travel to other planets. When he heard me tell my dream, he was definitely fascinated, but his questions went off in a direction I wasn't expecting. The first thing he asked was, "Were there any more people alive on the moon?" I hadn't really thought about it before, and I answered that I wasn't sure, but I didn't think so. Dylan paused for a moment, and I got the feeling that he was pretty sure there *were* other people on the moon, and his dad just hadn't seen them. "Were you scared?" Dylan asked next. "Not really," I said. I explained that I had been so excited at the thrill of scientific discovery that fear of where I was or what I was doing never entered my mind. As I told this to Dylan, I realized I was becoming mildly irritated. The reason I told him the dream in the first place was that I thought he would appreciate hearing a cool space adventure dream. But that wasn't where our conversation was going at all. "What makes you say that?" I asked "Do you think I *should* have been scared?" "Well," Dylan replied, choosing his words carefully, "I was thinking that the other people on the moon might get mad that you and the scientists were taking the skull because the moon people might still want to remember that dead person by keeping the skull." Slowly I began nodding my head. "That's a very, very good idea," I said after a long pause. "You know, I think you're right. The moon people definitely would want to keep that skull. I wasn't really thinking about that in the dream."

As the many new insights and possibilities opened up by Dylan's question rushed through my mind, I smiled at him the way I imagine a professional baseball player smiles at his son when he hits his first solid line drive.

Basic Principles of Dreamsharing

Talking about a big dream with someone you trust—a friend, a spouse, a sibling, a parent, a child—can be an extremely helpful means of discovering new and unexpected dimensions of the dream's meaning. Such conversations are best conducted in a comfortable, quiet place that has some degree of privacy and freedom from interruption. If there's too much noise or too many distractions, the conversation is almost certainly not going to go very far. Just as individual dream reflection requires a calm, peaceful frame of mind, dreamsharing with another person requires a calm and peaceful setting. The family breakfast table can provide a good atmosphere, and so can a car ride to school or work. Long walks on the beach or leisurely hikes through the woods are perfect settings, of course, but a late-night phone conversation can work just fine, and so can a long layover in an empty airport terminal.

The place to start is with the dreamer describing the whole dream, in as much detail as he or she can remember, in the present tense. It's important to use the present tense because this helps bring the dream back to life, reviving its immediacy for both the dreamer and the person listening to the dream. Compare "I was walking through a city, when I saw a man who suddenly started laughing at me" with "I am walking through a city, and I see a man who suddenly starts laughing at me." If you read the two sentences aloud, you'll hear the greater liveliness of the latter version of the same dream.

At this point it's best if the dreamer does *not* immediately say what he or she thinks the dream means. The value of sharing dreams depends on the listener developing his or her own ideas and insights into the dream's possible meanings. If the dreamer immediately gives an interpretation of the dream, the listener's ability to imagine other possibilities is greatly diminished, and the dreamer loses the opportunity to hear new perspectives on the dream. The dreamer should simply tell the dream, in the present tense, and then stop.

The listener will usually have some questions to ask about certain details of the dream that weren't clear in the first telling. "What did that room look like again?" "What kind of clothes were you wearing?" "Did you say you were feeling scared, or just annoyed?" Especially if the dream is long and complex, the listener may need to ask a number of these questions in order to form a clear mental picture of what the dreamer has described. The more fully and completely the listener can recreate a sense of the dream in his or her own imagination, the more likely it is that the listener will provide the dreamer with valuable insights and new perspectives.

These clarifying questions about the various details of the dream can easily shade into questions of specification like those described in chapter 5. "What kind of boat was it?" "Who's Uncle Jim? I've never met him before." "Where have you ever seen mountains like that?" "What exactly do you mean by a 'run-down neighborhood'?" The dreamer may be surprised at the details about which the listener chooses to ask questions of specification, and interesting new meanings in the dream may well emerge right here, before any further discussion is held. When I told my dream to Dylan, I certainly wasn't expecting him to focus his questions on the potentially frightening aspects of my expedition to one of Jupiter's moons. But when he did, I suddenly saw meanings in the dream that I had completely missed in my initial reflections.

The instant temptation for the listener is to try to guess what the dream means for the dreamer. Especially if he or she has a close relationship with the dreamer, the listener finds it almost irresistible to immediately speculate about how the dream is connected to some aspect of the dreamer's personal life. But the unfortunate effect of such speculation is to close off the listener's own reflections and, thus, to stop the discussion before it's even begun. Paradoxically, the dreamer will get the most out of the conversation if the listener doesn't make such guesses, but rather imagines the dream as if it were his or her *own* experience. Again, the great value of sharing dreams comes from stimulating the free play of the listener's imagination and from hearing the new ideas and insights that emerge as a result.

There's another important reason to avoid the "guessing game" approach to dreamsharing. Real mischief can be done by people who try to tell other people what their dreams mean. Going back to chapter 1, the cardinal principle of dream interpretation is that the dreamer is always in the best position to know what his or her dream ultimately means. Other people's insights can be very helpful, but the dreamer always remains the final authority on what the dream does and doesn't mean. The easiest way to keep this principle clearly in mind while sharing dreams is for the listener to use the prefacing phrase, "If it were my dream, . . ." This reminds both the dreamer and the listener to focus on the listener's spontaneous intuitions about what the dream might mean. It also creates an effective safeguard against people's tendency to try to play amateur psychoanalyst. Compare these two ways in which a listener could express an insight about a friend's dream: (1) "Your dream of a plane crash means you're out of control in your life, and you're about to crash." (2) "If I were to have that dream of getting in a plane crash, it would mean I'm afraid that I'm out of control in my life and that I'm about to crash." Not only is the second sentence a more polite and respectful way of saying the same basic thing, but it is also a more accurate way of saying it. The truth is that the listener does *not* really know what the dream means for the dreamer; all the listener knows for sure is what comes up in his or her own mind in the process of reimagining the dream. Saying, "If it were my dream," keeps everybody honest and helps protect against intrusive interpretations while promoting the greatest imaginative freedom for the listener.

Once the listener has shared his or her initial thoughts and reflections, it is a good time for the dreamer to say what he or she thinks the dream means. Now it might be the listener's turn to be surprised because the dreamer may have a very different understanding of what the dream is about. Sometimes the dreamer will describe some waking-life issue or experience that's directly related to the dream, and this may change the listener's whole understanding of the dream, initiating a brand new set of insights—"Wow, if that dream came to me on the one-year anniversary of my father's death, I think it would mean . . ." or "Hmm, if I'd had that dream two nights after breaking up with my boyfriend, my feeling would be . . . ," or "Well, if I'd just watched the movie *Titanic*, I think the dream would be saying . . ." Having started by opening the widest possible range of meanings for the dream's various images, the dreamer and the listener can now focus their conversation on those particular meanings that seem most relevant to their waking-life concerns.

Sharing dreams in the way I've outlined here is an open-ended process. The conversation can last five minutes, it can go on for an hour, or it can continue off and on for several days or weeks. In most cases the dreamer and the listener eventually reach a point where they both feel the conversation has run its course. Both people may feel a little awkward at this point because it may not seem they've found the "real" meaning of the dream. The awkwardness may possibly signal that they've hit a moment of mutual resistance. If they just pause for a few moments, staying patiently with the silence, the conversation may suddenly start up again and enter into even deeper realms of the dream's meaning. But it may simply be that the dreamer and the listener have gone as far as they can go with the dream, and the conversation is coming to a natural conclusion. If that's so, I think it's best if both people, the listener first and then the dreamer, take a last shot at formulating a one-sentence crystallization of what the dream means. A single summarizing sentence from both people brings a sense of closure to the discussion, and it helps the dreamer and the listener to integrate the broad range of the dream's possible meanings with the concrete realities of their waking lives.

The Surprising Value of Listening to Other People's Dreams

Depending on the circumstances, once the dreamsharing conversation comes to an end, it may be desirable to switch roles and to have the person who was initially listening take a turn sharing a dream. Once people have gotten warmed up talking about one dream, they often find that exploring a second one is even more fun, with the conversation flowing much more quickly and smoothly. However, there may not be the time or the inclination between both people to start a new discussion right away, so a two-way dreamsharing exchange may not be possible. If the conversation about the one dream has been satisfying for both people, that shouldn't be a problem.

Over time, though, it's best if there is some mutuality in who's telling the dream and who's listening. Alternating being the dreamer and the listener allows both people to hear interesting new perspectives on their dreams, and it allows both of them to enjoy the surprisingly thought-provoking experience of reimagining another person's dream.

This last point is one I'd like to emphasize. Dreamsharing is valuable not only for the dreamer, but also for the listener. Many people don't expect this when they first try talking about dreams with other people, and they're startled to find that they often learn more by hearing someone else's dream than by talking about their own dreams. The reason is that at a certain level all humans are dreaming about the same basic hopes, desires, fears, and conflicts. Thus the dream of one person may relate very directly and meaningfully to something happening in another person's life. Indeed, elements from one person's dream may actually enter into the dreams of another person. In a class I once taught, a woman named Grace described a very powerful dream in which she's standing on the beach and a huge tidal wave rises up and breaks directly on top of her; she's not scared at all, however, and she remains perfectly serene and tranquil as she's thrown and tossed by the surging water. In waking life Grace was a remarkably kind and gentle individual, and everyone in the class understood how well the dream expressed the deepest strengths of her personality. A few weeks later a student named Lucy, who was also quite nice but who was definitely a more anxious, high-strung person, told the class that she had just had a dream like Grace's. In Lucy's dream the tidal wave comes and breaks on top of her, and she starts to panic; but in the dream Lucy suddenly thinks to herself, "Wait a minute—Grace went through this and was fine; I can do that, too," and immediately her fear of the wave disappears.

Experimental Dreamsharing Groups

Sharing dreams in a more formalized group setting can be another rewarding path toward understanding and insight. The same basic principles outlined earlier still apply, but when there are more people involved, the dreamer has the opportunity to hear that many more new perspectives on his or her dream. For many years I've organized and led such groups in college and church settings, and I've found that with a minimal amount of guidance from me, the people in the group quickly develop the ability to make sensitive and insightful contributions to the discussion.

A dreamsharing group's conversations can go off in any of a number of different directions. The groups I've led in college settings have usually experimented with the various psychological theories they have been studying in class, for instance, reflecting on the dreams in terms of Jungian or Freudian symbolism. The groups I've led in church settings have revolved around explicitly spiritual issues and questions, exploring the relevance of dreams for questions of faith, revelation, and healing. I've also organized somewhat less formal dreamsharing groups among young children, and in these groups the conversations are less about what the dreams *mean* than about what can actively be *done* with them in terms of drawing, playacting, storytelling, and costume making.

Several of my colleagues have taken dreamsharing groups into new and very interesting territory, experimenting with the dreamsharing process as a means of promoting greater psychological and spiritual self-awareness among people who are suffering the harmful effects of problems caused by much bigger social forces and conflicts. Jane White-Lewis, a Jungian analyst and educator, teaches a class on dreams, symbolism, and literature to the students of an inner-city high school in New Haven, Connecticut. Many of White-Lewis's students come from families who are burdened by some combination of poverty, crime, substance addiction, and physical and/or sexual abuse. The students do their best to overcome these problems, working hard at their studies and actively seeking opportunities to escape the oppressive societal forces always threatening to pull them down. White-Lewis has found that the students' dreams definitely reflect the realities of their troubled social world. Images of police conflict, drug abuse, and teen pregnancy regularly come up in their dreams, and in discussing the symbolic meanings of these images, the students often find themselves openly sharing their feelings about the hardships of day-to-day life in their bleak, impoverished neighborhoods. In this way the initial focus on the dreams becomes a very effective means of helping the students expand their awareness of the social world around them. The insights gained from dreamsharing conversations give the students a much deeper understanding of how the problems of society affect them and how they can develop the strength to combat and overcome those problems.

In many of the students' dreams, White-Lewis has seen the emergence of classic "coming of age" stories, portraying with poignant and powerful symbolism the difficulties that nearly all adolescents, from whatever social background, experience in moving from childhood to maturity. A fifteen-year-old boy shared the following dream with one of White-Lewis's classes:

> I am lying on a mat in a cave with other kids my age. The cave is comfortable and warm. A man and a woman come and tell us that it is time for a hike up the mountain. I go along somewhat reluctantly. The mountain is steep, and I want to stop and go back to the cave. But that is not possible. We must continue. Besides, after we climb the mountain, we will have to do it again. I feel exhausted.

The boy who had this dream was a bright, hardworking student who was very motivated to do as well as he could in school. The mats in the cave reminded him of his nursery school, where the children wrestled around and took naps on large, comfortable mats. As the boy told this first part of the dream to the class, there was noticeable animation in his voice and features. Just as noticeably, this animation vanished when he got to the dream's second part about trudging up the mountain with the two adults. The contrast between the "happy" and the "depressed" sections of his dream became an opportunity for the students to talk about the anxieties they all felt about the process of growing up. The image of adulthood as an endless, exhausting climb up a mountain symbolically expressed fears all the students had that too many adults seem resigned to living pointless, meaningless lives. Starting from a discussion of the boy's dream, the class gradually shifted to a discussion of what it means to change from a child to an adult and how exactly each of the students could safely navigate their way through that turbulent developmental passage. Although at a conscious level the students were all striving to escape the problems that plagued their neighborhoods, they all shared a fear, at an unconscious level brought out by the boy's dream, about what they were striving *for*—what good was it to leave a troubled childhood behind if all you had was a meaningless adult life to look forward to?

White-Lewis is continuing to develop new ways of promoting dream education among adolescents from impoverished communities. Although it is no substitute for the three R's, a greater awareness and understanding of dream symbolism can clearly help teenagers make better sense of their deepest fears and desires and can give them new insights into the complex and conflict-ridden social world they will soon enter as full-fledged adults.

A different kind of experimental dreamsharing group has been developed by the Reverend Jeremy Taylor, a Unitarian Universalist minister from San Rafael, California. For many years Taylor's ministry has focused on the use of dreamsharing to promote psychological, social, and spiritual well-being. He has led dreamsharing groups in a wide variety of settings, including hospitals, prisons, AIDS clinics, schools, and churches. His work with prison populations is particularly interesting because it offers a new source of insight into the social dynamics of crime and punishment. Taylor once led a dream group for the inmates of San Quentin (California) State Penitentiary, a maximum-security facility reserved for especially dangerous convicts. One of the members of the group, a huge and very aggressive man named Frank, described with defiant bravado his childhood dreams of being chased by terrible giants whom he always managed to escape with ease. As the group discussed Frank's dream, Taylor said that if it were his dream, the giants would symbolize adults, who seem so big and powerful to children. Taylor also said that because he feels death in dreams often symbolizes growth and new life, if he had experienced Frank's dream, the part about continually escaping would indicate a deep unwillingness to change something about his personality. At this comment Frank leaned forward and angrily said, "Wait a minute! You saying I never grew up!" When Taylor said, "Yes, if it were my dream, that would certainly be one of its meanings," Frank "uttered a really foul expletive in a tone of surprise, then sat back, speechless, withdrawing into himself." As the group discussion moved on to discuss another inmate's dream, Frank suddenly returned to the conversation and, to everyone's surprise, made several incredibly insightful comments about the other man's dream. As the discussion continued and more dreams were shared, it turned out that nearly all the prisoners' dreams led back to stories about being beaten as children by their fathers and by other male relatives. Frank's dreams of the terrible giants became a kind of group symbol expressing a painfully formative experience that the prisoners suddenly realized they all shared in common.

Taylor has also led dreamsharing groups at two other prisons in California: the Federal Correctional Facility at Pleasanton and the California Medical Facility at Vacaville. Although it's difficult to measure the precise effects of the dream discussions on the prisoners, Taylor's work certainly suggests that group dreamsharing has something valuable to contribute to efforts to promote the mental health and the rehabilitation of prison inmates. In the case of Frank, Taylor later heard from prison staff members that Frank's behavior had changed significantly after the night he talked about his dream. "Although none of them [the prison staff] were willing to credit the dream work per se, they reported that Frank was suddenly much less volatile and more able to control himself."

Taylor's work also opens the possibility of new insights into the root causes of criminal behavior. The more society understands the long-buried conflicts and traumatizing childhood experiences that unconsciously motivate people to commit crimes, the better able it will be to help those people break free of the cycle of crime and punishment. This point is well illustrated by the experience of Bette Ehlert, a dreamsharing group leader who was originally trained by Taylor. Ehlert once led a group at a New Mexico correctional facility in which a man convicted of dealing crack cocaine described a terrible recurrent nightmare of being pressed down onto the floor by a dark, malevolent creature. As Ehlert and the other inmates reflected on the dream, the man admitted that as a child he had been sexually abused. The group's conversation soon focused on the symbolic connections between the man's childhood experience of "being pushed" and his adult criminal identity of "being a pusher" and on how the dream brings back feelings of helplessness that the crime of drug dealing seemed to try to overcome. Based on this kind of dreamsharing experience, Ehlert has formulated the following argument: "There is no such thing as *random* violence or crime. Victims become perpetrators, and perpetrators commit highly specific crimes. They commit crimes that are perfectly, metaphorically linked to their prior experiences of victimization or abuse. At the moment of the crime, the perpetrator experiences the precise form of mastery that was missing to him/her at the moment of victimization. Crimes are reparative attempts by victims." Ehlert admits that this is an "outlandish" claim that flies in the face of many prominent social scientific theories about crime and its causes. But if there's *anything* to her argument, the dreams of prison inmates are worth greater attention from criminologists and public policy makers, not to mention dream researchers.

Dreaming in Russia

One of the most educational dreamsharing experiences I ever had was during a 1991 conference titled "Dreaming in Russia," which was organized by Robert Bosnak, a Jungian analyst from the Boston area. The conference in Russia brought together for the first time dream researchers from the two opposing sides of the Cold War, and I was very much looking forward to a fascinating time of discussion, debate, and scholarly exchange. But sudden historical events came together to add a whole new dimension of intensity to the conference. Those of us flying to the meeting from the West arrived at the Moscow airport on the afternoon of August 19, the day a group of Red Army generals abruptly seized control of the Soviet Union from Mikhail Gorbachev and declared martial law across the country. As our tour bus left the airport and drove the twenty miles to our conference center just outside the city, we watched as streams of tanks and armored personnel carriers roared past in the other direction, heading to Moscow to forcibly prevent any resistance to the generals and their effort to return the Soviet Union to a hard-line communist form of government. For the next three days all of us at the meeting, the Westerners and the Soviets, were almost completely isolated at our conference center. The airport had been shut down, the phones didn't work, and all television and radio stations had been seized by the military and were broadcasting nothing but official announcements telling people to stay calm, to avoid the resisters, and to be patient until proper order had been restored in the country.

As frightening as the situation was for those of us from the West, who had no way to communicate with our relatives at home, it was much, much worse for the Soviets. From the bits and scraps of real news we could gather, it appeared there *was* a significant resistance being organized against the coup leaders, and sketchy reports of violent conflicts were coming in from various parts of the country, right near the homes of many of the Soviet attendees.

All of us at the conference agreed that because none of us could travel back home for at least several days, we might as well continue with our conference. Two moments from those strange, uncertain days at the conference center had an especially strong impact on me. One came during an exercise in "dream theater," a special kind of dreamsharing process in which the group "performs" one of the people's dreams as if it were a one-act play. We were acting out one of the Soviet women's dreams, and although I don't remember the dream itself, I still recall with vivid clarity the feeling of all of us *playing together*—we had practiced our different parts with great effort, and when we finally went through the whole dream together, I laughed aloud at how enthusiastically everyone threw themselves into their roles. For a brief but wonderful moment, we were all united in a realm of pure imagination.

The second moment I'll always remember occurred during one of the small dreamsharing groups we had each day. These groups were amazingly challenging and stimulating, even though the conversations could be extremely slow and difficult. Each group had members who spoke different languages, and the process of translating one person's dream imagery into another person's language often took great time and effort. One day in my group, a Lithuanian woman shared a dream of being attacked by a spider. We talked about her dream for a while, and then a Dutch woman said, "It's funny, but I once had a dream of being attacked by a spider, too." As we talked about this second spider dream, it gradually became clear that at a deep level the two women had experienced *the same basic dream*. There was a moment's pause as the members of the group realized that despite the vast differences of language, culture, and geography that separated us in so many ways, we all shared some kind of core humanity, some essential quality that united us as one species: You have dreams about being attacked by spiders? So do I.

Three days after it started, the attempted coup abruptly collapsed. The Red Army generals fled in disgrace, the Soviet Union collapsed as a governing entity, statues were smashed and streets hastily renamed, and a democratic movement led by Moscow Mayor Boris Yeltsin rose up to replace seventy years of communist dictatorship. The dream conference concluded a few days later, and each attendee traveled home with a radically transformed sense of what could be accomplished by sharing dreams across the boundaries of culture and political ideology. The effort required in trying to understand people from so many different backgrounds and in trying to make oneself understood to all of them brought out new interpretive abilities in each of us. Most important, the experience reaffirmed the faith that brought us all to the conference in the first place, the faith that sharing dreams with other people not only is a valuable source of personal insight, but also can be a powerful means of creating a deeper sense of human community.

New Adventures in Cyberdreaming

In recent years several researchers have been working on new ways to facilitate dreamsharing by the creative use of computer technology. As with everything related to the Internet, the quality of these efforts at "cyberdreaming" has been highly inconsistent. But enough progress has been made that the most important potentials, and the most serious limitations, are gradually becoming clear.

One major potential lies in dreamsharing chat rooms, in which a person posts a dream on a user group's bulletin board and invites other people to reflect on it. For some people this is their preferred method of sharing dreams with others. Particularly for people who live in geographically remote areas, dreamsharing via the Internet lets them meet and interact with a greater number and a wider variety of people than they ever could find in their local communities. Greater time flexibility is another big appeal of Internet dreamsharing; computers give people the freedom to participate in ongoing dream discussions whenever they have a few spare moments. And for people who are uncomfortable speaking up in group settings, the Internet makes it easier for them to express their ideas without fear or embarrassment. For all these reasons, Internet dreamsharing appeals to some people as a powerfully effective way of stimulating the intuitive creativity of both the dreamers and the listeners.

For other people, of course, the very idea of dreamsharing on the Internet is like fingernails scratching across a blackboard. The Internet is too impersonal, these people say; without actual face-to-face contact, there's no way to draw on the subtle meanings communicated by a person's facial expressions, bodily postures, and differing tones of voice. Worse, an Internet chat room is an inherently unsafe environment in which to share the often intimately personal details of one's dreams, an environment that offers no protection against other people intruding on the discussion and making inappropriate or even deliberately offensive comments.

Both sides of this debate are right, of course. Dreamsharing via the Internet has strong advantages and disadvantages, and different people are free to make different judgments about how the two balance out. I encourage people at least to give Internet dreamsharing a try, if only to prove that their suspicions about the Internet are grounded in fact and not fear. If, after some open-minded experimentation, people do decide that they prefer to share their dreams in more personal, face-to-face kinds of settings, they may still decide it's worth staying aware of new developments on the cyber-dreaming frontier. The technology is moving so quickly and the social norms governing how people behave on the Internet are evolving so rapidly that the limitations of today may well be overcome tomorrow.

The other major arena of computer-oriented dream research involves the development of software programs that can help people record, categorize, and analyze dreams in a variety of ways. Some of these programs are primarily designed for use with individuals' private dream journals. The programs give people the ability to index and cross-reference their dreams with great speed and ease, highlighting important symbols and clarifying recurrent themes. The use of such software programs can be a big help in practicing the methods of "following dreams" that I'll be describing in the next chapter.

Other software programs have been developed to help researchers sift through large databases and conduct statistical analyses of dream content. By far the most sophisticated of these programs is the one developed by G. William Domhoff, professor of psychology at the University of California, Santa Cruz, and Adam Schneider, formerly one of Domhoff's students and now a professional software designer. Their web site combines both the academic and the personal applications of computer technology to dream study. Visitors to the site can look through original dream reports gathered from thousands of research subjects, and they can enter in their own dream reports and have them analyzed for correlations with the whole research database. For example, you could go to the site and learn about the statistical differences in the contents of men's and women's nightmares, and you could enter in a series of your own nightmares and see how they compare with the nightmare patterns of typical men and women.

As with dreamsharing chat rooms, these software programs should be used with a due amount of caution. No software program can give a magic answer to the question of what your dream means, and fortunately most of the programs currently available are very explicit about what people can and can't learn from them. I draw on these programs much as I draw on the various dream symbol dictionaries I've collected over the years: They offer me different possibilities to consider as I reflect on what a dream means. Neither the software programs nor the symbol dictionaries have final authority over the dream, but they can both provide some new ways of thinking about certain images and themes that often help me come to new insights: "If it were *their* dream, that's what it might mean. Hmmm. . . ."

Dreamsharing and the Imagination

A common criticism of dream interpretation in general is that all theories of interpretation are obviously biased by the subjective interests and personal fixations of the theorists. In this view Freud was so obsessed by repressed sexuality and Jung was so befuddled by ancient mythology that their dream interpretations can have no real, objective validity. Their theories are nothing more than expressions of their own idiosyncratic personalities.

My response to this criticism is that subjective interests and private fixations can actually be a source of positive insight, *if they are recognized and utilized as such*. It's definitely true that Freud's personal experiences with sexuality colored his theory about dream symbolism; and it's also true that Jung's ambivalent relations with Christianity deeply influenced his approach to dream interpretation. But the mere fact that their theories have roots in their personal lives is not necessarily a problem. On the contrary, I believe it's the very reason why their theories are so interesting and powerful. Freud's vigorous struggle with the powers of sexual desire and Jung's painful effort to integrate the light and the dark sides of religion gave each of them a special sensitivity toward some of the most important and least understood regions of the dreaming imagination. Out of their personal experiences, they formulated theories that have helped many people shed new light on their own dreams. As long as their theories are understood as *their* perspectives on what dreams mean, people are free to listen to Freud and Jung as if they were members of a dreamsharing group: dreamers can invite their questions, reflect on their insights, and make personal judgments about which of those insights are most relevant to the experience of the dream.

The approach to dreamsharing that I've outlined in this chapter makes positive use of what I believe is a natural and ultimately inescapable tendency that all humans have to create their own imagined versions when they hear other people's dreams. *Humans cannot help doing this*—every time they hear another person describe a dream, their imaginations spring into action, with the crucial consequence that their responses are not to the other person's dream but to their own reimagined version of it. As long as people are open and honest about this, the ideas and insights that come up in imaginations may be of real value to dreamers. The only problem that can occur is if people forget to take responsibility for their own ideas, and shift from "If it were my dream . . ." to "Your dream means . . ."

I suspect the reluctance many people feel about sharing dreams with others is due to a concern over this very problem—a concern that if they share their dreams, other people are going to assume a know-it-all posture and tell them what the dreams *really mean*. Unfortunately this concern is often well founded, and I would always recommend that people be careful about when, where, and with whom they share their dreams, trusting their instincts about what is and is not a safe setting. But my hope is that the process I've outlined here can give people the ability to create a comfortable context in which to share their dreams with others. To summarize the steps in this process:

1. The dreamer starts by sharing the dream in the present tense.
2. The listener asks questions and offers "If it were my dream . . ." reflections.
3. The dreamer describes his or her own associations and reflections.
4. The dreamer and the listener engage in a back-and-forth conversation.
5. The conversation culminates in a final effort at one-sentence summaries.

It doesn't take a highly trained psychologist or an expert with multiple academic degrees to give you valuable insights into your dreams. If you give this dreamsharing process a try, I think you'll be surprised to find that some of your closest friends and family members possess dream interpretation abilities that would impress even Freud and Jung.

CHAPTER SEVEN

Following Your Dreams

Othello: *O monstrous! Monstrous!*
Iago: *Nay, this was but his dream.*
Othello: *But this denoted a fore-gone conclusion;*
          'Tis a shrewd doubt, though it be but a dream.
Iago: *And this may help to thicken other proofs*
          That do demonstrate thinly.
Othello: *I'll tear her all to pieces.*

—William Shakespeare, *Othello*

This chapter describes a series of methods that readers can use to follow dreams beyond the initial meanings that emerge through reflection and through sharing them with other people. Those initial meanings are important, but experience shows that big dreams always have additional levels of meaning that can be discerned only after further interpretive efforts are made.

The passage quoted from *Othello*, Shakespeare's darkest tragedy, serves as a dramatic illustration of the potential dangers of *not* following a dream beyond its immediate, seemingly obvious meaning. Iago has just told Othello about Cassio's adulterous dream of making love to Othello's wife, Desdemona. Iago tells Othello, "There are a kind of men so loose of soul that in their sleeps will mutter their affairs: one of this kind is Cassio." Iago then says that he recently overheard Cassio murmuring in his sleep, "Sweet Desdemona, let us be wary, let us hide our loves." As Iago lavishly imitates the pleasurable sighs he says Cassio emitted during his passionate dream rendezvous with Desdemona, Othello is whipped into a frenzy of jealous rage. The tragedy of this scene, and of the play as a whole, is Othello's failure to think critically about Iago's charge that Desdemona has been unfaithful to him. Once the malignant suspicion has been planted in Othello's mind, he is powerless against it; he interprets everything he sees and hears as further proof of the secret affair between Desdemona and Cassio. He even accepts a secondhand report of someone else's dream as reliable evidence confirming his wife's infidelity: "Tis a shrewd doubt," he says, "though it be but a dream."

A twofold danger is revealed in this passage for anyone engaging in the practice of dream interpretation. The first is the frightening ease of misinterpreting a dream because of a strong emotional bias. Othello immediately concludes that Cassio's dream validates his suspicions and "denotes a fore-gone conclusion" because his overwhelming jealousy prevents him from imagining any other possible meaning. Without critical self-awareness, Othello is helpless, unable to stop his emotions from predetermining the meaning he will perceive in the dream—he will see only what his jealousy allows him to see. The second danger revealed in this passage is that other people sometimes offer badly misguided advice about what a dream means. All of the encouragement I offered in chapter 6 about sharing dreams with others must be balanced with an appropriate degree of caution about how the emotional biases of those other people may negatively influence their comments. Othello never questions the trustworthiness of his long-time lieutenant Iago, but the audience knows that Iago has secretly pledged himself to Othello's destruction and that this "dream" of Cassio's is only one more piece of deception in Iago's cruel plot to defame Desdemona and drive Othello mad. Although people may pray that they never meet anyone as utterly evil and malevolent as Iago, they should still learn from Othello's tragedy always to be aware of the potentially mixed motives of those people with whom they share their dreams.

The methods of following dreams described in this chapter are aimed at helping people develop greater confidence in the interpretation of their big dreams. The methods are all variations on a basic effort to follow dreams *through time*. Time can reveal the limits of an initial interpretation and can bring out new and unexpected meanings that may well conflict with a person's first thoughts about the experience.

Keeping a Dream Journal

The single most important thing a person can do to follow a dream through time is to write it down. Keeping a dream journal provides the basis for many different kinds of advanced methods of interpretation. These methods work best if the journal is a record of *all* of a person's remembered dreams, "big" and "little" dreams alike. Sometimes a dream that at first did not seem terribly remarkable will, over time, grow in significance and relevance to waking life.

There are several ways to keep a dream journal, and readers should feel free to experiment until they find the way that works best for them. Most people begin by keeping a pad of paper and a pen next to their bed so they can write down whatever dreams they remember immediately on awakening. If a dream comes in the middle of the night, some people turn on a tiny lamp or a penlight so they can see to write legibly, whereas other people simply scribble a few key words and images in the darkness and then go back to sleep, waiting until morning to clarify and to fill in the rest of the dream. I've heard that a few people have tried keeping tape recorders by their bedsides so that they don't have to write anything when they wake up in the middle of the night with a dream. They just talk into a tape recorder, catching as many of the dream's details as possible. Because they can do this without any light and without even opening their eyes, their sleep is only minimally disrupted. However, the tape-recorder method does require the follow-up task of transcribing the dream, and for some people that's too time-consuming to be worth it.

Whatever method is used to make the initial recording of the dream (which is best written in the present tense, for the same reasons given on p. 152), the next step is to write out several pieces of waking-life information related to the dream. In most people's journals, this includes the date, the place where the dreamer was sleeping that night (or day, if the dream came during a nap), and some basic details about the dreamer's experiences the preceding day (e.g., "I had a pleasant lunch with a friend, I got stuck in a frustrating traffic jam, I watched a dumb comedy on television before going to bed"). Then it's helpful to give the dream a title, as if it were a short story or a movie. Titles make it much easier to refer back through the journal to find particular dreams, and titles also help focus the dreamer's attention on one particularly important aspect of the dream's meaning.

Improving Dream Recall

When people start keeping a dream journal they frequently worry about the adequacy of their recall. Most people remember an average of two to three dreams a month, which means they're *not* remembering any dreams at all for twenty-seven or twenty-eight nights a month. It can be very frustrating, after making the decision to keep a dream journal, to watch weeks go by without recalling anything to write down.

My advice is to focus less on the quantity of dreams you don't remember and more on the quality of your reflections on the dreams you *do* manage to recall. Although I know a few serious dream researchers who have compiled vast collections of their personal dreams, with journals containing thousands and thousands of entries, I would never suggest that theirs is the only or even the best way to pursue a deeper understanding of the world of dreaming. Several years ago I taught a class in which one of the students, a quiet, polite man in his late thirties, admitted with embarrassment that he could remember only one dream from his entire life. For the first few weeks of the quarter, while the other students avidly filled up their dream journals, this man continued to have zero dream recall each night. I told him not to worry, and to perhaps give some further attention to that one dream he could remember, which was in fact quite an interesting dream from a time of great change in his life several years earlier. The man did as I suggested, and he was surprised to find many new angles on the dream that he had never considered before. Then, just a couple of weeks before the end of the quarter, he came to class and with great pleasure reported that he had just remembered the second dream of his life. It had come during an afternoon nap that weekend, and it centered on an extremely vivid, highly animated figure of a Middle Eastern dancer who was spinning and whirling about with tremendous energy and beauty. Needless to say, the man found this to be a deeply meaningful dream, and by the end of the class I felt sure he had learned at least as much from his two dreams as the other students had from their journals of ten times that many dreams.

My belief, based partly on current experimental research and partly on my personal dream-journal experience, is that there is a natural ebb and flow to dream recall. Sometimes people remember many dreams, and sometimes they remember very few. I think it's best to trust that the dreams people do recall are worth their attention, and the ones they don't remember probably don't *need* to be remembered, at least not right now.

There are a variety of techniques that are definitely effective in helping stimulate greater dream recall. One good technique is to try moving more slowly when you get out of bed each morning. If you jump out of bed with the first sound of the alarm clock, whatever dreams you may have had are likely to vanish in an instant. (Alarm clocks are, from the perspective of dreams, one of the great evils of the modern world!) If you try instead to lie in the same position for a few moments, holding off any thoughts about what you're going to do when you get up, you may find that a few dream images or feelings are still lingering in your mind.

Another reliable technique is to try paying close attention to dream recall during middle-of-the-night awakenings. If you partly wake up during the night, whether it's to change sleeping positions or go to the bathroom, you have probably just left a REM-sleep phase and, thus, in all likelihood have been dreaming. If you can generate the presence of mind during these "micro awakenings" to ask if you've just had a dream, you'll probably discover that most of the time the answer is yes.

If you're serious about trying to improve your dream recall, it's very important to write down every little bit or piece of dream imagery you can remember, no matter how trivial or fragmentary it may seem. You might find that when you first wake up all you can remember is a little snatch of a dream—for example, "I am doing something with a friend." Although such wispy fragments may not seem worth the trouble to write down, if you do record them in your journal, you will frequently find that as you start writing, more details will slowly come to mind. "Something about being with my friend. Hmmm. . . . We're sitting together in a crowded place, I think—maybe outside a large house or on a school campus. There's a staircase near where we're sitting. My friend is talking with some other people. I'm listening. I'd like to talk with my friend alone, but there are too many people around. I'm not happy about that. But there doesn't seem to be anything I can do." In such cases what begins as a minuscule and seemingly random fragment turns out to be an opening into a fairly detailed dream.

Many people's dream recall is actually much better than they believe. All it takes for them to become more aware of their dreams is simply the effort to write them down.

Heeding the Call of Recurrent Dreams

Keeping a dream journal gives you the ability to follow your dreams in any of a number of different directions. One especially fruitful pathway leads into the realm of recurrent dreams. When asked the question, "What is your most memorable dream?" many people reply that it's not one single dream, but a recurrent dream they remember most clearly and vividly. It may be a nightmare they experienced several times during childhood, or it may be a dream that still comes periodically during adulthood. It may be a relatively "typical" recurrent dream scenario like being unprepared for a school exam or being naked in public, or it may be a strangely distinctive image that's unique to the dreamer. Recurrent dreams take a wide variety of forms, and researchers have devised an equally wide variety of theories about why recurrent dreams occur and what they mean. One point of general consensus among researchers is that recurrent dreams reflect the fundamental structures of the dreamer's life and personality. Recurrent dreams are

like psychological fingerprints—the appearance of the same setting, figure, or activity in several dreams across a period of time
indicates that those recurrent elements are deeply rooted in the
dreamer's mind. As a result, reflecting carefully on a recurrent
dream is a sure way to gain new personal insight and greater self-
awareness.

Jane was a thirty-four-year-old woman from a small farming
town in the Midwest who moved with her husband and two pug
dogs to a large West Coast city to attend a school for the ministry.
Jane enjoyed her seminary classes, particularly the ones on Christian spirituality, but she and her husband had real difficulties in
making a comfortable home in the school's rather shabby student-
housing facility. After her first year of school ended, Jane and her
husband began talking about moving out of student housing and
buying a condominium. Although they really disliked the small,
rundown apartment in which they were currently living, they also
worried deeply about the expense of buying a condo, the increased
time they would have to spend commuting, and the emotional and
financial commitment required to buy a house in the city. During a
two-week period early in the summer, Jane had a series of three
dreams that struck her as so vivid and memorable that she knew she
had to write them down:

*1. I see a dog named Stuart sitting passively in a big cornfield.
Although I know in the dream the dog's name is Stuart, I also
know that the dog is really Sam [one of their two dogs]. Suddenly
a big farming combine machine comes rumbling right at the dog
and scoops him up. I don't feel any particular fear, though. I walk
up to the combine, and I find that the dog has come out just fine.
Somehow I know that his name is back to being Sam again.*

*2. I'm in a garage, and Sophia [their other pug dog] is nosing
around under a car. There's a man in the car who wants to back
out, but he can't with the dog playing around under the car. I try
to find the dog and get her out, but I can't. I wake up feeling stuck
between the man and the dog.*

3. I have somehow become a dog, and I've found the keys to a car.
I bring the keys to the car and set them on the driveway right next
to the driver's side. But suddenly a workman dumps a load of
cement on top of the keys, and a moment later the cement is totally
dry, with the keys buried under it. Then my husband comes looking
for the keys to drive the car, but he's frustrated because he can't find
them. I become extremely worried that he's going to blame me for
letting the keys get buried.

Jane immediately saw the common images and themes recurring in each of the three dreams. Most noticeable were the dogs.
All three dreams centered around a dog, and the first and third
were particularly memorable to Jane because the dogs go through
such strange transformations. In the first dream her pug Sam
changes into "Stuart" and then back into Sam. In the third dream
Jane herself is changed into a dog. Another recurrent element in all
three dreams is the presence of a driving machine, first a farming
combine and then twice an automobile. And all three dreams share
a distinct kind of setting, a space outside of but in close proximity
to a home. Jane didn't clearly recognize any of the settings, but
they all felt vaguely familiar and somehow related either to her old
home in the Midwest (the cornfield) or her new home on the West
Coast (the garage, the driveway).

As Jane reflected on the dreams as a series, asking the same
questions of all three dreams and sifting through the interconnec-
tions among them, she slowly began to discern the distinctive
meanings of each one. The first dream expressed the deepest roots
of Jane's worries about buying a condominium: At base, she was
afraid of how big a change in her life such a move would represent.
Her dog Sam, whom she loved dearly, symbolized at one level the
emotional vulnerability she felt in making so strong a commitment
to living in the city and leaving her farm-town life behind. Initially
Jane had no idea why Sam would be named Stuart. After coming
up blank in her efforts to associate to that name, she realized its
unknown quality was exactly the point—she didn't know what was
going to happen. She feared that this impending process of major
life change (symbolized by the big farming combine rumbling

toward her) was threatening to turn her into something strange and unfamiliar, something with an unknown name. But to her surprise in the dream, Jane finds that the dog emerges from the combine in fine shape, with his familiar name restored. In reflecting on the dream Jane understood that a very hopeful meaning was being expressed in the figure of the dog: perhaps the looming changes in her life would not destroy her but would actually restore something vital and important in her life that she mistakenly thought she had lost.

Jane then saw that the second dream had taken this same basic theme and sharpened the waking-life connections in a way that re-emphasized the first dream's meanings. The second dream involves her other pug dog, Sophia, who is more willful, independent, and playfully curious than Sam. The conflict between Sophia and the man in the car struck Jane as a good metaphorical image of the struggle between herself and her husband over the decision to move. Jane realized that a part of her felt a stubborn resistance to any change in their living situation; given that she and her husband were already working hard at summer jobs, she worried that all the stress and strain involved in moving from their current apartment to a new condo would be overwhelming. As Jane reflected on this second dream and considered it in light of the recurrent elements from the first one, she suddenly thought of something she hadn't really understood before: *There are times when you have to back up before you can go forward.* Any process of change has moments of distress and hardship, and Jane suddenly felt more confident than ever that if she and her husband went ahead and moved, the end result would be worth whatever temporary setbacks and reversals might come along the way. The challenge, Jane realized, was some-how to reconcile the man and Sophia: How could she satisfy both his need to back the car out and the dog's desire to play and explore?

With this question in mind, Jane looked to the third dream, and she found a possible answer. In this dream the dog theme is carried to a new level—Jane is herself turned into a dog. She felt this symbolized her own inner potential to be playful, relaxed, and carefree; when she can integrate those qualities more fully into her waking life, she will find the "key" to driving the car and to getting the process of change under way. Jane realized this was a crucial part of the whole motivation behind moving—she, her husband, and Sam and Sophia would all have more room to play and relax in a new home. Some of the condominiums they were considering had their own little yards, which the dogs would love; she realized this might be a more important priority in deciding which one to buy than she had previously thought. But with this insight came two new concerns, and Jane understood that this was where she needed to focus her energies. First is the workman, who dumps a load of instant-drying cement on top of the keys, effectively paralyzing the moving process. Jane saw him as an expression of her financial anxieties, clearly indicating that nothing could happen until she found a proper, healthy balance between economic realities and playful desires. Second is the inability to communicate with her husband—in dog form, Jane cannot tell him what has happened to the keys, and he becomes angry and frustrated. Jane took this as a strong message to share with her husband the thoughts and feelings emerging in her "dog dreams" so that they could more openly and honestly figure out how to proceed with the move.

Jane's three dreams gave her valuable new insights into feelings, hopes, and anxieties she had not fully understood or appreciated before. She had been focusing so much of her energy on school and on the joys of the spiritual life that she had not focused enough attention on the more material concerns of her family's living condition. The three dog dreams helped Jane gain a much better sense of what the real issues were and how she and her husband might join together to deal with them.

As I mentioned earlier, recurrent dreams take a wide variety of different forms. In Jane's case the three dreams all came in a space of two weeks. Other people experience recurrent dreams in a much shorter period of time, sometimes having the same basic dream two or more times in a single night. Any time this kind of "instant recurrence" happens, you can be sure the dream is worth a good deal of conscious attention and reflection. The dreaming imagination will use rapid repetition of the same dream as a simple but effective means of emphasizing an especially important meaning. This is one of the points about dream interpretation that the Bible got right more than three thousand years ago. When Pharaoh told Joseph his dream of seven thin cows eating seven fat cows, followed immediately by a dream of seven thin ears of grain consuming seven plump ears of grain, Joseph explained that "the dream of Pharaoh is one": Both dreams express the same basic divine prophecy, that seven years of plenty in Egypt will be followed by seven years of famine. Joseph's comment that "the doubling of Pharaoh's dream means that the thing is fixed by God" corresponds to my point about recurrent dreams, that an immediate recurrence of the same essential dream is a strong indicator of its importance and value.

An entirely different form of recurrent dream involves the periodic repetition of a particular setting, character, or activity across a long stretch of time. Recurrent chasing nightmares are one common instance of this and so are anxiety dreams about being unprepared for a test. I've had two long-term recurrent dreams that have occurred every few months for many years now. In one I'm a player in an organized sporting event, such as a basketball game or a football game, and in the other I find myself starting college as a student once again. With both dreams the details can vary drastically from one instance to the other. With the sports dreams I sometimes play the game surprisingly well; at other times I make shockingly incompetent mistakes. With the college dreams I may feel extremely excited to be back at school, or I may feel terribly awkward and out of place. But the basic settings remain the same in every instance of these two dreams, and I've come to see them as "life frameworks" that help me to make sense of the ongoing flow of my experience. All through childhood and adolescence, I loved playing every sport in which I could get involved, and I feel the recurrent sports dreams are making use of those past experiences to frame and to make more understandable something going on in my current life. Thus, if I dream of playing basketball and not being able to make a basket because the ball has for some reason turned into a stack of dishes, I've learned to ask myself whether I may be more anxious than I know about a housekeeping problem in my family's home. When I have a dream of playing soccer (one of the few sports I never really played) and surprise myself by kicking the ball perfectly and scoring a goal, I know that somewhere in my current life I may be on the verge of developing a new ability. I also had the experience throughout childhood and adolescence of loving school. So when I have a dream of being excited to be a student at college again, I usually see it as an expression of a new enthusiasm I feel about something in my waking life. If, however, I feel weird or awkward in the dream about being back in school, I start to wonder if somewhere in my current life I'm regressing or getting stuck in a rut.

Here is where keeping a dream journal is crucial, because the real significance of life-framework dreams lies in the specific details that distinguish each dream from the others in the series. The deepest insights come from comparing the different dreams in the series and discerning the subtle patterns by which each dream expresses its own particular message. What I call life-framework dreams make use of important formative experiences from our past to help us make better sense of our present lives. For many people the dreams recur throughout their entire lives, and each appearance comes to feel like a visit from an old friend—"Oh, it's *that* dream again; I wonder what it has to say this time."

Yet another type of recurrent dream looks not to the past, but to the future. These could be called "rehearsal" or "anticipatory" dreams because their primary function seems to be to prepare the dreamer for something that's going to happen at some point in the future. Here's a good example that illustrates very powerfully the scientific point that such dreams have significant evolutionary value:

> *I am not sure of where I am exactly; however, that does not really concern me. It is not dark, yet not overly bright. I do realize I am indoors because though there is not a mirror visible to me, I know I am looking at myself and through my eyes. It is pleasantly warm and quiet; I even feel this in my arms, back, face . . . through my whole body. I may be reclined in a bed or a very soft and big easy chair. I am very comfortable and peaceful. I feel my abdomen, large and warm, and I know life is within me. Then I have the baby in my arms, and I am nursing the baby. It is so real that I feel the baby's gurgling and suckling physically. I have to emphasize the*

calm and the contentment, the overwhelming love I have for this
child welling up within me.

Andrea, the twenty-year-old woman who's had this same basic
dream half a dozen times in the past several years, had never actually conceived and borne a child. But some day she hopes she will,
and her recurrent dreams embody that hope in a wonderfully
intense experience of *what it will be like* when she has a baby of her
own.

Many people have recurrent dreams of experiences they have
not yet had but likely will in the future, experiences like graduating
from school, getting married, having children, and attending a
loved one's funeral. Such dreams can be thought of as emotional
practice runs, as the dreaming imagination's way of preparing the
dreamers for the future by envisioning different possible scenarios:
What will it feel like when I finish school? What will my wedding
be like? How will I deal with it when one of my parents dies? The
vividly realistic nature of these dreams gives the dreamer an extraordinarily revealing insight into his or her greatest hopes, and darkest fears, about the future.

When Movies, Myths, and Fairy Tales
Appear in Your Dreams

Another good method of following your dreams starts with paying
closer attention to the appearance of characters, settings, and plots
drawn from the cultural environment around you. In modern
Western society, movies and television programs are the most common cultural influences on people's dreams. I often hear descriptions of dreams in which people have personal encounters with
famous movie stars or find themselves in the middle of an episode
from their favorite television show. I also regularly hear of dreams
with a form and structure that have been directly influenced by
films and television—dreams in which the dreamer's perspective
zooms in and out like a video camera; dreams using standard film-
editing techniques like jump cuts, fade-outs, and slow motion; and
dreams containing classic cinematic set pieces, like the harrow-

ing car chase, the blazing gun battle, the torrid love scene, and the psycho killer stalking a helpless victim. There's a good reason, I believe, for this powerful shaping effect of movies and television on people's dreams. Wherever people live, in whatever kind of society, their dreaming imaginations make creative use of elements from the culture around them. Thus, the dreams of Native American people often refer to their tribe's traditional myths and legends; the dreams of medieval Christians frequently include images and themes from the Bible; and the dreams of modern Westerners regularly take the form of Hollywood movie productions.

As a practical method of dream interpretation, following your dreams into the broader realm of culture can be a tremendously illuminating experience because at a fundamental level culture expresses the dreaming imagination of a whole community. By tapping into that vast communal treasure-house of symbolic meaning, you will likely be surprised at how many new feelings and ideas related to the dream come to your mind.

Although this is not true of all dreams or even of all big dreams, people do occasionally experience dreams that speak directly to something going on in their culture, dreams that creatively respond to a special story, a haunting image, or a highly talented artist. The first step in following these dreams is to use a modified version of the questions of specification described in chapter 5. Why, out of all the possible cultural references available, did my dreaming imagination make use of *this* particular one? Why, to take a personal example, did I recently dream of the singer Alanis Morissette, out of all the famous cultural figures of whom I might have dreamed? What makes her different from all of them? What thoughts and feelings come to mind when I reflect on her songs, her appearance, her life story? How would the dream have been different if instead of Alanis Morissette I had dreamed of Whitney Houston, or Ella Fitzgerald, or Patti Smyth?

Taking a different example that I often hear reported by my students, why do you think your dream set you in a *Friday the 13th* movie rather than in any of the hundreds of other movies you've seen in your life? What is it about this particular movie that seems to have caught the attention of your dreaming imagination? How would you describe this film's basic plot to someone who had never seen it before? How is Jason Voorhees, the movie's hockey-mask-wearing villain, different from every other horror movie bad guy?

By asking these kinds of questions and following the insights they generate, important new dimensions of the dream's meaning come into focus. I've found that a good next step is to ask: What does the dream *do* with the specific cultural reference? Although it's exciting to discover that such a cultural reference is present in your dream, the truly important meanings come from looking more carefully at how exactly the character, theme, or image is *used* by your dreaming imagination. How does your dream modify the element, or change it, or adapt it to some new context?

A young artist named Sandra had this dream one night:

I am the seventeenth-century painter Rembrandt, wandering through the countryside looking for work. I come to a house, which is owned by the sixteenth-century painter Holbein, and I go inside only to find a big, strong wolf poised to attack me. I start fighting with the wolf, and then I am suddenly lifted up by an unseen female spirit hovering above and behind me. For a moment, I can see the wolf and myself [as Rembrandt] fighting below. Then I am thrust back into the battle.

The resurgent fear wakes up Sandra. Her dream has at least two different levels of cultural reference. First are the figures of Rembrandt and Holbein. By identifying her with Rembrandt, the dream expresses both her driving desire to be a great artist and her fear that the main obstacle to that goal is the excessively masculine tone of all her training: She's afraid that to become great she will have to learn how to "paint like a man." All of the teachers at the arts academy she attended were men, and Holbein was one of their great heroes. Sandra's dream takes the two cultural figures of Rembrandt and Holbein and uses them to express a deep conflict at the very heart of her effort to become a creator of culture herself. The dream also offers potential means of overcoming this conflict by using another cultural reference, this time to the classic fairy tale figure of the big, bad wolf. In *Little Red Ridinghood*, *The Three Little Pigs*, and several other well-known children's stories, the "big, bad wolf" is a terrifying creature (always a male) who uses both crafty intelligence and brute strength to capture and devour people. His appearance in Sandra's dream reemphasizes the idea that her growth as an artist is threatened by the masculine dominance of the arts academy, aptly symbolized by the inside of Holbein's house. Unlike a fairy tale, however, Sandra's dream ends on a decidedly ambiguous note. The wolf does not devour her, but neither does she escape him; the unseen female spirit doesn't really rescue Sandra from the danger so much as give her a new way of looking at it. By leaving her with this uncertain resolution to the classic fairy tale struggle, the dream made Sandra wonder if her growth as an artist might depend not on killing or escaping the wolf, but rather on somehow *dealing* with him as a real and inescapable part of her creative life.

Living in a truly multicultural world, and surrounded by an overwhelming variety of different symbols, meanings, and traditions, people today often find themselves asking where they fit in— "How can I figure out who *I* am, what symbols *I* believe in, which tradition *I* belong to?" One of my graduate school mentors, the historian of religions Wendy Doniger, wrote a book titled *Other People's Myths*, in which she described a dream relating these questions to her own life and experience:

> *I dreamed that I was at a meal in the common room of the divinity school at the University of Chicago, sitting at one of the long tables as I have so often done at formal and informal dinners, with friends on either side and across from me. And suddenly I looked up and realized that I was inside the Leonardo da Vinci painting of the Last Supper, that Jesus and the disciples had come forward in time to join us now at the table in Chicago. As I realized this, the person sitting beside me said to me, "But Wendy, what is your religion?" and I replied, "My myths are Hindu, but my rituals are Christian."*

She woke up from the dream wondering why she hadn't answered the person's question by saying, "My rituals are Jewish." Wendy's parents were both Jewish refugees from Poland; her sense of family and community was principally Jewish, and she usually attended a Passover celebration each year. But Wendy's dream locates her in a Christian ritual, and specifically within the single most famous artistic portrayal of that ritual, da Vinci's painting *The Last Supper*.

As she thought about the symbolic significance of this strange image in her dream she recognized similarities to the Hindu ceremony of *prasada*, in which food left over after an offering to the gods is distributed to the worshipers, and also to a Hasidic tradition of gathering for the third meal on the day of the Sabbath. These similarities led her to see the dream as an expression of her own distinct identity at a point where all these cultural and religious traditions intersect:

> For the myth of the communal meal served me simultaneously as a Jewish Seder, a Christian Eucharist, a Hindu *prasada*, and a University of Chicago dinner. My dream incorporated my four rituals (three religious and a transcendent fourth): Jewish, Christian, Hindu, and academic. The fourth, the academic, provided a kind of metareligion that transcended religions, a framework that made possible the bricolage of the other three. Of course, this was only a *dream* of a ritual, a story that I told myself about a ritual—a myth. I had not converted to a new ritual, merely dreamed that my usual rituals had taken on a new mythic dimension. But the Christian (particularly Catholic) and Hindu myths had come to play a very important role in my religious thinking, to answer needs that were not answered by the ritual community into which I had been born, with implications that I had not yet come to terms with until I had that dream.

Using Dreams to Inspire Prayer and Meditation

In both Eastern and Western religious systems, and in smaller indigenous spiritual traditions from all over the world, dreams have long been used to enhance the practice of prayer and meditation. Rituals of "dream incubation" are the most widespread form of this kind of religious dream practice. In a dream incubation ritual, people first perform various purification ceremonies and then go to sleep in a special, sacred place like a cave, a mountaintop, a graveyard, or a temple, praying to their tradition's divinities to send them a revelatory dream. Such rituals can be found in nearly every religion in the world, with Christians praying for dreams from Jesus and the Saints, Native Americans seeking dreams from their ancestral spirits, Muslims calling to Allah, ancient Greeks petitioning the healing god Asclepius, Chinese Buddhists inviting an appearance from their temple gods, and so on. These practices may seem quaintly superstitious to people in modern society, but I would suggest readers not dismiss them before giving them a try. The basic logic behind dream incubation rituals is that a strong and sincerely expressed waking-life question can actually evoke a response from the dreaming imagination. It's not that you simply say, "I'd like to dream of *X*," and then magically you do. Rather, what can happen is that deep, focused prayer or meditation on something truly important in your life will stimulate a dream directly related to that waking-life concern.

Bryn was a woman in her late twenties who had drifted from job to job since graduating from college and who was feeling increasingly anxious and uncertain about ever finding a career for herself. Having been raised in a Christian family, Bryn prayed regularly as part of her religious life; but now Bryn suddenly found that every time she prayed, waves of desperate emotion flooded through her, leaving her crying and trembling. Not knowing where else to turn for direction, she looked to her dreams and wrote the following prayer in her journal: "Dear God, my biggest concern right now is my career. Please give me some guidance. I will try to give you my will. Let some direction come in my dreams tonight. I am your servant. In Jesus' name, Amen." Three nights later she had this dream:

> I am in high school or college. I have missed many of my calculus classes, but I am also to star in a school play. I have just found out I am to play the role of Christine in Phantom of the Opera. I am thrilled and frightened at the same time, and I tell the director (a woman) that I don't think my voice is good enough. She replies that "He" has chosen me for the part, and I discover I have already auditioned and the director won't be able to undo anything "He" has done. She reassures me I am exactly right for the part. I am skeptical, never having acted or done a musical.

Bryn awoke from the dream a bit puzzled, but definitely more hopeful about her career anxieties. She felt the dream had definitely responded to her prayers, and she now had a deep confidence that a new and better future was already taking shape in her life. She didn't have to do or achieve anything new; she had already "auditioned" and gotten the part. The contrast between doing poorly in the calculus class and doing well in the play accurately reflected her waking-life dissatisfaction with her current work (in a data processing company) and her desire to find a new job in which she could better use her creative and intuitive abilities.

Of course, the dream did not automatically solve all of Bryn's troubles. It took her three more years before she found a company in which she could truly "star," and even then it took another year before she developed a good relationship with her new boss, whose "controlling mentor" personality was perfectly foreshadowed by the *Phantom of the Opera* reference in her dream. But all through this time, the dream remained a clear, vivid presence in Bryn's mind; and rather than "solving" her problems, it responded to her prayer by giving her the deep spiritual guidance she so desperately wanted in making her own decisions about what to do with her life.

The relationship among dreams, prayer, and meditation can work in the opposite direction, too. Just as focused meditation on a particular waking-life concern can evoke a dream response, so a special dream can inspire new developments in one's prayer life. People often find that if they just sit quietly in a comfortable, private place, close their eyes, and try to remember an especially vivid dream, the dream literally comes back to life—the images, the characters, and the feelings from the dream reenter conscious awareness to reveal new meanings, new insights, and new intuitions that were not previously recognized or appreciated. In this regard prayer and meditation can be thought of as the creation of a mental space in which the energies of dreaming and the concerns of waking life are invited to meet each other and to have a mutual, open-ended conversation.

Let me close this chapter by repeating the fundamental importance of keeping a dream journal. If you truly want to follow your dreams into their deeper realms of meaning and value, there is no substitute for keeping a written journal of your experiences and reflections. Dream journals allow people to track their dreams through time in both directions: into the future, by disclosing the evolution of various recurrent images, themes, and characters; and back into the past, by highlighting the historical roots of present-day issues and concerns. It can be a surprisingly revelatory experience to go back through your journal and to find that past dreams have accurately anticipated and responded to a major conflict in your current life.

A dream journal's ultimate value is to serve as an honest and intimate witness of your journey through life. Nothing else can give you as clear a picture of your hopes and desires, your fears and anxieties, your most painful wounds from the past and your most cherished wishes for the future.

CHAPTER EIGHT

Creating Your Dreams

We are such stuff as dreams are made on.

—William Shakespeare, *The Tempest*

This last chapter carries the process of dream interpretation to its ultimate conclusion: the transformation of dreams into waking-world realities.

The most immediate effect of a big dream on a person's life is to *seize* his or her conscious awareness. Certain dreams are so powerful, so numinous, so incredibly, intensely vivid and realistic that they absolutely *force* the dreamer to pay attention. Dreamers may not know right away what their experiences mean, and they may never be able to translate their dreams' amazing images and unforgettable sensations into rational language. But at a fundamental level, the simple *presence* of the dream in the dreamer's consciousness is what matters most. This entrance of the dream into waking-world awareness is itself a kind of creative process, a transformation of the dream from one dimension of reality to another. All big dreams are driven by an essential desire to *create*: All big dreams seek an ever greater presence in the dreamer's life, and all big dreams strive to bring new realities into existence. The final stage of interpreting a big dream is doing whatever you can to satisfy this creative energy welling up from within the dream.

Creativity and Problem Solving

A great deal of research has been done on the relationship between dreaming and creativity, and the basic findings of this research are fairly easy to summarize. Dreaming appears to be one of the crucial elements in a four-stage process of problem solving. This process occurs whenever a person faces a challenge requiring a creative solution, whether it's a challenge involving a personal relationship, an intellectual puzzle, an issue at work, or an attempt at making a piece of art.

- The *first stage* of the process involves an intense focus and concentration on the problem at hand. The person studies the problem, examines it, analyzes it, and tries as hard as he or she can to figure it out.
- In the *second stage* the person, unable to solve the problem by purely rational concentration, simply lets go of it. Exhausted and frustrated, the person gives up for a while and goes on to think about something else.
- The *third stage* occurs outside of waking consciousness, when the person goes to sleep and begins to dream. The unconscious faculties of the mind continue to work on the problem, and suddenly a dream appears that offers the person a novel solution to the problem.
- In the *fourth stage* the person awakens and tests the creative new solution to see if it does indeed work. Sometimes it does; but even when it doesn't, the dream often jars the person's previous way of conceptualizing the problem, and this in itself can lead to the discovery of a new solution.

Researchers have identified this four-stage process of dream-inspired problem solving in a wide variety of settings. Artists, of course, make frequent use of the creative power of dreaming—a musician may struggle to play a certain song well and then has a dream that reveals a new technique that dramatically improves the performance of that song. Scientists, too, have found that dream images can disclose new insights into the thorniest difficulties of their work, suggesting new possibilities for their theories, equations, and experiments. Numerous inventors have discovered that some of their strangest dreams have provided breakthrough ideas in designing and building new tools and mechanical devices. In the realm of religion, dreams can be regarded as problem solvers par excellence—people from all over the world have experienced dreams of divine revelation that healed their sufferings, relieved their despair, and creatively reoriented their lives. Perhaps the most commonly experienced form of problem solving through dreams comes in the context of personal relationships—when a person is having serious troubles with a family member or a romantic partner, a special dream will sometimes come that gives the person a creative new way of working through the troubles.

The best explanation that researchers can give for the problem-solving power of certain dreams is that dreaming allows for a more flexible and wider ranging mode of thinking than is ordinarily possible in waking consciousness. In dreaming, the mind is looser, more fluid, more playful. Dreaming is a realm of pure freedom, and this liberation from the constraints of external social reality allows the mind to try out a greater variety of possible solutions to the given problem. *Brainstorming* is the word people use when they want to describe this mode of thinking in a waking state. Current research suggests that dreaming is the original form of brainstorming and that, in fact, no attempt by waking consciousness can ever match dreaming for sheer creative energy and dynamism.

When learning about these important research findings on dreams and creativity, people sometimes neglect the importance of the fourth stage of the problem-solving process. A dream cannot in and of itself solve a waking-life problem; what is always necessary is the willingness of the dreamer to pay conscious attention to the dream, to test its workability, and finally to act on its guidance. It is tempting to think that simply having a powerful dream will turn an ordinary person into a famous artist or a revolutionary scientist, but, for better or for worse, it doesn't work that way. Artists and scientists are able to make use of their dreams in special ways because they have the practical training and the technical skills necessary to do so. Dreams inspire those who are prepared to be inspired and who are able to do the practical work to transform their inspirations into realities.

In my view the key finding of current research on this subject is that dreams serve a creative, problem-solving function in *all* people. Wherever people live, whatever kind of work they do, whatever kinds of challenges they face, their dreams offer them a true wellspring of creative possibility. Although there are many wonderful examples of famous people having creative inspirations in their dreams, I believe such examples can actually obscure the most important point here—that *non*famous people, too, have dreams of astonishing creative power. All people have this power within them, a power that can change the way they think, feel, and behave in waking life.

Cultivating a Harmony of Conscious and Unconscious Desire

Sometimes people get so excited when they first discover the problem-solving power of dreaming that they eagerly try to *use* their dreams to further their waking-life goals. This can be a tricky business, however. I am very skeptical about efforts to manipulate dreams to give people new business ideas, to improve their sex life, to help them lose weight, to fix a bad relationship, or to pick stock market winners (to name just a few of the things I've heard people try to do with their dreams). The reason these efforts rarely work is that dreams have their *own* goals, their *own* aims and intentions; and these usually do not correspond with people's more materialistic and egocentric wishes. The creative power of dreaming emerges only when there's a harmony of conscious desire and unconscious desire, when the object is something so vital and important that the person's whole being strives to reach it. Such a harmony cannot be forced or imposed; this is why dreams will never be a quick path to getting rich or becoming famous.

Arlene was a woman in her midthirties who had spent most of her childhood on the Hawaiian island of Molokai but who had lived for the past ten years on the American mainland, pursuing a career as a producer in the music industry. Although Arlene had achieved a great deal of success, she was coming to a turning point in her life, and she realized she wasn't sure which way she wanted to go. Many different professional opportunities beckoned to her, all of them offering money, excitement, and prestige. But the more Arlene thought about it, the more she found herself thinking about her home on Molokai, her friends and family members there, and her memories of the magical environment of the island. One night as she was pondering her various career possibilities, Arlene had this dream:

> I'm at a music club—jazz, I think. Then a voice says, "It's time to leave." All the patrons are asked to leave. The music isn't playing anymore, it's like the end of a set or something. So we walk out of this club, and then I'm joined by some of my Molokai cousins. Now we're in an open, wooden house on the island, talking and laughing and having a really good time. They bring in their beach towels and hang them on the rafters of the house. And then suddenly I see this huge Kuan-yin. She's red, and fiery, and brilliant, and her robes are flowing. She's incredible. I can feel her presence. She's really big and right in front of me. So then I ask myself, "Where can I put her?" She must be from my mother or someone. The only place I have space for this Kuan-yin—her figure seems to be made of pure energy—is in my kitchen. I put her in the kitchen, near where the refrigerator would go.

Arlene's family had lived on Molokai for several generations. They originally came from China, and they had brought with them many cultural and religious traditions from their homeland. Kuan-yin is a Buddhist goddess of compassion, wisdom, and nurturance who has been reverently worshiped for many centuries. Many Buddhist families have an image of Kuan-yin somewhere in their home, and as Arlene grew up, she became used to seeing the figure of the goddess in the kitchen of every relative's home. When she awoke from her dream, Arlene could still feel the vivid presence of Kuan-yin, not the presence of a wood or stone sculpture but of the goddess herself, radiating energy, love, and goodness. For several days afterward, the dream remained clear in her mind, and as Arlene worked through her career decision, she relied on Kuan-yin's energy for guidance during the process. Arlene now knew, with a certainty and confidence she did not have before the dream, that she needed to move back to Hawaii. She realized that her conscious concerns about money and status were only part of the equation; she also needed to satisfy her deep spiritual desires to "find a place for Kuan-yin" and to reconnect with the glorious beauty and lush vitality of Molokai. Arlene turned down the many job offers she had on the mainland and began actively exploring career opportunities in Hawaii. Within a few months she found a good job, and she flew back to create a new life for herself.

Arlene's dream did not *make* her decide to return to Hawaii; she was already thinking along those lines, and she may well have moved even without the dream. But her dream came at a key moment in her decision-making process, and it gave her a much deeper understanding of what was at stake for her both professionally and spiritually. She respected the dream's relevance to her current life situation, and she allowed Kuan-yin to play a creative role in her problem-solving efforts. As a result, when Arlene did decide to move back to Hawaii, she knew, with deep and total self-confidence, that it was the right thing to do.

One of the most moving and thought-provoking accounts I've ever heard of how dreaming can help create greater conscious-unconscious integration comes from an acoustic biologist named Katy Payne. Her experience, like Arlene's, suggests that big dreams can be trustworthy companions in a person's ongoing effort to create meaning and value in life. Payne was originally trained as a research scientist, and for the first fifteen years of her career she carefully studied the songs of humpback whales. She then turned her attention to the question of how elephants, the largest living land mammals, communicate with each other. As she got involved with this new research, her investigations took a totally unexpected turn when one day she found herself remembering a childhood experience of being in her church's choir and physically *feeling* the deepest notes of the organ as it played. Payne suddenly realized she had felt similar bodily sensations while in the presence of the elephants. She and her colleagues quickly made a series of sophisticated audio recordings, and to her amazement their analysis of the recordings proved she was right: The elephants were indeed communicating via infrasound—powerful vibrations pitched too low for human ears to detect. The night after analyzing the data and validating her surprising insight, Payne had this dream:

> *I am lying in a deep, damp, warm grassy sward in the faint light of predawn. Close, in fact, looming over me, is a swaying, silent circle of elephants. They are large and small, and several are reaching out with their trunks to sniff me where I lie, tiny and helpless. They sway hugely, breathing over me for a long time, and then the largest female speaks in a voice that I hear the way you can sometimes hear in a dream, without vocal features, language, or sound. "We do not reveal this to you so you will tell other people."*
>
> *I lie silent, holding my breath, waiting for more. But there is only the sound of the elephants' breathing and their strange eyes looking down, down, and down at me—me at the very bottom of all those trunks and all those gazes—with the serious, inscrutable expression that I associate uniquely with elephants.*

Payne awoke from the dream just before dawn. It was Thanksgiving morning, and as she had planned, she got out of bed and drove to a Quaker Friends' meeting to celebrate the holiday. Inside her she could still feel the dream "drumming on my heart." When she got to the meeting, she sat down among the other Friends; but before she knew it, she stood up and was sharing her experience with the others. "The gathered Friends listened as people do when sound comes out of deep silence." Then she sat down again, noticing as if from a great distance that there were tears running down her face.

Payne and her colleagues published their findings on elephant communication in the scientific journal *Behavioral Ecology and Sociobiology*. Their research was immediately received with tremendous public interest and attention, and the *New York Times* published an especially detailed account of Payne's work. Looking back at her dream in light of these articles, Payne became aware of a painful gap between them:

> The articles announce a discovery in which Bill, Liz [her scientific colleagues], and I are agents and the elephants are objects. The dream announces a revelation in which elephants are agents

and I am a receiver. The articles refer to a world in which animals and people are separate and secret from each other, poorly acquainted and without common birthright. The dream refers to a world where we are of one blood. . . . In such a world animals reveal things to each other, and even occasionally to people like me: their attention to us is commensurate with ours to them.

Payne began to realize in a way she never had before that her training as a scientist had not prepared her for the kind of research she now felt called to pursue. If she wanted to learn more about how elephants speak with each other, she could no longer treat them as mere objects and herself as a detached observer. She realized she had to find a way to relate to them as fellow creatures, as beings who share with her an intrinsic dignity and worth. Over the next several years Payne continued her research in Kenya, Namibia, and Zimbabwe. As she increased her scientific understanding of the elephants' communication patterns and social behavior, she also developed a passionate determination to do whatever she could to protect them from the destructive encroachment of human civilization. She became a leading international voice in conservation efforts aimed at preserving the natural habitat of the elephants, and she organized a number of research projects that provided further information about how to create a peaceful new relationship between elephants and humans.

At a surface level, Payne's dream of the elephants circled around her could be seen as a warning to her to say nothing about her discovery of infrasound communication. From that perspective, her journal article and her subsequent research would be a direct violation of that warning. But I think Payne understood that her dream was expressing deeper and more complex meanings than that. The elephants in her dream told her what *not* to do with her discovery—but they said nothing about what she *should* do with it. The dream left her with that crucial question; and in consciously reflecting on the contrast between the dream and the published articles, Payne realized that her waking-world challenge was to honor the revelation she had received from the elephants by teaching other humans to honor them, too. From that point on, her research aimed at proving to people that elephants are not mere "objects," but rather are sentient beings with their own distinctive forms of wisdom and intelligence. Payne argued that only by bridging the conceptual gap between subjects and objects, only by eliminating the assumption that humans are the supreme form of life, could any true understanding be developed between people and those other living creatures with whom they share the planet.

Payne's dream became a true creative touchstone for her, a powerful source of moral guidance, scientific inspiration, and life purpose. Her experience is all the more remarkable because it illustrates how even in the realm of scientific research, where reason and logic reign supreme, the greatest creativity comes from a deep harmonization of conscious desire and unconscious desire.

Dream Creativity in Daily Life

A harmony of conscious desire and unconscious desire cannot be forced, but it can definitely be nurtured. If you take the time to use the methods described in this book, and if you're patient enough to let the dream interpretation process unfold at its own pace, I think you'll find that a closer relationship develops rather quickly between the conscious aspects and the unconscious aspects of your self.

There's a simple principle that can help this process along, a principle that modifies a line of John F. Kennedy's: *Ask not what your dreams can do for you, but what you can do for your dreams.* Instead of looking in a utilitarian fashion at how your dreams can be used to improve your waking life, try considering what you in your waking life can do to satisfy the yearnings of your dreams. There's nothing terribly complicated about following this principle; it can be satisfied by very easy and small-scale kinds of activities. For example, if you have a dream of an old friend you haven't seen in a while, try the next day giving that friend a call on the phone. If you have a dream about a bear, try reading a magazine article or an encyclopedia entry on bears to see what you can learn about them. If you have a dream about a certain kind of cake, try ordering it the next time you go to a restaurant, or try making that same kind of cake yourself. If you wake up with a particular song running through your mind, make a point that day of playing the song on your stereo.

Following the "what *you* can do for your dreams" principle has the effect of inviting your dreams to become cocreators of your life. This does not (to repeat a point made several times in this book) require you to surrender all conscious volition and abandon yourself to the whims of your dreams. On the contrary, this principle challenges you to develop a truly *mutual* relationship between the conscious aspects and the unconscious aspects of your self, a relationship in which neither side dominates or is enslaved by the other. It is true that creating such a relationship can be a frightening and even painful process, especially if a person's conscious goals and attitudes are rigidly fixed or excessively one-sided. Dreams are always pushing us forward in our growth, and if we become too attached to our current way of being, the transformational powers of dreaming may appear dark and threatening, as an evil, malevolent force endangering our very lives. But becoming more open to our dreams does *not* mean repudiating all of our waking-life beliefs and ideals; it simply means learning to respect our dreams as *real*, honoring their tremendously creative energies and acknowledging their value and relevance to the most important waking-life questions and concerns.

Some years ago, I had a dream (another instance of my recurrent sports dream) that gave me a very specific method of dream interpretation that has helped me greatly in this process of harmonizing dreaming and waking life:

I am at a softball game, and in the game I'm playing terribly: I make some awful throws, I can't catch the ball when it's hit to me, and in general I just can't seem to keep my attention focused on the game. I feel so stupid and incompetent that I finally break down and cry.

Now I see my sister at a hospital with a newborn boy; I'm very happy for her, but there's nothing I can do to help, and again I feel empty and depressed.

Now I'm at a horribly run-down public housing project, with dozens of little children running around. At first I feel afraid of the dark, strange building and also painfully guilty about having

neglected to help these poverty-stricken children. But to my surprise,
I see that the children are actually doing pretty well—they're happy,
energetic, and playful.

Finally I find myself at a conference workshop trying, and fail-
ing, to understand a particular dream. A small Chinese woman,
who has been leading the workshop, comes over and helps me with
the dream. I listen as she teaches me a way of putting dreams in
poetic form, a way that seeks to express the essential patterns of
meaning emerging in each dream. She tells me this method will
help me remember the dream and "keep it close" [her words] in
my waking life.

When I woke up from this dream, I initially felt frustrated because I couldn't remember the exact poetic formula the small Chinese woman had taught me. I knew it was somehow related to haiku (the Japanese method of writing poems in three lines, one each of five, seven, and five syllables). Like haiku, the Chinese woman's method focused on using the shortest and clearest images from the dream to create the poem; but there was something different about her way, and it bothered me that I couldn't remember more exactly what she had taught me. Finally, I decided to trust in the value of what I *did* remember, and I realized that perhaps the precise form of the poem was less important than making the creative effort to express the spirit of the dream.

Looking back at the rest of this dream, I slowly came to understand each scene as an image of what happens when I focus too much on my conscious efforts on *making something happen* and not enough on what's happening with the broader creative process of which my consciousness is but one part. In the softball scene I get so caught up in my own performance that I forget I'm playing a game; the harder I *try*, the worse I do. When my sister has a baby, all I can think of is my own helplessness and inadequacy; I neglect to realize that I'm a part of this, that I now have a new nephew and the responsibility of helping bring him into the world. The third scene of the dream starts, like the previous two, with very negative emotions: As I stand before the run-down housing project, I feel frightened for my personal safety and terribly upset and guilty at my own failure to prevent such a tragedy from happening. But when I see that the children in the project are relatively happy, I get my first glimpse of the possibility that perhaps I (my conscious self) can't control every situation and fix every problem—I realize that perhaps there are *other* powers at work here, and maybe I should find some way to better relate to them.

The final scene of the dream starts with another experience of frustration and incompetence, but this time the dream goes on to offer me a creative new way of dealing with this recurrent problem. The little Chinese woman's dream poetry method, and her advice to "keep the dream close," is an inspiration to gently loosen the excessively harsh and obsessive control that my conscious mind sometimes wields over my waking-life activities. The more I can keep the essential images and feelings of my dreams present in my day-to-day awareness, the better able I'll be to see and appreciate what I can, and cannot, accomplish by the force of my conscious will.

I'm a person who loves words, so it makes sense that dream poetry would appeal to me as an especially good way of creatively expressing my dreams, "keeping them close," as the little Chinese woman suggested. But everyone is different in this regard, and I would encourage readers to think about what forms of artistic creativity give them the greatest sense of comfort and ease and to try using those artistic forms to express the various meanings of their big dreams. For example, people with a more visual bent can try drawing or painting images from their dreams. More physically-oriented people can try expressing their dreams through movement, dance, and athletics. People who know a lot about music can try putting their dreams into a song. The goal of making these creative efforts is not to produce a grand work of high art, but to bring the dream's meanings more clearly and more fully into the dreamer's life—the same goal that motivates all efforts at dream interpretation. A drawing that other people would regard as crude and amateurish might, *for the dreamer*, perfectly express a whole realm of new meanings that other modes of interpretation had not revealed. It's very important in exploring your dreams in this way to ignore what other people think is or is not art and to simply focus yourself on giving free expression to the creative energies welling up from your dreaming imagination.

I would also encourage people to experiment with forms of artistic expression they *don't* have a lot of experience using. Sometimes an unfamiliar approach is the best way to recognize unusual kinds of meaning. It's the same idea as the one behind the method of the "surprise reverse" (p. 143). If you deliberately surprise yourself by trying an entirely different way of approaching a dream, you will often discover important new meanings that fill out and enrich your understanding of the dream. This was certainly my experience at the Russian dream studies conference with the process of dream theater. I had never participated in any kind of dramatic production before, and because I am a rather shy and introverted person, I became nervous at the very idea of acting out dreams in a large group. But to my surprise I found that it was actually a lot of fun, as well as an excellent means of discovering new aspects of a dream's meaning. You may find the same to be true if you try taking a special image from one of your big dreams and expressing it through an unfamiliar artistic medium. The very fact that you "don't know what you're doing" when you try to paint, or act, or sing, or write poetry means that you're offering your dream a brand new creative channel and giving your dream the freedom to express its meanings with as little conscious control or influence as possible.

Flying

For many people the most exhilarating dreams they ever experience are flying dreams. The amazing physical sensation in these dreams of actually soaring through the air is almost always accompanied by feelings of joy, pleasure, and liberation. Flying dreams regularly occur in childhood, and decades later people still have fresh, vivid memories of what those dreams felt like. Here's an account from the novelist Stephen King:

> The dreams that I remember most clearly are almost always early dreams. And they're not always bad dreams. I don't want to give you that impression. I can remember one very clearly. It was a flying dream:
>
> *I am over the turnpike and I am flying along wearing a pair of pajama bottoms. I don't have any shirt on. I'm just buzzing along*

*under overpasses—kazipp—and I'm reminding myself in the dream
to stay high enough so that I don't get disemboweled by car anten-
nas sticking up from the cars.*

That's a fairly mechanistic detail, but when I woke up from this
dream, my feeling was not fear or loathing but just real exhilaration, pleasure, and happiness.

One of the most remarkable facts about flying dreams is their
universality: They have come to people in cultures all over the
world. These dreams are not the product of experiences with modern technology—people were having flying dreams long before
the invention of airplanes, helicopters, and rocket ships. The earliest example I've found is in the *Oneirocritica* by the second-
century A.D. dream researcher, Artemidorus. Artemidorus records
an account of "a man who was living in Rome [who] dreamt that he
flew around the city near the rooftops and that he was elated by his
adept flying." Many examples of flying dreams are also reported
by anthropologists working in non-Western cultures with communities of people who have never been in or even seen a modern air-
plane. In these cultures, flying dreams are revered as important
spiritual revelations because they usually involve amazing encounters with powerful ancestors, sacred animals, and otherworldly
beings.

As with a few other classic dream types, flying dreams are a
truly cross-cultural and transhistorical phenomenon. Twentieth-
century psychologists have naturally asked the question of where
these dreams come from. Freud offered the thought that perhaps
the original basis for flying dreams is the childhood experience of
being playfully thrown in the air by one's parents. In Freud's view,
flying dreams are built up out of people's memories of that common childhood experience, and the joy and exhilaration that so
often accompany the dreams are symbolic expressions of sexual
pleasure. By contrast, sleep laboratory researchers dismiss Freud's
theory and argue instead that flying dreams are caused by the
extreme activation of the central nervous system during REM
sleep. When people enter REM sleep, their minds are so overwhelmed with internally generated stimulation that they may fanci-
fully imagine they're flying, just as they imagine at other times that

they are standing naked in a public place, or are lost in a forest, or are back in their third-grade classroom.

In my view neither of these explanations does real justice to the experience of flying dreams. Neither of them gives careful enough attention to the quality that the dreamers themselves invariably emphasize: the *realness* of the feeling of flight. Whether or not the dreams are tied to early childhood memories or fantasies of sexual desire, the feature that always grabs the dreamers' attention is the feeling of really and truly *flying*. The rushing of the air, the joyful movement of the body, the elevated perspective on the world below—these are the elements that astonish and amaze the dreamers, and these are the elements that make the dreams so incredibly memorable.

It seems pretty obvious that flying dreams would have some connection to the brain's activity during sleep. But the important question is: Why, out of all the possible scenarios the brain could imagine, does it choose to imagine flying? The specific flying motions that people tend to experience in dreams (soaring, swooping, hovering, gliding) usually have no relation to any physical sensations they've ever had in their waking lives—in other words, the dreams are not built up out of memories of actual waking-life experiences. This means that in such dreams the brain is imagining *something new*. Instead of using the memory of a past experience to make sense of the stimuli generated by REM sleep, the brain is imagining a brand new scenario, creating an experience that not only *has* not happened to the dreamer, but *could* not happen to the dreamer in any normal sense of reality. Flying dreams are visions of the impossible—they reach beyond what we are to imagine what we might become.

This line of reflection leads to another key question: Why do flying dreams so often come with the extraordinary sensations of joyfulness and exhilaration and with that vivid feeling of *realness*? It's remarkable not just that the dreams portray an impossible activity, but that they portray it with such a stunning sense of reality. What could be the meaning or purpose of this? Why does the dreaming imagination generate this extra charge of energy and intensity in the sensory experience of flying dreams?

Scott was fourteen years old when he had this dream:

Some relatives and I are socializing on a patio, a brown wooden patio that hangs out from the side of what appeared to be a two-story house. The setting of the dream is a clear, sunny day, with white clouds in the background. I am drinking some punch, and it is a family-reunion-type party. With me on the porch are two of my older relatives, who are grandmas. They are both wearing full-length flowered red dresses and one of them is carrying a cane. Suddenly I realize that the patio doesn't appear to be two stories off the ground any longer, and I begin to feel like gravity no longer exists. I spread my arms slowly and steadily begin to rise away from the patio. I'm flying! The thrill is exciting, and I am happy as I look back at my relatives who are still on the patio and appear to be getting farther and farther away. I climb and climb in the sky until I finally come to a point where a gold or bronze flute appears. The flute is floating through the air while the music of the flute is playing. I may have grabbed the flute and played it, but in any case the music was truly harmonious and nice sounding. Then my two grandmas pop into the clouds as they fly through the air holding hands. As the music plays, they fly side-by-side to a higher elevation than mine and disappear into the clouds. I begin to descend back to earth. I land behind a building in a city. It's a very nice day, and the building is creating shade and keeping me out of view of the traffic. I soon attempt to take flight again. I do the typical Superman "Up, up, and away!" effort but have no luck. I do this several times and the dream comes to an end.

Scott's experience illustrates what I believe is one of the most powerful meanings expressed by flying dreams: the discovery within oneself of amazing and previously unknown creative powers. As is common in these dreams, Scott felt the most intense and memorable part of the experience was the sensation of actually flying. As he began to rise up in the air he felt a joy, power, and freedom he'd never known before. For an adolescent boy, on the brink of leaving childhood and entering adulthood, such a dream can be seen as a kind of symbolic initiation, a transformation from the warm, nurturing environment of his family up into the sky of his own infinite potential, into his own creative future. Flying is a perfect symbol of this kind of personal transformation because it shows the dreamer that what seems impossible now, at the present stage of growth, will truly become possible in the future, at the stage just ahead. The incredible intensity of the flying experience has the function of emphasizing the vital importance of that meaning—the dreaming imagination makes absolutely sure that the dreamer knows these seeming impossibilities are *real* potentials in his or her waking life.

Many flying dreams take that basic message even further and reveal additional truths about the process of future growth and development. As Scott soars into the sky, he sees a gold or bronze flute playing beautifully harmonious music; this only intensifies his wonder and amazement at the creative potentials opened up by his newfound ability. Then Scott sees his two grandmas flying through the clouds with him, and he realizes that he's not the only one who has the power to fly. This is a crucial point, because too often people (especially adolescent boys) assume that growing up means breaking free from one's family and leaving all childhood ties behind. Scott's dream suggests to him that his future growth does not require him to break his ties with his family; rather, his upward flight may lead him to form a higher relationship with the traditions of his family, symbolized by the hand-holding grandmas who are also able to fly with surprising ease and skill.

At the end of the dream, when Scott is back on the ground and trying to take flight once again, he makes another valuable discovery: The creative powers blossoming within him cannot be controlled or manipulated by conscious will alone. Trying to be Superman, and ordering himself to "Up, up, and away!" won't work. If he wants to fly again, Scott would somehow have to combine the power of his individual will with *other* forces and *other* powers. The dream leaves Scott, as so many big dreams do, with a deeply challenging question about the fundamental nature of his life and the path of his future growth: How can the joyful energy and exhilarating freedom he experienced in this remarkable dream become a part of his waking life?

In many of the world's religious and spiritual traditions, the experience of flying is regarded as a potent symbol of the infinite creativity with which all humans are born. The Night Flight of the Prophet Muhammad, the visionary travels of Central and South American shamans, the Ascension of Jesus, the levitational abilities of Buddhist mystics, the moonlit rides of broom-wielding witches— the ability to fly symbolizes transcendence of the limitations of the ordinary world and entrance into the realm of the sacred and the divine. *Dreams* of flying give a brief but unforgettable sense of this transcendence. These rare but deeply impactful dreams granted the dreamers a momentary experience of the glorious power of their own creative freedom, a freedom that extends beyond gravity, beyond their ordinary assumptions about what is and isn't possible, beyond all conventional beliefs about what human existence is and can become.

CONCLUSION

We Are All Big Dreamers

Hermia (awaking): *Help me, Lysander, help me! Do thy best*
To pluck this crawling serpent from my breast!
Ay me, for pity! What a dream was here!
Lysander, look how I do quake with fear.
Methought a serpent eat my heart away,
And you sat smiling at his cruel prey.
Lysander! What, removed? Lysander! Lord!
What, out of hearing? Gone? No sound, no word?

—William Shakespeare, *A Midsummer Night's Dream*

In this book I have tried to portray the primary features and the central qualities of big dreams in as broad a fashion as possible, without relying on any one theory, perspective, or worldview. I've tried to respect the many different attitudes people bring to the subject of dreams, and I have done my best to address the concerns and the interests of *all* readers. Whatever your views, whatever your background, I hope this book has spoken to your deepest questions about the nature, the meaning, and the functions of human dream experience.

In these final pages I will offer the basic elements of my own theory about dreams and dreaming. The value of making theories is

206

that they create a conceptual framework in which people can clarify their perceptions, organize their thoughts, and answer their questions. The danger of making theories is, of course, that they can inadvertently narrow people's perceptions, constrict their thoughts, and close their minds to the possibility of asking *new* questions. This danger is especially great when it comes to dream theories, and I confess that it's more than slightly absurd to try to devise a theory about something as infinitely varied and wildly diverse as dreaming.

As I've been writing this book, the image has frequently come to my mind of the delightfully ridiculous croquet game Alice tries to play during her adventures in Wonderland, where the mallets are live flamingos, the balls rolled-up hedgehogs, and the wickets bent-over card soldiers. None of these creatures are at all happy about being forced by the tyrannical Queen of Hearts to serve as props in this game, and all of them keep moving and shifting around so much that Alice finally realizes it's impossible for her to play a "normal" game of croquet. Dreams, I have found from long experience, are a lot like those flamingos, hedgehogs, and card soldiers in Alice's Wonderland: Dreams are just as adverse to externally imposed rules, just as resistant to being defined and categorized, just as filled with lively and unpredictable willfulness. Any theory that fails to acknowledge this is doomed to frustration.

Snake Dreams

Let me come at my theory via a brief digression into the symbolism of another classic, cross-cultural type of dream: snake dreams. Throughout history, from cultures all over the world, people have reported extraordinarily memorable dreams of snakes and serpents. These dreams occur with great frequency even in modern society, even with people who have never had any direct contact with a snake.

The passage quoted from *A Midsummer Night's Dream* marks one of the early turning points in that wonderfully farcical romantic comedy. Hermia and her lover Lysander have just snuck away from Athens to escape her father's decree that she give up Lysander

and marry another man. After fleeing into the dark forest surrounding Athens and making sure no one is following them, the
two youths lie down to take their rest. Lysander does his amorous
best to seduce Hermia right then and there; but she chastely re-
minds him that until they are formally married, they must sleep a
little ways apart from each other. Lysander reluctantly agrees.
While he and Hermia slumber under the trees, the mischievous
wood fairy Puck flits by and pours a magic love potion in Lysander's
eyes. As a result of this potion, when Lysander is awakened by
another young Athenian woman who happens to be fleeing through
the woods (the plot gets very complicated here), he suddenly falls
passionately in love with her. Looking down at the sleeping Hermia, Lysander scornfully repudiates all his past feelings for her, and
he runs off into the woods to pursue the other woman. Hermia
awakens at this point, startled into consciousness by her frightening dream of the snake eating her heart while the smiling Lysander idly watches. She receives a second jolt when she realizes that
Lysander is gone, and she is now alone in the strange, fairy-
haunted forest.

The snake in Hermia's dream has at least two levels of symbolic
meaning. At one level, the snake clearly reflects the treachery of
Lysander for abandoning her. It's likely that the sleeping Hermia
was able to hear Lysander's cruel words repudiating his love for
her, and so it would seem her dreaming imagination has symbolically expressed her reaction to those words. The image of the snake
evokes in her intense feelings of surprise, pain, fear, and betrayal
toward her lover. At another level the dream can be understood as
an expression of Hermia's feelings about Lysander's romantic
urgency before they went to bed, with the snake serving as an apt
symbol of the intrusive aggression of his sexual desire. (People
were making symbolic connections between serpents and the male
genitals long before Freud!) At both levels, then, Hermia's dream is
a sharp warning to her to beware of Lysander. The extreme vividness and intensity of the dream is a call to her to *pay attention*, to
look more closely and reflectively at what's going on with her relationship with the man she hopes to marry. The snake serves to
symbolize deep, and deeply conflicted, feelings about this man,
feelings that Hermia has yet to consciously acknowledge.

A snake is also the major figure in one of history's most famous problem-solving dreams. Friedrich von Kekule was a professor of chemistry in Belgium in the late 1800s. Like other chemists of the time, he was struggling to understand how exactly the benzene molecule of carbon and hydrogen atoms was structured. No conventional linear arrangement seemed to work, but no researcher had come up with any good alternatives. Then Kekule suddenly saw the answer—in a dream. He described his discovery to the astonished attendees of a scientific convention in 1890, explaining that one day he had fallen asleep in his chair and started dreaming:

> [T]he atoms were juggling before my eyes. . . . My mind's eye, sharpened by repeated sights of a similar kind, could now distinguish larger structures of different forms and in long chains, many of them close together; everything was moving in a snake-like and twisting manner. Suddenly, what was this? One of the snakes got hold of its own tail and the whole structure was mockingly twisting in front of my eyes. As if struck by lightning, I awoke.

Kekule immediately went to work testing the symbolic insight of his dream, and his calculations proved that the dream was indeed correct: By constructing a model of the benzene molecule as a closed *ring*, rather than as a straight line, with an atom of carbon and hydrogen at each point of a hexagon, Kekule instantly solved a problem that had vexed chemists for decades. His discovery of the "benzene ring" marked a fundamental advance in the scientific understanding of the chemical processes underlying all organic life. Kekule concluded his conference presentation by telling the attendees, "Let us learn to dream, gentlemen, and then we may perhaps find the truth."

Although Kekule said nothing specific about the snake itself, I don't think it was a coincidence that his scientific insight emerged in this particular symbolic form. The image of a snake biting its own tail is a classic mythological symbol of infinity, of the endlessly circular nature of time, space, and being itself. The twisting, writhing serpent in Kekule's dream granted him a glimpse of this realm, an insight into the deepest structures and forces of life. At the very edge of human understanding, far beyond the reach of conventional thought, these strangely vibrant creatures offered the Belgian scientist a radically new way of looking at the world.

Snakes are considered in many Native American spiritual traditions to be powerful figures of wisdom and intelligence. Shamans regularly receive sacred teachings and healing powers from dream encounters with snakes. One example of this comes from the Paviotso people of the American Southwest, where a shaman named Rosie Plummer described to an anthropologist how her father had gained his powers by means of a series of snake dreams: "[R]attlesnake came to him [my father] in dreams and told him how to cure snakebites. He was told to catch rattlesnakes and take out two fangs until he had ten, and to get ten stone beads the color of rattlesnake eyes. He made a string of beads with the stones and fangs to use in curing people bitten by rattlesnakes. He could treat other illnesses as well." Plummer went on to tell the anthropologist that after her father died, he began to appear in her own dreams, always with the message of encouraging her to become a shaman. Then Rattlesnake himself came to Plummer in her dreams and told her to gather various healing ingredients—eagle feathers, white paint, wild tobacco—and to sing certain songs to help cure people of their illnesses. At first Plummer was reluctant, but after the snake came three or four times, she finally accepted the spiritual calling and became a shaman. From that point on, she received regular dream visits from Rattlesnake, each time receiving a new song or healing technique.

Plummer's dream interactions with Rattlesnake gave her the ability to help her relatives and neighbors deal with a very real waking-world danger. The Paviotso people shared their desert homeland with a sizable population of actual rattlesnakes, and getting bitten by one of the poisonous creatures was a constant threat. Many Paviotso knew, however, that through her dreams Plummer had formed a close and mutually respectful relationship with the spirit of Rattlesnake. When they were bitten, they went to her for help, trusting in the power of her healing methods and drawing comfort from the depth of her religious wisdom.

The last snake dream example I'd like to offer comes from a contemporary setting. Nora was a forty-one-year-old woman who had recently gotten divorced and was now back in college, finishing the degree she had given up on when she married her husband. Nora was still sad and mournful about the ending of her marriage, and although she was excited to be back in school, she also felt anxious about trying to start her whole life over again. She was also worried about having started a new romantic relationship, which was rekindling all her old fears about love and intimacy. One night she had this dream:

> *I am standing alone at the edge of a freshwater pond in the woods during the late afternoon in midsummer. It is very warm, there is a slight breeze from tall trees, lots of shade in this cove, and the water is clear and calm. There is no sense of other life: no animals, birds, fish, or people. The sunlight sparkles on the water twelve to fifteen feet from shore.*
>
> *A large snake slithers nearby, over my feet and around my ankles. It is very large, six feet long, five inches in diameter, greenish silver with gold bands of color. Its body is warm and smooth, and its eyes are gray. It makes no sound, and the air parts as it moves around the shore then into the water.*
>
> *It beckons me to swim with it; I understand its thoughts, an intuitive language. I leave my clothing on the ground and swim out toward the sunlight. The water is clear, cool, and refreshing, not murky or cold. I swim out a ways, dive down, backstroke, float. The snake swims nearby companionably, winds around my belly, thighs, around my legs. I have no fear or sense of threat from the snake, only a pleasant silence. The snake swims to shore and goes into the underbrush by the trees. I fall asleep floating on my back in the sunlight.*

Nora had never experienced a dream like this before. The large and vividly colored snake immediately caught her attention. She had never previously dreamed of a snake, nor had she ever even held one in her waking life. She knew snakes were cold-blooded animals, but the one in her dream was definitely warm to the touch.

In reflecting on the dream Nora wondered why she wasn't afraid of such a strange creature rubbing against her body. She also wondered about the magical energy she felt radiating from the pond. The warm sunlight sparkling on the water had an irresistible allure, and the incredible serenity and peacefulness of the whole setting was so great that it was hard for Nora to describe it in words.

Very slowly, an understanding of this powerful dream began to emerge in Nora's mind. She realized the dream was calling her to let go of her fears, to trust in herself, and to allow a process of rebirth to begin. Nora came to see the remarkable snake as a figure of great intelligence and power; she understood that she could put her faith in the snake and trust it to care for her. In the dream Nora, like a snake herself, sheds her outer garments and enters the warm, clear water of the pond—a nice symbolic expression of the new life she had begun since the end of her marriage. Although the figure of the snake definitely had an element of masculine sexuality, it also conveyed to Nora a symbolic encouragement to grow, to change, to shed the old, and to embrace the new. Nora felt that in waking life she would almost surely feel frightened and endangered if she saw or touched such a creature; but in her dream the snake fills her with a renewed sense of trust, hope, and faith in the future. Indeed, it was precisely this surprising reversal of Nora's ordinary waking-world assumptions that enabled the dream to generate such a transformational impact on her life.

In very general terms, the universal occurrence of snake dreams can be given a clear scientific explanation. Zoologists have found that fear of snakes is instinctive in all Old World primates, including our species of *Homo sapiens*. Like their chimpanzee, gorilla, and orangutan relatives, humans are born with a tendency to avoid snakes. The evolutionary reason for this innate fear is simple: venomous snakes are, and have always been, a real danger wherever humans live, so there's a definite survival value to feeling a strong and immediate aversion to these creatures. Such an instinctive fear will naturally express itself in dreams; and it stands to reason that the more frequently people have frightening nightmares about snakes, the better prepared they'll be to avoid these dangerous animals in waking life.

Scientific explanations are *not* currently available, however, for the special meanings of vivid and highly charged snake dreams such as the ones described earlier. Evolutionary psychology can state that at one level snake dreams are aimed at promoting our physical survival. But what about the other levels of meaning that clearly aim at something *more* than physical survival? The serpent dreams of Hermia, Friedrich von Kekule, Rosie Plummer, and Nora can hardly be reduced to mere warnings of actual snakes in their waking-life environment. Even Plummer's dream goes beyond the danger of waking-world snakes and opens up to her new realms of cultural tradition, spiritual experience, and self-knowledge.

All four of these snake dreams are driven by an energy that seeks to promote other aspects of the dreamer's well-being, aspects that cannot be simply reduced to the biological concept of sur-vivability. This, I believe, is the fundamental challenge for a theory of dreams: How can these *other* aims, goals, and intentions that emerge in people's dreams best be understood and explained? What is the teleology of dreaming? Where are dreams pointing, and why?

Dreaming Provokes Greater Consciousness

Taken as a whole, the current evidence from psychology, neuro-science, religious studies, history, and anthropology strongly indicates that dreams do *more* than promote physical survival. I believe that *more* is best understood as the growth and expansion of con-sciousness. I like this particular phrase "dreaming provokes greater consciousness" because of the interplay between two different senses of the word *provoke*. The most literal sense of the word is "to call forth or give voice to" (in Latin, *pro* + *vocare*), a sense that relates it to "vocation" and to one's "calling" in life. The second and more common meaning of the word is "to spur, prod, or incite," all verbs that imply a forceful impetus toward action and movement. I believe dreaming "provokes" in both of these ways. It calls new voices into the dreamer's conscious awareness, voices that serve to guide and inspire the dreamer, and it actively stimulates the dreamer to consider new thoughts, to acknowledge new feel-ings, and to take new actions in waking life.

In my scholarly writings I've used the term "root metaphors" to describe in a more precise way the transformative effects certain types of dreams have on consciousness. I've focused my research specifically on those extraordinarily vivid and powerful dreams that become spiritual touchstones in people's lives, dreams that provide awe-inspiring metaphorical visions of reality that reach far, far down into the deepest roots of existence. My present conclusion (which I hope will continue to change and evolve as I keep on with this work) is that although these dreams come in many different forms, the basic effect of all "big" or "root metaphor" dreams is to provoke greater consciousness—to renew, revitalize, and reorient people's fundamental feelings and beliefs about themselves, about the world around them, and about their ultimate relationship to reality.

It makes me very happy to see that people in contemporary society are becoming increasingly aware of the psychological and spiritual values of reflecting on dreams. Thanks to the work of many dedicated dream researchers and psychotherapists and thanks to the educational efforts of organizations like the Association for the Study of Dreams, many people are developing a solid and well-grounded knowledge of what dreams are, how they can be interpreted, and what potentials can be discovered within them. This growing sophistication in society's understanding of dreams leads me to wonder about the future. What might happen some day as an outgrowth of such widespread dream awareness? What kinds of effect might this have on society as a whole? Could it be that one of the greatest potentials of dreaming is to provoke the growth not just of individual consciousness, but of communal consciousness as well?

As I bring this book to a close, let me leave you with the following vision, a kind of "dreamer's utopia" that imagines one possible answer to those questions:

> *The world is pretty much the way it is now . . . the way it always has been and always will be. People have babies, raise families, celebrate holidays, get old, and pass away. People get up each morning and go to work, they eat and sleep, they play games and do chores around the house. In so many ways there is nothing different about this*

future world, nothing except for the one small detail that everyone heeds the call of their dreams. Everyone in this world listens, everyone ponders and reflects, everyone keeps the call of their dreams fresh in their minds and close to their hearts. No one is a slave to their dreams, nor does anyone seek to be master over their dreams. Dreams are their companions, their confidantes, their friends.

In this world that is so similar to our own, the people understand from their own personal experience that human life is most fulfilling when it is lived in service to a dream. They've discovered for themselves that the glory of human existence comes in the passionate devotion to a dream, in throwing one's whole life into the creative process of making new realities out of the ideals of the imagination.

The people of this world fight with each other, all the time; there's none of that "lion laying down with the lamb" business in this utopia. The people struggle with each other continuously; they endlessly argue and debate and criticize. They do this because it's fun, because it's deeply enjoyable to wrestle with fellow humans in the eternally mysterious process of transforming imagination into reality.

In this world the people know their dreams, and thus they know the profound power that dwells within each individual, a power capable of infinite nobility, goodness, and love. And because the people know their nightmares, too, they know that in each individual lurks true darkness, a potential for monstrous violence and destruction. Knowing these things, the people do whatever they can to help one another cultivate that inherent nobility, and discipline, as much as is humanly possible, that ever-present darkness. "We are all dreamers," the people teach their children in this utopia. "Every one of us, the high and the low, the young and the old, the healthy and the sick, the mighty and the weak, every one of us is a dreamer." And the children will laugh because they know this is true. Indeed, the children knew this before they knew anything else. They were born with this knowledge. We are all born with this knowledge. And we are all born with the hope that the day will come soon when its truth will finally flower in every single human soul.

The study of dreams is still in its infancy, and I'm sure that future researchers will make discoveries that will revolutionize our current understanding. In a way I feel that we dream researchers are like those ancient astronomers who many thousands of years ago stood under the brilliant night sky and did their best to make sense of what they could see in the heavens above them. Like the astronomers of ages past, we dream researchers have only begun to map out the vast imaginal realm that is revealed in human dreaming experience. We are just now starting to discern with real clarity the deeper patterns and fundamental symbolic structures that underlie people's most extraordinary and memorable dreams. My hope is that the evidence we are gathering today will help those researchers in the future who share our passionate desire to explore, to understand, and to celebrate the tremendous dream-creating power that dwells *in potentia* in all of us.

Notes

Introduction

1   *But almost every religion in the world*   For scholarly evidence in support of this point, see K. Bulkeley, *Spiritual Dreaming: A Cross-Cultural and Historical Journey* (Mahwah, N.J.: Paulist Press, 1995). Sources for the given examples are provided in that work.

2   *Psychologist Carl Jung referred to these*   C. G. Jung, *Dreams* (Princeton, N.J.: Princeton University Press, 1974), p. 36.

Chapter 1. Dreams of Reassurance

10   *In recent years psychological researchers*   For a more detailed scholarly discussion of current psychological research on REM sleep and dreaming, see K. Bulkeley, *An Introduction to the Psychology of Dreaming* (Westport, Conn.: Praeger, 1998), chapters 5 and 6.

13   *"In this model, attempting to remember"*   F. Crick and G. Mitchison, "The Function of Dream Sleep," *Nature* (1983) 304, p. 114.

14   *the most interesting dreams*   J. Allan Hobson, quoted in the Discovery Channel documentary *The Power of Dreams*, in the segment titled "The Search for Meaning."

20   *Sigmund Freud, the founder of*   For a more detailed discussion of Freud's dream theory, see K. Bulkeley, *An Introduction to the Psychology of Dreaming*, chapter 2.

21   *This is why the ancient Greek philosopher Aristotle said*   Aristotle, *The Collected Works of Aristotle*, edited by R. McKeon (New York: Random House, 1941), p. 630.

22   *There are better and worse interpretations of a dream*   For a more detailed discussion of the philosophical issues involved in distinguishing better from

217

worse dream interpretations, see K. Bulkeley, *The Wilderness of Dreams: Exploring the Religious Meanings of Dreams in Modern Western Culture* (Albany, N.Y.: State University of New York Press, 1994).

24   *For many researchers the idea that*   I am thinking here of Freud, Calvin Hall, David Foulkes, and J. Allan Hobson. I have examined their antireligion theories in more detail in *The Wilderness of Dreams*.

27   *The "dreamer religions" that sprang up*   See C. E. Trafzer and M. A. Beach, "Smohalla, the Washini, and Religion as a Factor in Northwestern Indian History," *American Indian Quarterly* (1985) 9:3, pp. 309–24.

27   *"He traveled to the spirit world"*   Trafzer and Beach, p. 312.

Chapter 2. Dreams of Making Love

31   *One of the most surprising findings of modern laboratory research*   This point, and many of those made in the following pages, draw on information presented in the entry "Sex and Sleep" from *The Encyclopedia of Sleep and Dreaming*, edited by M. Carskadon (New York: Macmillan, 1993).

32   *As one researcher described*   *The Encyclopedia of Sleep and Dreaming*, p. 536.

33   *"But in my sleep"*   Augustine, *Confessions*, 10.30.

33   *A monk named Antiochus Monachus*   P. Mayerson, "Antiochus Monachus' Homily on Dreams: An Historical Note," *Journal of Jewish Studies* (1984) 35:1, pp. 51–56.

41   *Here are two sample passages from* Oneirocritica   Artemidorus, *Oneirocritica*, translated by R. J. White (Park Ridge, N.J.: Noyes Press, 1975), pp. 65, 61.

48   *In the summer of 1992, I started a research project*   For a more detailed discussion of this project on dreams and politics, including references to Calvin Hall's views, see K. Bulkeley, "Political Dreaming: Dreams of the 1992 Presidential Election," in *Among All These Dreamers: Essays on Dreaming and Modern Society*, edited by K. Bulkeley (Albany, N.Y.: State University of New York Press, 1996).

Chapter 3. Nightmares

56   *In recent years researchers have looked closely at the psychophysiological elements of nightmares*   For more information on nightmares, see E. Hartmann, *The Nightmare: The Psychology and Biology of Terrifying Dreams* (New York: Basic Books, 1984), and H. Kellerman, ed., *The Nightmare: Psychological and Biological Foundations* (New York: Columbia University Press, 1987).

57   *Nightmares are most frequently experienced by young children*   For more information on children's dreams and nightmares, see A. Siegel and K. Bulkeley, *Dreamcatching: Every Parent's Guide to Understanding and Exploring Children's Dreams and Nightmares* (New York: Three Rivers Press, 1998).

61   *Carl Jung had a nightmare like this*   For Jung's report and interpretation of this childhood nightmare, see his autobiography, *Memories, Dreams, Reflections* (New York: Vintage, 1965), pp. 11–13.

63   *Researchers aren't clear yet on how exactly this experience of fading*   For more information on dreams and trauma, see D. Barrett, ed., *Trauma and Dreams* (Cambridge, Mass.: Harvard University Press, 1996).

63   *A recent study conducted by sleep laboratory researchers in Israel*   P. Lavie and H. Kaminer, "Dreams That Poison Sleep: Dreaming in Holocaust Survivors," *Dreaming* (1991) 1:1, pp. 63–74.

64   *"For God speaks in one way, and in two"*   Job 33:14–18.

67   *"Some years ago, I was a heavy cigarette smoker"*   W. Dement, *Some Must Watch While Some Must Sleep: Exploring the World of Sleep* (New York: W. W. Norton, 1972), p. 102.

68   *"Only the dream can allow"*   Ibid.

69   *"the ego is only a bit of consciousness"*   C. G. Jung, ed., *Man and His Symbols* (New York: Dell, 1964), p. 4.

76   *In Hindu mythology there are numerous stories*   See W. D. O'Flaherty, *Dreams, Illusion, and Other Realities* (Chicago: University of Chicago Press, 1984).

79   *Current research suggests that these frightening experiences*   See the entry on "Psychophysiology of Dreaming" in *The Encyclopedia of Sleep and Dreams*.

82   *One of the leading theories of modern scientific research*   See J. Allan Hobson, *The Dreaming Brain* (New York: Basic Books, 1988).

83   *Here is classicist Edith Hamilton's description of the Titans*   See E. Hamilton, *Mythology: Timeless Tales of Gods and Heroes* (Mentor, 1969), pp. 64–65.

Chapter 4. Dreams of Death

87   *In* Theogony, *his lyrically rendered myth of creation, Hesiod*   Hesiod, *Theogony*, lines 211 and 212.

87   *In cultures all over the world, sleep has been regarded as a close kin to death*   For more information on the relations among sleep, death, and dreams, see K. Bulkeley, *Spiritual Dreaming*, chapter 1.

88   *According to one medical researcher*   *The Encyclopedia of Sleep and Dreaming*, p. 165.

95   *On April 29, 1997, the Norristown, Pennsylvania, police*   The account of the case of Craig Rabinowitz is taken from newspaper reports from the Associated Press (10/30/1997) and the *Legal Intelligencer* (10/1/1997).

97   *some scholars have gone so far as to argue*   See E. Tylor, *Primitive Culture* (New York: H. Holt, 1889).

99   *In early April of 1865, Abraham Lincoln*   See S. B. Oates, *With Malice Toward None: A Life of Abraham Lincoln* (New York: HarperPerennial, 1977), pp. 425–26.

106   *As one researcher put it, dreams "enable us"*   R. Cartwright and L. Lamberg, *Crisis Dreaming* (New York: Harper Collins, 1992), p. 269.

114   *In sociological terms this type of loss is called* secularization   For a more detailed discussion of secularization, see K. Bulkeley, *The Wilderness of Dreams*, chapter 19.

Chapter 5. Reflecting on Your Dreams

122   *This is an issue that dates back at least as far as Aristotle*   For a more detailed discussion of Aristotle's views of dreams, see K. Bulkeley, *An Introduction to the Psychology of Dreaming*, chapter 1.

124   *what the poet John Keats called "the negative capability"*   See C. Rycroft, *The Innocence of Dreams* (New York: Pantheon, 1979), p. 50.

134   *In the view of many researchers, when a neurochemical burst*   See the entry on "PGO Waves" in *The Encyclopedia of Sleep and Dreaming*.

135   *One of the more counterintuitive findings of modern dream research*   See K. Bulkeley, *An Introduction to the Psychology of Dreaming*, chapter 6.

138   *Some researchers have called this "the dyadic instinct"*   See E. O. Wilson, *Consilience: The Unity of Knowledge* (New York: Knopf, 1998), p. 153.

143   *One of my favorite stories from Freud's* The Interpretation of Dreams   S. Freud, *The Interpretation of Dreams* (New York: Avon, 1965), pp. 184–85.

Chapter 6. Sharing Your Dreams

148   *Sharing dreams in a family context is a practice anthropologists*   See K. Bulkeley, *Spiritual Dreaming*, p. 158.

153–54 *use the prefacing phrase, "If it were my dream"* I learned this technique from Jeremy Taylor, who describes it in greater detail in his book *Dream Work* (Mahwah, N.J.: Paulist Press, 1983).

157 *Jane White-Lewis, a Jungian analyst and educator* See her essay "Dreams and Social Responsibility: Teaching a Dream Course in the Inner-City" in K. Bulkeley, ed., *Among All These Dreamers*. The dream example described here comes from her article "Entering the Imaginal World of Adolescence," *Dream Time* (1998) 15:1–2, pp. 8–11.

159 *A different kind of experimental dreamsharing group has been developed by the Reverend Jeremy Taylor* See J. Taylor, *Where People Fly and Water Runs Uphill* (New York: Warner Books, 1993), pp. 147, 150.

160 *This point is well illustrated by the experience of Bette Ehlert* See her essay "Healing Crimes: Dreaming Up the Solution to the Criminal Justice Mess," in K. Bulkeley, ed., *Among All These Dreamers*, p. 209.

165 *By far the most sophisticated of these programs is the one developed by G. William Domhoff* The current address of Domhoff and Schneider's Web site is www.dreamresearch.edu.

Chapter 7. Following Your Dreams

183 *One of my graduate-school mentors, the historian of religions, Wendy Doniger* See *Other People's Myths* (New York: Macmillan, 1988), pp. 132–33.

184 *Rituals of "dream incubation"* For a more detailed discussion of these rituals, see K. Bulkeley, *Spiritual Dreaming*, chapter 11.

Chapter 8. Creating Your Dreams

189 *A great deal of research has been done on the relationship between dreaming and creativity* See the entry "Creativity in Dreaming" in *The Encyclopedia of Sleep and Dreaming*.

193 *an acoustic biologist named Katy Payne* The following account of Payne's experiences comes from her book *Silent Thunder: In the Presence of Elephants* (New York: Simon & Schuster, 1998), pp. 28–29, 41.

200 *Here's an account from the novelist Stephen King* Quoted from N. Epel, *Writers Dreaming* (New York: Carol Southern, 1993), pp. 141–42.

201 *The earliest example I've found is in the* Oneirocritica For a more detailed discussion of this example and of other flying dreams, see K. Bulkeley, *Spiritual Dreaming*, chapter 6.

Conclusion: We Are All Big Dreamers

208   *Friedrich von Kekule was a professor of chemistry*   See R. Van de Castle, *Our Dreaming Mind* (New York: Ballantine, 1994), pp. 35–36.

210   *One example of this comes from the Paviotso people*   See W. Z. Park, "Paviotso Shamanism," *American Anthropologist* (1934) 59, p. 101.

Annotated Bibliography

Adams, Michael V. 1996. *The Multicultural Imagination: "Race," Color, and the Unconscious* (New York: Routledge). The first book to address the question of how racial and ethnic factors influence people's dreams.

Barrett, Deirdre, ed. 1996. *Trauma and Dreams* (Cambridge, Mass.: Harvard University Press). A collection of excellent essays by therapists and researchers on how working with dreams can help people overcome the devastating effects of traumatic experiences like sexual or physical abuse.

Beradt, Charlotte. 1966. *The Third Reich of Dreams* (Chicago: Quadrangle Books). Hard to find, but a fascinating portrait of the dream life of people living in Germany from 1933 to 1939, the years in which Hitler and the Nazi party were coming to power.

Bosnak, Robert. 1996. *Tracks in the Wilderness of Dreaming: Exploring Interior Landscape through Practical Dreamwork* (New York: Delacorte Press). The latest work by one of the most gifted dreamworkers currently in practice.

Bynum, Edward Bruce. 1993. *Families and the Interpretation of Dreams: Awakening the Intimate Web* (Binghampton, N.Y.: Harrington Park Press). The only book on dreams that seeks to integrate the rich traditional wisdom of Africa with modern psychological dream theory.

Delaney, Gayle, ed. 1993. *New Directions in Dream Interpretation* (Albany, N.Y.: State University of New York Press). An edited anthology by a leading dreamworker that illustrates several different methods of dream interpretation.

Domhoff, William G. 1996. *Finding Meaning in Dreams: A Quantitative Approach* (New York: Plenum). For people interested in what the quantitative study of dream content has taught about the nature of dreams, this is the book.

Epel, Naomi. 1993. *Writers Dreaming: Twenty-Six Writers Talk about Their Dreams and the Creative Process* (New York: Crown). A wonderful collection of conversations with prominent writers like Isabel Allende, William Styron, and Stephen King about how dreams influence their creative work.

Freud, Sigmund. 1965. *The Interpretation of Dreams* (New York: Avon). Although originally written 100 years ago, Freud's monumental work still has much of value for contemporary people; skip the long first chapter, though.

Gackenbach, Jayne, and Stephen LaBerge. 1988. *Conscious Mind, Sleeping Brain: Perspectives on Lucid Dreaming* (New York: Plenum). The best source of research on the phenomenon of lucid dreaming.

Garfield, Patricia. 1991. *The Healing Power of Dreams* (New York: Fireside). All of Garfield's books are a delight to read, but this one has special relevance for people who have experienced some kind of physical or emotional problem and want to look to their dreams for help.

Hartmann, Ernest. 1998. *Dreams and Nightmares: The New Theory on the Origin and Meaning of Dreams* (New York: Plenum). One of the true elders of the dream research community, Hartmann presents a grand theory of dream function in this impressive book.

Hill, Clara. 1996. *Working with Dreams in Psychotherapy* (New York: Guilford Press). An excellent introduction to the use of dreams in psychotherapeutic contexts; remarkably clear and straightforward.

Hobson, J. Allan. 1989. *The Dreaming Brain: How the Brain Creates Both the Sense and Nonsense of Dreams* (New York: Basic Books). A very readable introduction to contemporary neurological studies of dreams, with a powerful and controversial theory about the "nonsense" of dreaming.

Hunt, Harry. 1989. *The Multiplicity of Dreams: Memory, Imagination, and Consciousness* (New Haven, Conn.: Yale University Press). A difficult but ultimately rewarding investigation of the deep cognitive processes at work in the formation of dreams.

Irwin, Lee. 1994. *The Dream Seekers: Native American Visionary Traditions of the Great Plains* (Norman, Okla.: University of Oklahoma Press). The best book available on the incredibly rich and sophisticated dream traditions of various Native American cultures.

Jung, Carl G. 1965. *Memories, Dreams, Reflections* (New York: Vintage Books). Although this book isn't a how-to manual of Jungian dream interpretation, it does provide a memorable portrait of Jung's life and work, and it shows how his dream theories originated from his own dream experiences.

Kelsey, Morton. 1981. *God, Dreams, and Revelation: A Christian Interpretation of Dreams* (Minneapolis, Minn.: Augsburg Fortress Publishers). The best book on Christian dream traditions, with a strongly Jungian bent.

Krakow, Barry, and J. Niedhardt. 1992. *Conquering Bad Dreams and Nightmares* (New York: Berkley Books). A good how-to approach for dealing with troublesome nightmares.

LaBerge, Stephen. 1985. *Lucid Dreaming: The Power of Being Awake and Aware in Your Dreams* (New York: Jeremy P. Tarcher). The breakthrough book on the subject of lucid dreaming.

Miller, Patricia Cox. 1994. *Dreams in Late Antiquity: Studies in the Imagination of a Culture* (Princeton, N.J.: Princeton University Press). A highly academic but immensely interesting study of the dream beliefs and practices of Greek, Roman, and early Christian traditions.

Moffitt, Alan, Milton Kramer, and Robert Hoffmann, eds. 1993. *The Functions of Dreaming* (Albany, N.Y.: State University of New York Press). An outstanding collection of high-quality research on the question of what function(s) dreaming may serve.

O'Flaherty, Wendy Doniger. 1984. *Dreams, Illusion, and Other Realities* (Chicago: University of Chicago Press). A mind-bending exploration of theories and myths surrounding the "realness" of dreams, with an emphasis on Hindu and Buddhist perspectives.

Rinpoche, Tenzin Wangyal. 1998. *The Tibetan Yogas of Dream and Sleep* (Ithaca, N.Y.: Snow Lion Publications). A well-written introduction to the dream yoga traditions of Tibetan Buddhism.

Rupprecht, Carol Schreier, ed. 1993. *The Dream and the Text: Essays on Literature and Language* (Albany, N.Y.: State University of New York Press). A wide-ranging collection of essays about the role of dreams in various works of world literature.

Siegel, Alan. 1990. *Dreams That Can Change Your Life* (New York: Jeremy P. Tarcher). Describes the important role of "turning-point dreams" for people dealing with various kinds of life crises.

Sullivan, Kathleen. 1998. *Recurring Dreams: A Journey to Wholeness* (Freedom, Calif.: The Crossing Press). The only book available that deals specifically with the puzzling phenomenon of recurring dreams.

Taylor, Jeremy. 1998. *The Living Labyrinth: Exploring Universal Themes in Myths, Dreams, and the Symbolism of Waking Life* (Mahwah, N.J.: Paulist Press). A masterly survey of the most important archetypal themes that commonly occur in people's dreams, written by one of the foremost leaders of contemporary dreamwork.

Tedlock, Barbara, ed. 1987. *Dreaming: Anthropological and Psychological Interpretations* (New York: Cambridge University Press). A highly sophisticated collection of essays examining the role of dreams in various non-Western cultures, particularly in Central and South America.

Ullman, Montague, and Nan Zimmerman. 1979. *Working with Dreams* (New York: Jeremy P. Tarcher). A clear, accessible introduction to exploring dreams both individually and in group settings.

Van de Castle, Robert. 1994. *Our Dreaming Mind* (New York: Ballantine Books). A vast, sweeping survey of what people have thought about dreams, from ancient times right up to the present.

Von Grunebaum, G. E., and Roger Callois. 1966. *The Dream and Human Societies* (Berkeley, Calif.: University of California Press). An amazing collection of scholars from many different academic fields discuss the historical and social roles of dreaming; hard to find, but worth the effort.

Young, Serinity. 2000. *Dreaming in the Lotus: Innovation and Continuity in Buddhist Sacred Biography* (Somerville, Mass.: Wisdom Publications). A beautifully written study of the profound role that dreams have played in the history of Buddhism.

Index of Dreams

Chapter 8. Creating Your Dreams

Conclusion: We Are All Big Dreamers

Index